Shaheed Bhagat Singh

Shaheed Bhagat Singh

Patriotism, Sacrifice and Martyrdom

Edited by

S. Ram

Commonwealth

Shaheed Bhagat Singh

Edition : 2026

ISBN : 81-7169-951-0

Published by :
COMMONWEALTH PUBLISHERS (P) LTD.
4831/24, Govind Lane,
Ansari Road, Darya Ganj,
New Delhi - 110002
Ph. : 23242541, 23272541
e-mail : commonwealthpublishers2016@gmail.com

Distributed by :
ARJUN PUBLISHING HOUSE
4831/24, Govind Lane,
Ansari Road, Darya Ganj,
New Delhi - 110002
Ph. : 23242541, 23272541
e-mail : arjunbooks2001@gmail.com

Laser Typesetting by :
Dimple Computers
Delhi

Printed at :
Balaji Offset
Delhi

Preface

In the long drawn political struggle Shaheed Bhagat Singh and his comrades played a significant role for the attainment of complete independence. Undoubtedly they had to struggle very hard to achieve their aim. Their patriotism and sacrifice was par *excellence*. Their sense of organisation was unique and they operated with discipline. They had deep involvement in anti-*Raj* activities and as the machinery of the *Raj* had been pursuing them, their involvement in the Lahore Conspiracy Case led to the final martyrdom.

The theme has been weaved into twelve comprehensive chapters. Its deep thrust is on the early life of Bhagat Singh, his inclination and much interest to wage a 'war' against the *Raj* and achieve *Swaraj* at any cost. The death of Lala Lajpat Rai on the eve of the arrival of Simon Commission at Lahore led to the murder of J.P. Saunders, throwing of bomb in the Central Assembly, arrest of several young patriots and ultimately their death by hanging in the verdict of the Lahore Conspiracy Case. In fact, the work contains several aspects of the life of Bhagat Singh.

The material has been collected from several centres of research. These are National Archives of India, Sapru House Library, Nehru Memorial Museum and Library, Delhi University Library, Central Secretariat Library, Jawaharlal Nehru University Library and Indian Council of Historical Research Library. I indeed feel beholden to the members of these institutions who supported me in several ways during my researches. I am grateful to eminent authors whose writings have been used in the text.

Dr. S. Ram

Contents

1 Revolutionaries and the Raj

I

In the Punjab, the revolutionary movement sprouted in the shape of Bharat Mata society founded and organised with the initiatives of Sardar Ajit Singh, Sardar Kishan Singh, Sufi Amba Parshad Mehta, Anand Kishore, Pindi Das, Kidar Nath and last but not the least, Banke Dayal. Founded in 1907, it did function as a secret youth movement in various areas of the Punjab. Their personal contacts with the people, speeches, meetings and gatherings and patriotic literature greatly helped them in inculcating a renewed spirit of sacrifice amongst the people, which prepared them for the struggle ahead.

The revolutionary activities of the Babbar Akali Movement in the Punjab had significant impact on the youth of the region and the uneducated village folk, which greatly helped in numerous ways for the success of this movement[1]. The rise of the movement is ascribed to the pernicious[2] activities of Sardar Mota Singh of Patara, small village at a distance of about three kilometers form Jalandhar Cantt. It was he who called into being the party of Sikhs in the Doaba who believed in violence and who hoped to make government impossible by a campaign of murder and terrorism to be spread, eventually, throughout and beyond the province[3].

Associated with Mota Singh was Sardar Kishan Singh Gargaj, a pensioned Havildar of the 2/35th. Sikh and from a village, baring, in Jalandhar district who had been concerned in the Akali Conspiracy Case of 1921 in which the murders of Mr. Bowring of C.I.D. and of other officials were contemplated.

The only effect of this was the formation of a band of Sikh desperadoes who undertook to protect Sardar Mota Singh at the cost of their lives and who acted as his bodyguard, when he attended and spoke at meetings. No one among the public was prepared to assist in his arrest and the local police was unable to effect it for some time. Mota Singh was ultimately arrested in June 1922 and was lodged in the Nagpur Jail[4].

In August 1922, appeared the paper called the Babbar Akali Doaba. The leaflets, which contained violently senditious stuff, were distributed free of charge. There was no lack of sympathisers and active helpers and by the winter of 1922 an absolute region of terror had been established in Hoshiarpur and Jalandhar districts. In February, a dacoity was committed at Rahon by the Babbar Jatha and a few days later a zaildar of the Kapurthala State was brutally murdered for having assisted the state authorities in the suppression of Akali agitation. Besides, there were a few other murders and daring dacoities[5].

The Sikhs generally sympathised with the Babbars and the few who did not were too afraid to help the officers of the government. It was, therefore, decided to throw a wide net and simultaneous raids were made in 39 villages on 22 April, 1923 and as a result of this raids 71 persons were arrested. These arrests proved a serious blow to the organisation[6].

Enquiries were, however, carried to the Montgomery district where it was found that Sardar Jawala Singh and other had committed a murder for robbery and the nucleus of another Babbar organisation had been formed. This scheme was nipped in the bud by the proof of the murder and by action under the preventive sections of the Criminal Procedure Code. In January 1924, the first supplementary case with 36 accused was sent for trial, the accused including certain men of the army charged with supplying ammunition and bombs to the gang. With the death of Sardar Waryam Singh the only operation to be undertaken had been 'clearing up'. The total number of accused against whom evidence had been collected of active participation in the conspiracy was 169 of whom 8 were still at large. Of these accused no less then 54 were men who had served in the army and 8 were returned emigrants. The enquiries had resulted in the working out of 32 cases committed by the 'Babbar gangs' besides 9 miscellaneous cases of murder, dacoity, etc. Action was taken under Section 107, Criminal Procedure Code against more than a hundred persons in the Doaba, and ninety-six cases under

Section 216 of the Indian Penal Code. Apart from stolen property in the shape of jewellery etc. the recoveries included four mills bombs, six shot guns, eleven revolvers, six swords, five chhavis, 285 cartridges of different kinds and one detonator[7].

In the second decade of the twentieth century, the scene of India's struggles and sufferings shifted to the heart of the Punjab. The region, well known for its alluvial soil, rich culture and traditions, had been the gateway of India for foreign invasions in the last few centuries. Its material race, however, bore these onslaughts and faced them with courage, conviction and determination. The struggle against the Raj was, however, consistent and long, and it was a mixed episode tinged with non-violence and violence.

As the strains and stresses were greater in the Punjab, the agitation there was more extensive than in other province. There was greater fervour, more strident emotions, large gatherings of crowds and all this tended to rowdy demonstrations, alarm of authorities and frequent clashes. Punjab had achieved a reputation of turbulence since the agrarian troubles of 1907. The conditions had greatly deteriorated since then. The province was feeling a sense of deep frustration........[8].

The incidents of *Komagata Maru* which became an historic event in the second decade of the twentieth century had a romantic setting. It left the sea-shores of the Hong Kong port on 4 April, 1914 with one hundred and sixty-five immigrants. One hundred and eleven joined them in Shanghal, eighty-six at Moji and fourteen at Yakohama.[9] The ship reached Vancouver on 23 May. The trouble started when the immigration authorities at Vancouver raised serious objection in connection with the immigration laws of the country. For example, they were asked to show their health certificates; to show two hundred dollars in cash and to fulfil other conditions. As the immigrants failed to do so, the *Komagata Maru* remained anchored and this kind of behaviour of the sea-shores officials led Indians of Vancouver to form a 'Shore Committee' which moved the Supreme Court. On 7 July, the Supreme Court gave its judgement that the new Orders-in-Council prevented it from interfering with the decisions of the Immigration Department, and that was the end of their hope of getting justice and legel redress of their grievances.[10]

At the legal decision, the authorities asked the Komagata Maru to vacate the Canadian shores. And at last it sailed back for Yakohama on 23 July, 1914.[11]

The functioning of the Ghadr Party in the Punjab was unique and historic in its content. Manned by most devoted, sincere and selfless workers imbued with the patriotic zeal and fervour of the highest order, the party owed its origin from San Franciso on 18 August, 1913, about a year prior to the outbreak of the First World War which had deeply involved the British government and its colonies all over the world. Its presidentship was entrusted to a sincere, intelligent and painstaking youngman, Lala Har Dayal and secretaryship to Sohan Singh Bakhna, a fiery speaker and devoted worker. Through their weekly, *Ghadr*, they propagated their ideas for winning independence after ousting the British bureaucracy from India with a revolution. The party had much impact on thousands of emigrants from the Punjab to Canada. They were indeed unhappy over various rules and regulations which governed their very existence in a way which was repulsive in its nature.

The episode of *Komagata Maru* and the insults hurled on its passengers, resulting into the fatal incidents of about 20 Ghadrites and injuries to numerous others, added fuel to the fire. With all kind of anger, resentment and dissatisfaction and with no hope for the future, these Ghadrites came back to the Punjab with the blessings of their devout leader, Sardar Gurdit Singh of Sarhali village in Amritsar district. Soon their anti-Raj propaganda worked well in the rural areas and the people began to feel that a great change was coming in the near future.

The revolutionary activities of the Ghadrites included looting of banks, and government treasury; attacking police stations, railway stations and other agencies controlled and administered by the government. They established bomb factories both at Lahore and Amritsar, and they committed a large number of outrages, murdered officials and wrecked trains and communications. They printed and distributed considerable revolutionary literature and their declared object was Ghadr i.e. revolution. In January-February 1915, they organised disturbances on a large scale in south-western Punjab and a considerable number of murders and decoities involving much destruction of property were perpetrated. The peasantry also played its own part in this respect and some of them propagated amongst the people that the British government had come to an end and that they owed allegiance to the German Kaiser and the Amir of Afghanistan.[12]

Michael O'Dwyer in his speech in September 1917 in the Legislative Council said as follows, 'Hon'ble members are doubtless familiar with the serious dangers which menaced the security of the province during the first two years of the war, the Ghadr conspiracy and other real and covert movements, engineered by the King's enemies within or without India, with the object of subverting the Government, but, perhaps they are less familiar with the action, the prompt, vigorous and decisive action taken by the people of the Punjab, Muhammadans, Sikhs and Hindus, to range themselves on the side of law and order and to stamp out sedition and anarchy. There was no hesitation, no sitting on the fence, no mawkish sympathy with red-handed crime, no insincere apology for so-called misguided youths pursuing noble ideas, no subtle distinction between evolutionary and revolutionary patriotism.

This type of violent agitational approach of the Ghadrites was taken serious note of by the government which was fully armed with a new law, known as the Defence of India Act, which armed the police and the bureaucracy with a wide range of powers to deal with the insurgency caused by them. With no strong and deep linkage with one another; lack of resources and a well-organised leadership; bereft of mass support; out-break of the war and involvement of whole nation in it and last but not the least, the superior resources and striking power of the British government—all these factors proved suicidal for the continuance of their revolutionary activities for a long time. Consequently, during the second year of the First World War, their rendezvous were smashed very severely as a result of which many were imprisoned and convicted; some were transported for life and about twenty of them were sentenced to death.

This kind of model of self-sacrifice had deep-rooted effect on the minds of the people who were greatly worried over the economic situation, which had completely broken their backbone. Their thinking and line of action, at a later stage, had a deep linkage with the repulsive prevailing situation in the Punjab.

Principal Chhabil Das of National College, Lahore and a prominent member of the servants of the people society, reminisced thus:

'Among Ghadrites who came back to India to arouse the people against British imperialism, Bhai Parmanand was also one of those persons, who was inspired along with Dr. Har Dayal and other Ghadrites. Then he was charged with high treason and was sentenced to death, but at the intervention of Pandit Madan Mohan Malaviya and Mr. C.F. Andrews, his sentence was commuted to transportation for life. Later on, at the expiry of about five or six years, he was released'.[13]

Although crushed with an iron hand, the Babbar Akali Movement had significant impact in reawakening the peasantry and apprising them of their fundamental rights. By their speeches, writing and personal contacts with masses of the Punjab, they succeeded in inculcating anti-Raj feelings in them and a sense of hopefulness for winning independence after ousting the British from their motherland.

The most shocking tragedy of the struggle was enacted on April 13, the Baisakhi day, the Hindu new year in the north. About 1,600 rounds were fired and the firing ceased only when the ammunition was exhausted. Hundreds more were injured and left to die without medical attendance or even water. This indeed was the most shocking tragedy of the freedom struggle in twentieth century.

Martial Law was imposed on the whole of the Punjab. What followed was reign of terror. All leaders of the people, whether in political life or not, were arrested and thrown into prison. Every effort was made to humiliate the people. In one street in Amritsar, they were compelled at the point of the bayonet to crawl on their bellies. There was strict censorship of the press. No reports of the happenings were allowed to go out of the province. But as days passed, rumours about the diabolical doings of the authorities spread throughout the country.[14]

'The Amritsar massacre caused an unparalleled indignation not only in India but also among all fair-minded people in England. But the steps taken by the Government to compensate the sufferers and to punish the wrong—doers were extremely inadequate.'[15]

E.S. Montagu was fully aware of the fact that the policy of ruling India by the sword alone was impossible and he had the realisation that 'the Government—foreign or indigenous, could not rule a people for any length of time without the willing support of unquestioning acquiescence of a section of the effective classes of the people. Besides, he had a personal stake in the Indian affairs. He had worn himself out to process the Reforms and was naturally most anxious for their success. He made up his mind and in the budget debate on May 22, gave a promise to hold an enquiry.'[16]

The reaction of the people rose to phenomenal height. The *Satyagraha* pledge to be taken by the people said, 'Being consciously of opinion that the (Rowlett) Bills.... are unjust, subversive of the principles of liberty and justice, and destructive of the elementary rights of individuals on which the safety of the community as a whole and the State itself is based, we solemnly affirm that, in the event of these Bills becoming law and until they are withdrawn, we shall refuse civilly to obey these laws and such other laws as a committee to be hereafter appointed may think fit, and we further affirm that, in this struggle, we will faithfully follow truth and refrain from violence to life, person or property.'

Although Punjab was isolated and cut off from the rest of India demands were made for the recall of O'Dwyer and Chelmsford. Indemnity for the prisoners was pressed and enquiry in the Punjab happenings urged, both in England as well as in India. During this period the leaders of the Home Rule League and the Liberal Federation showed activity in giving evidence before the Joint Parliamentary Committee. Among them were Vithalbhai Patel, Bal Gangadhar Tilak, Bipin Chandra Pal, Mrs. Annie Besant, Surendranath Banerjea, Tej Bahadur Sapru, Srinivasa Sastri and others. They all impressed upon the secretary of State the urgency of an enquiry into the recent events in order to pacify public opinion.

The Bharat Naujawan Sabha, the Communist Party, Kirti Kisan Party, the Socialist Party, the Students Unions and the Bal Bharat Sabha played their role in the freedom struggle. Undoubtedly Youth Association of Bengal did a commendable work in this regard. After his return from England in 1921,

Subhas Chandra Bose to whom the present movement owes its origin to a great extent put in his efforts to bring together all young students in schools and colleges on a common platform and inculcated in them the nationalistic and patriotic fervour for the country. Later on, when he gave a call to young girls to join it, its name was changed to 'All Bengal Youth Association.' Its main aim was to consolidate and extend its power both by open propaganda and secret organisation. It was also to work for the eradication of social evils and uplift of depressed classes. Bose personally appealed to youngmen and was able to secure their support in all 'open and secret' work. He was of the opinion that, 'Youth movements are not reformatory but revolutionary. The youths of India are no longer content with handing over all responsibility to their older leaders and sitting down with folded hands or following like dumb-driven cattle. They have realised that it is for them to create new, free, great and powerful India.'

Besides, the All-Bengal Students' Association, formed in 1924, had a well-disciplined organisation and cadre of young workers in various areas of the province. Pramod Kumar Ghosalan and Birendra Kumar Das Gupta were elected its President and General Secretary. The association aimed at inculcating the spirit of selfless sacrifice and patriotism amongst the youths of the province and also to spread its objects beyond the borders of Bengal.

The work of the revolutionaries was wholly secret. The prime function of the leadership was to spot out potential, sincere and devoted comrades and then pursue them relentlessly with literature and arguments till they gave their assent to join them. They took precaution not to approach youths with a bad reputation or a family background, which had no reputation in accordance with their standards.[17]

So revolutionaries had to be really handpicked. Ugly surprises would always occur; nevertheless we had to take certain precautions. When I spotted out a possible comrade, I gave him books. In the beginning historical novels with patriotic tilt such as Bankim's and Ramesh Chandra Dutt's novels and patriotic poems of Navin Sen, Maithilisharan and Rajni Sen were given... I gave him lives of patriots like those of Rana Pratap, Shivaji, Garibaldi, Mazzini, Wallace, etc... The life of the Indian revolutionary martyrs constituted the last course. In between the youth was fed on the history of the Chinese revolution (1912), Zaghlul Pasha's struggle for Egyptian independence etc.[18]

"Prolonged discussions took place in our ranks about what to do to break this stagnant calm. Socialist literature was trickling in, the triumph of the November revolution, the consolidation of the socialist regime in Russia and more than anything else, the aid given by the Soviet Union to Asian countries like Turkey and China against imperialist powers attracted us towards the new Socialist state and towards the ideas and principals it embodied."[19]

Bhagat Singh was indeed very active in the Punjab. With his efforts and cooperation of his comrades was formed the Naujawan Bharat Sabha, a militant youth organisation to propagate Socialist ideas and above all preach anti-Raj sentiments. The Sabha became a very popular political organ, which played a significant role in the radicalisation of the youths of the country.

The background of the events, which had led to the martyrdom of Bhagat Singh and raised him to the pantheon of India's greatest heroes, was provided by the general despondency among the youths in India after the suspension of the Non-cooperation Movement in February 1922. The nationalist movement seemed to be paralysed on the one hand by dissensions among the top leaders, and on the others, by the growing communal bickerings and riots.

It was in this atmosphere that many youngmen in various parts of the country came to the conclusion that the methods followed by Gandhi and the Congress were not capable of carrying the country forward and preparations must be made for an armed struggle to wrest power for British hands. And in order to prepare the people for such a struggle it would be necessary to carry on propaganda through brave deeds of heroism and effective protest against the barbarities perpetrated by the British.[20]

II

Bhagat Singh's ancestors were Sandhu Jats and were settled since generations in a small but prosperous village, Khatkar Kalan, situated at a distance of about thirty kilometers from Phagwara railway station. Geographically it is in the Jalandhar district. The Doab was a renowned belt of revolutionaries and was always humming with patriotic fervour. Khatkar Kalan, now a place of pilgrimage, could not remain in isolation and, with the passage of time, the spirit of selfless work, patriotic fervour and supreme sacrifice for the country was kindled in a small house of this village.[21]

In the first half of the nineteenth century, some members of Bhagat Singh's family had served in various capacities in the army of Maharaja Ranjit Singh and had shown distinction in their service careers. They were well-conversant with the onslaughts of Pathans from North-West Frontier as well as the speedy expansion of the British commercial and political interests in India. And above all, the British annexation of the Punjab and the subsequent administration in the provine had deep imprint on the patriotic fervour of his ancestors.

Like any other villager of his time, Bhagat Singh's grandfather, Sardar Arjan Singh led a simple life, his main avocation being the medical practice of Unani system. His clients were the common village folk who had complete faith in the efficacy of his medicines and his verbal advice to be followed with meticulous discipline by the patients. Imbued with the knowledge of Urdu, Punjabi, Persian and Sanskrit, the doctor kept himself fairly busy in various kinds of social and religious work in his area, which made him a popular figure.

During this time, the Arya Samaj movement, with his firm socio-religious base, had gained much momentum in many cities and towns of North India. To be its member or worker was in, in fact, a big gain in the social life of any person. So Arjan Singh became a member of his organisation and showed so much activity in it that he preached its gospel amongst the simple illiterate villagers. His powerful influence coupled with the reforming zeal had much impact in the suburbs.

In the first decade of the twentieth century, when the British government declared Lyallpur as the 'canal area' and made the offers of land to the people of the Doaba, many families of the region migrated to the land of the alluvial soil, far away from their homes. Sardar Arjan Singh also migrated with his family and settled in a small village at Banga in district Lyallpur.[22]

Educated in Sain Das Anglo-Sanskrit High School at Jalandhar, indeed one of the premier Arya Samaj institutions in the Doab, Sardar Kishan Singh was imbibed the sense of nationalism at a very young age by the renowned teacher and a selfless Arya Samaj worker, Lala Sundar Dass. This type of education with its main emphasis on simplicity, dedication, sacrifice and love for his country paid him rich dividends as he, later on, imbibed such feelings in each and every member of his family.

Soon after coming out of the school, Kishan Singh involved himself in a private job which could fetch him a bare pay enabling him to maintain his family with honest means worthy of the tradition of his ancestors. The well-established industrial Prudential Company with its headquarters in Mumbai offered him an opportunity of service in its branch located in Punjab. But this kind of work merely for his subsistence and maintenance of the members of his family did not interest him much. He did find some time for more fruitful activity–both social and political-in the years to come.

Thus, Kishan Singh proved himself instrumental in helping and organising relief work for the backward famine-stricken people of Central Provinces and the victims of the severe earthquake in Kangra. He also worked shoulder to shoulder in helping Lala Lajpat Rai for the cause of the destitute and helpless orphans. His involvements in social sphere soon crossed the slow moving borders into an active field of political activities for which the family was destined in the coming few decades of the twentieth century. So in 1906, all the three brothers had a meeting with Sufi Amba Prasad, Sardar Kartar Singh and Mahasha Ghaseeta Ram and decided to raise their patriotic fervour against the condemned and much criticised Colonisation Act and the Bari Doab Canal Act. These acts of the government had greatly damaged the interest of the peasantry in the canal areas of the Punjab and it did need the services and sacrifices of more and more prominent, sincere and dedicated persons for its cause in the movement already launched with full force. The foundation of political party known as Bharat Mata Society with the help and cooperation of Sufi Amba Prasad and others offered him a platform for his political and agitation approach against the measures of the government. Next year, when he took an active part in the anti-government agitation in connection with the peasantry of the canal region, he found himself in jail along with numerous colleagues of the movement.

Kishan Singh's political activities, however, did not abate at this end. They were rather intensified with the passage of time. During the First World War the activities of the Ghadrites were greatly intensified on the Indian political horizon. As was expected him, he did not hesitate to support this anti-government movement in every possible way. So far so that Kartar Singh Sarabha, one of the prominent members and hero of the Ghadr movement reported regarding the receipt of one thousand rupees in the form of financial support coupled with his other political activities which were thought to be ant-government and it could not remain a secret for a long time. The police could unearth this kind of activity sponsored and supported by Kishan Singh at a time when the Ghadr movement was being crushed with very strong measures by the Punjab government. In such measures of the government, Kishan Singh was also the victim of police rules and regulations. He was, therefore, labelled as a dangerous element and a supporter of anti-government agitation and movement. For all this, he was punished : he was interned in his village for some time during First World War. Thus, his political activities which he carried with a sense of true nationalism and patriotic fervour in his veins, brought him numerous personal troubles both in jails and outside it. His sacrifice for the motherland and above all, the family tradition maintained by his younger brother, Sardar Ajit Singh; and his son Sardar Bhagat Singh are worthy of emulation.

Sardar Kishan Singh used to live in Nawan Kot, Lahore and from there he shifted to Kucha Nihal Chand in 1920. The atmosphere in his house, according to Jaidev Gupta, a class-fellow of Bhagat Singh, became very tense after the tragedy in Jallianwala Bagh as all types of people used to come there and talked about martial law and its effects on the people of the Punjab.[23] These prominent leaders were Bhai Parmanand, Kedar Nath Sehgal, Lala Pindi Das and others.[24]

It is strange coincidence that when Bhagat Singh was born, this father who was lodged in Lahore Central Jail in connection with an agitation against the Colonisation Bill and his uncle, Ajit Singh whose sacrifice for the national cause is proverbial, was in Mandalay jail, were released on the same day. It is commonly believed that the child Bhagat Singh was initially named as *Bhaganwala* by his grandmother as the birth of the new baby brought good luck and fortune to the members of the family. Later on he was named Bhagat Singh. From the very childhood, he had the signs and traits of a great man who became later on an unforgettable hero of the Indian nation.

When Bhagat Singh was only three years old, he happened to go to a farm in the village alongwith his father. While Sardar Kishan Singh was busy with his friend, the child got himself engaged in a typical kind of work i.e. he began to insert straw in the land. And when his father asked him what he had been doing, he replied innocently, '*Babooke Bo raya hun*'. The child could not pronounce the word. *Bandook* i.e. gun. But the idea was very clear. For a few generations, the ancestors of Bhagat Singh had been busy in the anti-raj activities in order to get freedom for the motherland. Therefore, this kind of thinking was a natural instinct with the child.[25]

Bhagat Singh received his primary education in the District Board Primary School, Banga. Needless to say, he was an intelligent, well disciplined and a popular student. His teachers were happy with his performance, in the class. He had to shift to D.A.V High School, Lahore when his father came to settle there along with members of his family.[26] In the new school, Bhagat Singh's academic performance was quite satisfactory as it is clear from the following letter.

On 22 July, 1918, when Bhagat Singh was only eleven years old, he wrote a letter in Urdu to his grandfather giving details about his performance in the class. It is as follows:

Respected Babaji,

Namaste

I respectfully inform you that I received your letter. I was very happy to read it. I could not write to you about my examination as I did not receive any intimation at that time. I have received the results of English and Sanskrit. I am successful in them. In Sanskrit, I have got 110 out of 150 marks and in English, 68 out of 150. Anybody getting 50 marks of a total of 150 is declared successful. By getting 68 marks, I have done well. Do not worry about me. Marks in other subjects are not yet told. My holidays would commence on 8th August. When will you come here? Please do write.[27]

Yours affectionately,

Bhagat Singh

The D.A.V. High School, Lahore was undoubtedly the best educational institution affiliated to the Punjab University. Besides, the members of teaching staff in each and every subject were highly qualified, well trained and, above all, sincerely devoted to their profession. The institution attracted the best students belonging, both to the elite class as well as middle class families. The crop of the talented students, it produced in the Middle School Examination as well as the High School Examination used to become a feeder for the well-known D.A.V. Coll%ge, Lahore Bhagat Singh did well in almost all the subjects.

As a student in the D.A.V. High School, Lahore, Bhagat Singh devoted more time for the study of extra-curricular literature which afforded him a vivid and glaring insight into the doings of numerous patriots and nationalists of India and foreign countries. His mind and thought were greatly influenced by the ideology and speeches of the leaders in the first decades of the twentieth century. These leaders were no less than Lala Lajpat Rai, Sufi Amba Prasad, Lala Pindi Dass, Mehta Anand Kishore and other prominent leaders of the Doab region. Besides the Ghadr movement leaders like Sardar Kartar Singh Sarabha, Rash Behari Bose and other heroes of this anti-government movement had much impact on his young mind. Sardar Kishan Singh's house at Banga was the frequented rendezvous of these leaders who often sought his advice and financial support. All these incidents were being watched with great interest and comprehensiveness by young Bhagat Singh who soon chose the career of violent defiance against the policies of the British government and launched a movement, which was unparalleled in the annals of Indian history.

Besides the life sacrifices of Sardar Kartar Singh Sarabha surpassed all other influences on the political philosophy of Bhagat Singh. The impact of *Shaheed* Kartar Singh Sarabha's heroism and sacrifice on Bhagat Singh can also be judged from the fact, that when the latter was arrested, a photograph of the *Shaheed* Kartar Singh was recovered from him. He carried Sarabha's photo in his pocket and derived great inspiration from him. Moreover, he used to show that photograph to his mother and say, "Dear mother, This is my hero, friend and compansions." While at home, Bhagat Singh used to sing the following couplet-favourite with Kartar Singh Sarabha:

Seva desh di jindarye bari aukhi
Gallan Karnian dher sukhalian ne
Jinhan desh seva wich pair paya
Unhan lakh musibtan Jhallian ne[28]

It is very easy to talk, but to serve one's motherland in the real sense, is extremely difficult, O my little soul. They who took upon themselves the task of serving their motherland had to undergo lacs of life's pangs and agonies.[29]

In an interview Jai Dev Gupta has recorded about the attitude of Sardar Kishan Singh and Lala Lajpat Rai in connection with the participation of student in the political movement of the day. He narrates how Bhagat Singh and he were confronted with these two prominent personalities—one being the guardian of a young student who was yet to show his remarkable acts of bravery and courage and the other leader of all-India fame with a huge following of the youth. Before leaving the school, Bhagat Singh was very shy to tell his father. So he asked me to convey him our decision. When I told his father about our decision, he was very angry. He said, "What would you do, if you do not study? *Mazdoor Banoge Kya? Dhhakke Khaoge? Pahle parh to lo*. Then, of course, I told him we would join National College....". Similarly, when we went to Lala Lajpat Rai and told him of our decision, he was very angry with us. He told us that we should first study and became learned men, and then only we could think of joining the national movement and being our political career. We could not say anything because he was so angry.[30]

The period between 1914–19 was indeed a difficult period for India as well as the world. The main reason was the outbreak of the First World War, which had involved not only Europe but also many Asian and Middle-Eastern countries. The very fact that it continued intermittently for about six years, it shattered the economy of the countries which had direct involvements in this grand venture. Its aftermath created serious problems of unlimited magnitude, hitherto unheard of in India, especially in Punjab. The acute unemployment, the role of *Ghadr* movement[31] leaders, the harsh and cruel treatment by the British bureaucracy, the passage of the Rowlett Act, the patriotic fervour and peaceful agitation and resentment shown by the people in respective of their affiliation to any caste, creed and community; mob fury at some places causing damage to government buildings and property; unwanted transfer of civil control to military authorities; firing at the Jallianwala Bagh resulting into the deaths of hundreds of innocent persons assembled in a peaceful gathering on a sacred day; promulgation of the notorious, cruel, unwanted highly criticized martial law in Amritsar, Lahore, Gujranwala, Kasur, Gujarat, Layallpur and other areas; the in-human crawling order, flogging in public of innocent persons, arrests and convictions of old and infirm persons, barristers, pleaders, doctors, teachers, students, shopkeepers, labourers and numerous others without hearing their points of views and without affording them any kind of legal assistance to plead their innocence;[32] the administration of fancy punishments by young British military officers; indiscriminate bombing, resulting into scores of deaths of innocent and peaceful villagers of Gujranwala region; physical and mental tortures of inhuman and uncivilised nature unethical interference in the functioning of numerous educational institutions including the prestigious Medical College, Lahore and infliction of punishments to the students in the hottest days of May 1919 without the permission and assent of the educational authorities; firings at numerous places,[33] in the name of law and order, resulting into the deaths of many innocent persons; the posting of punitive police; the exactions of illegal fines on the areas as a whole; the looting of valuables by the personnel of police and army; procuring numerous articles like milk, ghee, eggs, fruit, vegetables, etc. by the army personnel without any kind of payment to the shopkeepers; compelling innocent people to give false evidence to support government's version and support its cases and last but not the least, the hanging of numerous persons who had participated in the anti-government agitation at one time or another, had serious impact on the minds of the people of the Punjab. They felt their peaceful lives being disturbed and perturbed.

The Amritsar session of the Indian National Congress held in December 1919 under the presidentship of Pandit Motilal Nehru enthused the people of India with new dimensions of political ideology which soon emerged into a different model for launching an all-India movement in the next year. This model indeed was a new phenomenon which gave birth to a mass movement under the leadership of Mahatma Gandhi who had emerged as a respected leader at the commencement of the First World War and began gaining his ascendancy in the hearts of the people of India after about half a decade.

The presidential speech of Motilal Nehru traced out the history of the British Raj in many facets. He was indeed critical of the ways and methods followed by the British bureaucracy in India and expressed a sense of dissatisfaction with the non-fulfilment of promises made by the Home Government.

The inauguration of the first Non-cooperation Movement under the leadership of Gandhi, after the Amritsar session of the Indian National Congress, brought about a revolutionary change in the thinking of the people of India. Whereas this movement took up the political issues like the Punjab wrongs, *Khilafat* along with the boycott of councils, schools and colleges, propagation of swadeshi, etc., as its main programme, it spelt out a new modal of education out of the sphere of the British system of education. The idea was to establish a chain of *Vidya Piths*[34] i.e. national schools and colleges in different parts of the country with a new type of curricula, which laid much emphasis on history, culture, tradition, philosophy, etc. with Indian bias. The main motive was to shun and boycott the government-managed and government-aided institutions and also attract the youths of the country to join them so that the patriotic sentiments could be inculcated in them.[35] Such national institutions were established in Calcutta, Patna, Ahmedabad, Aligarh, Delhi, Banaras, Lahore, and other places. The well-known institutions were the Kashi Vidya Pith, Gujrat Vidya Pith, Aligarh Muslim University, Bihar Vidya Pith, the Bengal National University, the Tilak Maharashtra Vidya Pith and, last but not the least, the Punjab Qaumi Vidya Pith, Lahore.

Such a call had much effect on young Bhagat Singh who considered it his best opportunity to serve the motherland by joining the National College, Lahore.[36] Founded, managed, organised and nurtured by the prominent leaders of the Punjab, Bhai Parmanand and Lala Lajpat Rai, this institution attracted numerous youths of the north-western region of India who, later on, were in the forefront of the first and second Non-cooperation, Movements, Quit India Movement and the revolutionary movement launched by Bhagat Singh, Rajguru and Sukh Dev, along with their numerous associates who made superb and supreme sacrifices for the attainment of independence.

Bhagat Singh also joined the prestigious National College, Lahore where he was greatly influenced by the teachings of his professors, but mainly by that of Professor Jai Chandra Vidyalankar who taught history to the students. Vidyalankar did lay much emphasis on the revolutionary cult by citing examples from the marvellous successes achieved by the people of Russia against the Czar in 1917. It was indeed a theme, which awakened the spirit of patriotism amongst the students including young Bhagat Singh. Even precious life could be given to free one's country from the shackles of centuries of old slavery in the form of British colonialism in India. Such was the main theme of teaching in the Vidya Piths and the National College, Lahore.

As a student, Bhagat Singh was intelligent, active, smart and above all well-disciplined. He respected and obeyed his teachers and the latter showed immense love for him. His academic results were fairly good as he never shirked his studies. Besides, he was superb actor and a dramatist. A regular member of the local National Club as he was, he often acted the historical roles of the great Mauryas, Guptas and Maharana Pratap. His immense success in this extracurricular activity was mainly because of the fact that he maintained an enviable typical Punjabi youthful physique and a commanding voice which always enabled him to dominate the stage by successfully performing the role of a hero in the drama or one-act-play. He had a natural command in Punjabi, Urdu and English. Besides, he knew Hindi and Sanskrit well. With all these qualities, Bhagat Singh had gained much prominence amongst the students and teachers not only of his own college but of other local colleges.[37]

Principal Chhabil Das of National College reminisced, besides them being my students we had good personal relation too. In the evenings we could meet and talk informally on so many subjects. We spent several nights on the bank of the River Ravi and spent moonlit nights, boating and rowing there giving expression to our innermost feelings on any subjects.... In the year 1928, when Bhagat Singh heard that I was I going to be married, he approached me and asked me if it was true? I replied in the affirmative. He insisted that I should not marry. I said "Bhagat Singh, if I could get a really very good life companion who, instead of retarding my activities, would invigorate them, what would be your view? In the same breath I quoted three concrete examples of Mrs. Sun-Yat-Sen..... wife of Lenin and...companion of Karl Marx." (At this) Bhagat Singh replied,

'Guruji who can vanquish you in any argument, so he yielded'.[38]

There were no books at hand. So it was for the teachers to select book from the libraries and give the relevant portions to the students...in our National College, we used to talk about Mazzini and Garibaldi. We used to talk about Ireland, about Sinn Fein movement of De Valera and other movements and about the Russian Revolution.[39]

The proposal of marriage for young Bhagat Singh was a turning point in his career. Like other provinces of India, early marriage both for a boy and a girl was a common prevalent custom in the Punjab also. Often the grandfather or the grandmother had the upper hand in the decisions of arranging marriages. They indeed loved their grandsons immensely. Such was a case in Sardar Kishan Singh's home where his old mother expressed her desire for the betrothal and marriage ceremonies of Bhagat Singh who was hardly nineteen years old. Kishan Singh contacted Sardar Teja Singh Mann of village Mannawala in district Sheikhupura for his sister's engagement with his son. But before in any final decision was made in this regard, Bhagat Singh was duly informed. He not only reacted to it very strongly, but communicated to his father his firm and bold resolve not to marry till the aim of his life was achieved. And this noble aim was the burning desire of independence for India. He indeed sought the blessings of his farther and grandmother so that he could have the strength, noble ideas, a firm determination and an enviable strength of character to achieve the cherished aim of his career. His father and other members of the family did not approve of the decision communicated by Bhagat Singh. All efforts to bring him round his own decision having failed, Kishan Singh was left with no alternative. Soon Bhagat Singh made the final decision to discontinue his study, leave the college forever and also leave Lahore for Kanpur, which had become a center of revolutionary activities in north India.

Before leaving Lahore, Sardar Bhagat Singh left a letter in the drawer of a table lying in his father's room.

Respected father,

Namaste

The mission of my life has devoted for the attainment of freedom for motherland. Therefore, I do not give any kind of preference to rest and worldly desires.

You must remember when I was a child, my grandfather announced at the time of my thread ceremony that my life would be dedicated for the cause of motherland. I am, therefore, fulfilling the commitment made at that time. I trust you would excuse me.[40]

Yours affectionately,
Bhagat Singh

About Bhagat Singh's views on marriage, his class fellow Jai Dev Gupta reminisced thus. '..... I asked Bhagat Singh, why he was not marrying? He told me (in a frank way) that he had chosen a path which was full of many possibilities. His two uncles had gone that way and they had left two widows. Should he also leave another widow for weeping and wailing? He told me that he was not going to spoil the life of any young lady. He said, "My determination is this and let these people say anything.... The path he chose was fraught with serious consequences, even death. So marriage would be an obstacle in his way. But his father and other members of his family were bent upon this. So one day, when he was pressed by them very much, he left Lahore".[41]

As mentioned earlier, Professor Jai Chand Vidyalankar was the mentor and guide of Bhagat Singh. It seems probable that Bhagat Singh made the final decision and took the vow not to marry and instead to devote the rest of his career to attain independence for the motherland mainly with the help, advice, guidance and support of Professor Vidyalankar. It is also true that Bhagat Singh was advised by him to keep in touch with Ganesh Shanker Vidyarathi of Kanpur who had been busy doing secret work with great patriotic fervour. He was running a small press, known as the Pratap Press.

With the letter of introduction from Professor Vidyalankar, he found no difficulty in leaving Lahore and coming to Kanpur where he introduced himself to Ganesh Shanker Vidyarathi who was much impressed by the unquestioned sincerity of Bhagat Singh. He tutored him about the basic and elementary tenets of leading a difficult, uneasy and uncomfortable life and not bowing before the alien authorities even if he had to lay down his precious life. For all this, Bhagat Singh was mentally prepared and, therefore, it took him no time to agree to what Vidyarathi advised him.

It was indeed a novel and a most romantic experience of a youngman of about seventeen years old who had come to an other province–a few hundred miles away from home and had chosen a path of life which had not the approval of his father and other members of his family. To conceal his true identity he changed his name to Balwant, and began working in the Pratap Press. It was just a small work, probably to assist Vidyarathi. He found time in studying the history of the countries, which had passed through bloody revolutions. He also read much about socialism as a system of government and had deep study of the pitiable plight of nations under surveillance and the colonial rule. This type of study had greatly heightened and elevated his mental faculties and made him realise the fundamental rights of the oppressed people. He, therefore, began to feel that the alien rule must come to an end the teeming millions must enjoy the basic rights given to an individual in a welfare state.

Ganesh Shankar Vidyarthi's house was the centre of political activities of numerous young revolutionaries with whom Bhagat Singh formed deep connection in the common cause of fighting the violent war for independence. He became a member of the Hindustan Republican Association an organisation run by the revolutionaries in north India, but mainly in the United Provinces. Already, some well-known and devoted youngmen like Batukeshwar Dutt, Chandrashekhar Azad, Jogesh Chandra Chatterjee, Bejoy Kumar Sinha and a few others were the active members of this organisation.

Ajoy Kumar Ghosh reminisced, I believe it was sometime in 1923 that I met Bahgat Singh for the first time. A young boy of about my age—I was fifteen at that time—he was introduced to me by B.K. Dutt in Cawnpore. Tall and thin.... very quiet, he seemed a typical village lad lacking smartness and self-confidence... One day in 1928, I was surprised when a youngman walked into my room and greeted me. It was Bhagat Singh but not the Bhagat Singh that I had met two years before. Tall and magnificently proportioned, with a keen, intelligent face and gleaming eyes, he looked a different man altogether. And as he talked, I realised that he had grown not merely in years.[42]

During this period, Sardar Bhagat Singh did much spade work in the political field in some districts of U.P. He personally toured these areas, contacted numerous young persons, apprised them of the aims and objects of the Hindustan Republican Association. He indeed prevailed upon them to join this organisation whole-heartedly and work in the villages for the independence of the country. The main plank of his philosophy was to propagate for the armed revolution in the country against British imperialism by distributing various kinds of leaflets containing patriotic poems and songs. He also began to attend the local *melas* attended by thousands of uneducated people including peasants, farmers, labourers and school-going children. The main refrain on the leaflets was *jago mere desh ke logo*, viz. wake up my fellow countrymen.

At some occasions, Bhagat Singh and his associates were closely pursued by the police, but they were quite experts including the police and the latter failed miserably to lay their hand on them.

With all this kind of touring work, Ganesh Shankar Vidyarathi wished to fix up Bhagat Singh in a job where he could be more effective in enthusing the young minds and prepare the youth for the national cause. This meant the headship for him in a national school near Aligarh which he accepted and performed his duties towards the students efficiently and diligently. His organising capacity in this respect was quite remarkable.

The long separation from his parents was a source of painful agony for them, speçially his grandmother showed her much keenness to see her grandson. But deeply engrossed and involved in the national work, as Bhagat Singh was, any kind of message from his parents to return home did not prove effective for the time being. Sardar Kishan Singh entreated his son time and again and apprised him of the grave physical condition of his grandmother as well as his assurance that he had his mother would never compel him for marriage. It is said that through the good offices of Maulana Hasrat Mohani, Bhagat Singh staged his back to Lahore early in 1925.

But any kind of domestic love or affectionate paternal treatment would not divert his attention towards any other avocation except the revolutionary activities to which he was deeply and sincerely wedded. He would move out of his home at Lahore and met young boys whom he apprised of the violent revolution to be launched against the British Raj for achieving the sacred goal of independence.

During the period, he migrated to Delhi where he found the atmosphere quite congenial to work in one capacity or the other. It is said that he worked in a daily newspaper, *Vir Arjun* for about six months. But he did not disclose his identity to anybody and functioned, without any kind of fear, under an assumed name, viz. Balwant Singh. Thus, he found no difficulty in carrying on his political activity in Delhi. But he was yet to work in a wider field of political activity by launching anti-government measures. And for this, he thought it proper to come back to Lahore where he wished to have contacts with leaders and parties busy in revolutionary activities.

Soon after his arrival in Lahore, Bhagat Singh formed active connections with the Kirti Kisan Party which was functioning under the supervision, advice and guidance cf Sardar Sohan Singh Josh. Bhagat Singh also worked for some time on the editorial staff of the *Kirti*—a reputed journal with socialist leanings edited by Sardar Sohan Singh Josh.

REFERENCES

1. Home Poll, file. 200, 1936.
2. It is a typical bureaucratic phraseology.
3. Home Poll, File 200, 1926
4. *Ibid.*
5. *Ibid.*
6. *Ibid.*
7. *Ibid.*
8. Tara Chand, *History of the Freedom Movement in India, Vol. III,* New Delhi, 1972, p. 478.
9. Of them only 25 were Muslims and rest were Sikhs.
10. A.C. Bose, *op. cit.,* p. 63.
11. Khushwant Singh and Satindra Singh, *Ghadar,* 1915, New Delhi, 1966, pp. 28-29.
12. About 28 persons were hanged and 100 transported.
13. Transcript of interview with Chhabil Das, Nehru Memorial Museum and Library, New Delhi.

14. J.B. Kripalani, *Gandhi: His Life and Throught*, New Delhi, 1970, pp. 82-83.
15. Subhas Chandra Bose, *The Indian Struggle, 1920–1942*, Mumbai, 1967, p. 26.
16. Tara Chand, *op. cit.*, pp. 481-82.
17. Manmathnath Gupta, *They Lived Dangerously: Reminiscences of a Revolutionary*, Delhi, 1969, p. 92.
18. *Ibid.*, p. 93.
19. See 'Bhagat Singh and His Comrades' an article by Ajoy Ghosh in *New Age*, 22 March, 1931.
20. See an article, 'Remembering Bhagat Singh' by Bimal Prasad in the *Mainstream*, 28 March, 1981.
21. See Virendra Sandhu, *Amar Shaheed Bhagat Singh*, Delhi, 1974, p. 1.
22. Sardar Arjan Singh had three sons. Sardar Kishan Singh, Sardar Ajit Singh and Sardar Swaran Singh.
23. Transcript of interview with Jai Dev Gupta, Nehru Memorial Museum and Library, New Delhi.
24. *Ibid.*
25. Virendra Sandhu, *op. cit.*, p. 1.
26. His elder brother Sardar Jagat Singh was a student in the same school.
27. Virendra Sandhu, *op. cit.*, pp. 7-8.
28. Quoted in Gurdev Singh Deol, *Shaheed Bhagat Singh: A Biography,* Patiala, 1969, p. 14.
29. *Ibid.*
30. Transcript of interview with Jai Dev Gupta, N.M.M.L.
31. It was indeed a patriotic movement against the British *Raj*.
32. No *appeal*, no *vakil*, no *dalil*, had become a common saying amongst the people of the Punjab.
33. The situation could easily be brought under control without resorting to firing.
34. Centers of education.
35. The initiative in this regard was taken by Gandhi, C.R. Das, Bhai Parmanand, Lajpat Rai and others.
36. This institution was affiliated to the Punjab Qaumi Vidya Pith, Lahore.

37. Bhagat Singh left the National College in 1924 when he was hardly seventeen years old.
38. Transcript of interview with Chhabil Das, Nehru Memorial Museum and Library, New Delhi.
39. *Ibid.*
40. Virendra Sandhu, *op. cit.*, p. 14.
41. Transcript of interview with Jai Dev Gupta, *op. cit.*
42. Ajoy Kumar Ghosh, *Bhagat Singh and His Comrades*, Bombay, 1945, pp. 1-4.

2 Emergence of Bhagat Singh

Bhagat Singh evolved a novel method of propagating the ideology of his party amongst the masses. His frequent tours at various obscure places in north India afforded him an ample opportunity of meeting common people and telling them the line of action he and his associates had undertaken and also the kind of government and the society India would have after the British had left our country. Even he used the jail and the court where he was lodged as a political prisoner and where he was tried as the places for propaganda of his political ideology. He was a staunch believer of socialism. Like Mazzini, Garibaldi and Cavour, he always held that it was the martyr's blood that ripened ideas. He was a voracious reader and had studied all kinds of literature on Marxism.

Bhagat Singh's political ideology revolves round a very pertinent point i.e. his faith in God. What were the reasons for adopting a particular kind of faith which had taken him far away from the belief in the supreme being. A true and sincere revolutionary in the best traditions of Marx, Engels and Lenin, he explains his belief with a comprehensive straight forwardness in his views and reasoning in an article 'Why I am an Atheist.'[1]

In the first place, I have altogether failed to comprehend as to how undue pride or vain gloriousness could ever stand in the way of a man in believing in God. I can refuse to recognise the greatness of a really great man provided I have also achieved a certain amount of popularity without deserving it or without having possessed the qualities really essential or indispensable for the same purpose. That much is conceivable. But in what way can a man believing in God cease believing due to his personal vanity? There are only two ways. The man should either begin to think himself a rival of God or he may begin to believe himself to be God. In neither case can he become a genuine atheist. In the first place, he does not even deny the existence of his rival. In the second case as well he admits the existence of a conscience being behind the scene guiding all the movements of nature. It is of no importance to us whether he thinks the supreme conscious being to be somebody apart from himself. The fundamental is there. His belief is there he is by no means atheist. Well, here I am. I neither belong to the first category nor to the second. I deny the very existence of that Almighty Supreme being. Why I deny it shall be dealt with later on. Here I want to clear one thing, that it is not vanity that has actuated me to adopt the doctrines of atheism. I am neither a rival nor an incarnation nor the Supreme Being Himself. One point is decided, that it is not vanity that has led me to this mode of thinking. Let me examine the facts to disprove this allegation. According to these friends of mine I have grown vain glorious perhaps due to the undue popularity gained during the trials—but Delhi Bomb and Lahore conspiracy cases. Well, let us see if their premises are correct. My atheism is not of so recent origin. I had stopped believing in God when I was an obscure young man, of whose existence may above-mentioned friends were not even aware. At least a college student cannot cherish any sort of undue pride, which may lead him to atheism. Though a favourite with some professors and disliked by certain others, I was never an industrious or a studious boy. I could not get any chance of indulging in such feeling as vanity. I was rather a boy with a very shy nature, who had certain pessimistic dispositions about the future career. And in those days, I was not a perfect atheist. My grandfather under whose influence I was brought up is an orthodox Arya Samajist. An Arya Samajist is anything but an atheist. After finishing my primary education I joined the D.A.V. School of Lahore and stayed in its Boarding House for full one year. There, apart from morning and evening prayers, I used to recite *"Gayatri Mantra"* for hours and hours. I was a perfect devotee in those days. Later on, I began to live with my father. He is a liberal in as much as the orthodoxy of religions is concerned. It was through his teaching that I aspired to devote my life to the cause of freedom. But he is not an atheist. He is a firm believer. He used to encourage me for offering prayers daily. So this is how I was brought up. In the non-cooperation days I joined the National College. It was there that I began to think liberally and discuss and criticise all the religious problems, even about God. But still I was a devout believer. By that time I had began to preserve the unshorn and unclipped long-hair but I could never believe in the mythology and doctrines of Sikhism or any other religion. But I had a firm faith in God's existence.

Later on I joined the revolutionary party. The first leader with whom I came in contact, though not convinced, could not dare to deny the existence of God. Oh my persistent inquiries about God, he used to say, "Pray whenever you want to". Now this is atheism less courage required for the adoption of that creed. The second leader with whom I came in contact was a firm believer. Let me mention his name—respected comrade Sachindra Nath Sanyal, now undergoing life transportation in connection with the Karachi conspiracy case. From the every first page of his famous and only book, "Bandi Jivan" (or Incarcerated Life), the Glory of God is sung vehemently. In the last page of the second part of that beautiful book his mystic– because of vedantism— praises showered upon God form a very conspicuous part of his thoughts. "The Revolutionary leaflet" distributed throughout India on January 28, 1925, was according to the prosecution story the result of his intellectual labour. Now, as is inevitable in the secret work the prominent leader expresses his own views—which are very dear to his person and the rest of the workers have to acquiesce in them——in spite of differences, which they might have. In that leaflet one full paragraph was devoted to praise the Almighty and his rejoicings and doing. That is all mysticism. What I wanted to point out was that the idea of disbelief had not even germinated in the revolutionary party. The famous Kakori martyrs— all four of them—passed their last days in prayers. Ram Prasad Bismil was an orthodox Arya Samajist. Despite his wide studies in the field of Socialism and Communism, Rajen Lahiri could not suppress his desire of reciting hymns of the Upanishads and the Gita. I saw only one man amongst them, who never prayed and used to say, "Philosophy is the outcome of human weakness or limitation of knowledge." He is also undergoing a sentence of transportation for life. But he also never dared to deny the existence of God.

Up to that period I was only a romantic idealist revolutionary. Uptil then we were to follow. Now came the time to shoulder the whole responsibility. Due to the inevitable reaction for some time the very existence of the party seemed impossible. Enthusiastic comrades—nay leaders—began to jeer at us. For some time I was afraid that some day I also might not be convinced of the futility of our own programme. That was a turning point in my revolutionary career. "Study" was the cry that reverberated in the corridors of my mind. Study to enable yourself to face the arguments advanced by opposition. Study to arm yourself with arguments in favour of your cult. I began to study. My previous faith and convictions underwent a remarkable modification. The romance of the violent methods alone which was so prominent amongst our predecessors, was replaced by serious ideas. No more mysticism, no more blind faith. Realism became our cult. Use of force justifiable when restored to as a matter to terrible necessity: non-violence as policy indispensable for all mass movements. So much about methods. The most important thing was the clear conception of the idea for which we were to fight. As there were no important activities in the field of action I got ample opportunity to study various ideals of the world revolution. I studied Bakunin, the anarchist leader, something of Marx, the father of Communism and much of Lenin, Trotsky and other men who had successfully carried out a revolution in their country. They were all atheists. Bakunin's "God and State", though only fragmentary, is an interesting study of this subject. Later still I came across a book entitled 'Common Sense' by Nirlamba Swami. It was only a sort of mystic atheism. This subject became of utmost interest to me. By the end of 1926, I had been convinced as to the baselessness of the theory of existence of an Almighty Supreme being who created, guided and controlled the universe. I had given out this disbelief of mine. I began discussion on the subjects with my friends. I had become a pronounced atheist. But what it meant will presently be discussed.

In May 1927, I was arrested at Lahore. The arrest was a surprise. I was quite unaware of the fact that the police wanted me. All of a sudden while passing through a garden I found myself surrounded by police. To my own surprise, I was very calm at that time. I did not feel any sensation; neither did I experience any excitement. I was taken into police custody. Next day I was taken to the Railway Police lock-up where I was to pass full one month. After many days' conversation with the police officials I guessed that they had some information regarding my connection with the Kakori Party and my other activities in connection with the revolutionary movement. They told me that I had been to Lucknow while the trial was going on there, that I had negotiated a certain scheme about their rescue, that after obtaining their approval, we had procured some bombs, that by way of test one of the bombs was thrown in the crowd on the occasion of Dussehra 1926.They further informed me, in my interest, that if I could give any statement throwing some light on the activities of the revolutionary party, I was not to be imprisoned but on the contrary set free and rewarded even without being produced as an approver in the court. I laughed at the proposal. It was all humbug. People holding ideas like ours do not throw bombs on their own innocent people. One fine morning Mr. Newman, the then Senior Superintendent of C.I.D., came to me. And after much sympathetic talk with me imparted—to him—the extremely sad news that if I did not give any statement as demanded by them, they would be forced to send me up for trial for conspiracy to wage war in connection with Kakori Case and for brutal murders in connexion with Dussehra bomb outrage. And he further informed me that they had evidence enough to get me convicted and hanged. In those who days I believed—though I was quite innocent—the police could do it if they desired. That very day certain police officials began to persuade me to offer my prayers to God regularly both the times. Now I was an atheist. I wanted to settle for myself whether it was in the days of peace and enjoyment alone that I could boast of being an atheist or whether during such hard times as well I could I stick to those principles of mine. After great consideration I decided that I could not lead myself to believe in and pray to god. No, I never did. That was the real test and I came out successful. Never for a moment did I desire to save my neck at the cost of certain other things. So I was a staunch disbeliever: and have ever since been. It was not an easy job to stand that test. 'Belief' softness the hardships, even can make them pleasant. In God man can find very strong consolation and support. Without Him man has to depend upon himself. To stand upon one's own legs amid storms and hurricanes is not a child's play. At such testing moments, vanity—if any—evaporates, and man cannot dare to defy the general beliefs. If he does, then we must conclude that he had got certain other strength than mere vanity. This is exactly the situation now. Judgment is already too well-known. Within a week it is to be pronounced. What is the consolation with the exception of the idea that I am going to sacrifice my life for a cause? A God-believer Hindu might be expecting to be reborn as a king, a Muslim or a Christian might dream of the luxuries to be enjoyed in paradise and the reward he is to get for his sufferings and sacrifices. But what am I to expect? I know the moment the rope is fitted round my neck and rafters removed, from under my feet, that will be the final moment—that will be the last moment. I, or to be more precise, my soul, as interpreted in the metaphysical terminology, shall all be finished there. Nothing further. A short life of struggle with no such magnificent end shall in itself be the reward if I have the courage to take it in that light. That is all, with no selfish motive, or desire to be awarded here or hereafter, quite disinterestedly have I devote my life to the cause of independence, because I could not do otherwise. The day we find a great number of men and women with this psychology who cannot devote themselves to anything else than the service of mankind and emancipation of the suffering humanity; that day shall inaugurate the era of liberty. Not to become a king, nor to gain any other rewards here, or in the next birth or after death in paradise, shall they be inspired to challenge the oppressors, exploiters and tyrants, but to cast off the yoke of serfdom from the next of humanity and to establish liberty and peace shall they tread this—to their individual selves perilous and to their noble selves the only glorious imaginable—path. Is the pride in their noble cause to be misinterpreted as vanity? Who dares to utter such an abominable epithet? To him I say either he is a fool or a knave. Let us forgive him for he cannot realise the depth, the emotion, the sentiment and the noble feelings that surge in the heart. His heart is dead as a mere lump of flesh, his eyes are weak, the evils of other interests having been cast over them. Self-reliance is always liable to be interpreted as vanity. It is sad and miserable but there is no help.

You go and oppose the prevailing faith, you go and criticise a hero, a great man, who is generally believed to be above criticism because he is thought to be infallible, the strength of your argument shall force the multitude to decry you as vain glorious.

This is due to the mental stagnation. Criticism and independent thinking are the two indispensable qualities of revolutionary. Because Mahatmaji is great, therefore, none should criticise him. Because he has risen above, therefore, everything he says—may be in the field of Politics or Religion, Economics or Ethics—is right. Whether you are convinced or not you must say. "Yes, that's true". This mentality does not lead towards progress. It is rather too obviously reactionary.

Because, our forefathers had set up a faith in some supreme being—the Almighty God—therefore, any man who dares to challenge the validity of that faith, or the very existence of the supreme being, he shall have to be called an apostate, a renegade. If his arguments are too sound to be refuted by counter arguments and spirit too strong to be cowed down by the threat of misfortunes that may belief him by the wrath of the Almighty—he shall be decried as vain glorious, his spirit to be denominated as vanity. Then why to waste time in this vain discussion? Why try to argue out the whole thing? This question is coming before the public for the first time, and is being handled in this matter of fact way for the first time, hence this lengthy discussion.

As for the first question, I think I have cleared that it is not vanity that has led me to atheism. My way of argument has proved to be convincing or not, that is to be judged by my readers, not me. I know in the present circumstances my faith in God would have made my life easier, my burden lighter and my disbelief in Him had turned all the circumstances too dry and the situation may assume too harsh a shape. A little bit of mysticism can make it poetical. But I do not want the help of any intoxication to meet my fate. I am a realist. I have been trying to overpower the instinct in me by the help of reason. I have not always been successful in achieving this end. But man's duty is to try and endeavour, success depends upon chance and environments.

As for the second question that if it was not vanity, then there ought to be some reason to disbelieve the old and still prevailing faith of the existence of God. Yes; I come to that now Reason there is. According to me, any man who has got some reasoning power at his command always tries to reason out his environments. Where direct proofs are lacking philosophy occupies the important place. As l have already stated, a certain revolutionary friend used to say that philosophy is the outcome of human weakness. When our ancestors had leisure enough to try to solve out the mystery of this world, its past, present and the future, its whys and wherefores, they having been terribly short of direct proofs, everybody tried to solve the problem in his own way. Hence, we find the wide differences in the fundamentals of various religious creeds, which sometimes assume very antagonistic and conflicting shapes. Not only the Oriental and Occidental philosophies differ, there are differences even amongst various schools of thoughts in each hemisphere. Amongst Oriental religions, the Muslim faith is not at all compatible with Hindu faith. In India alone Buddhism and Jainism are sometimes quite separate from Brahmanism, in which there are again conflicting faiths as Arya Samaj and Sanatan Dharma. Charwak is till another independent thinker of the past ages. He challenged the authority of god in the old times. All these creeds differ from each other on the fundamental question; and everybody considers himself to be on the right. There lies the misfortune. Instead of using the experiments and expressions of the ancient Savants and thinkers as a basis for our future struggle against ignorance and to try to find out a solution to this mysterious problem, we lethargical as we have proved to be raise the hue and cry of faith, unflinching and unwaring faith to their versions and thus are guilty of stagnation in human progress.

Any man who stands for progress has to criticize, disbelieve and challenge every item of the old faith. Item by item he has to reason out every nook and corner of the prevailing faith. If after considerable reasoning one is led to believe in any theory or philosophy, his faith is welcomed. His reasoning can be mistaken, wrong, misled and sometimes fallacious. But he is liable to correction because reason is the guiding star of his life. But mere faith and blind faith is dangerous: it dulls the brain, and makes a man reactionary. A man who claims to be a realist has to challenge the whole of the ancient faith. If it does not stand the onslaught of reason it crumbles down. Then the first thing for him is to shatter the whole down and clear a space for the erection of a new philosophy. This is the negative side. After it begins the positive work in which sometimes some material of the old faith may be used for the purpose of reconstruction. As far as I am concerned, let me admit at the very outset that I have not been able to study much on this point. I had great desire to study the Oriental Philosophy but I could not get any chance or opportunity to do the same. But so far as the negative study is under discussion, I think I am convinced to the extent of questioning the soundness of the old faith. I have been convinced as to non-existence of a conscious supreme being who is guiding and directing the movements of nature. We believe in nature and the whole progressive movement aims at the domination of man over nature for his service. There is no conscious power behind it to direct. This is what our philosophy is.

'As for the negative side, we ask a few questions from the believers'.

(1) If, as you believe, there is an almighty, omnipresent, omniscient and omnipotent god—who created the earth or world, please let me known why did he create it? This world of woes and miseries, a veritable, eternal combination of numberless tragedies: not a single soul being perfectly satisfied.

Pray, don't say that it is his law: If he is bound by any law, he is not omnipotent. He is another slave like ourselves. Please don't say that it is his enjoyment. Nero burnt one Rome. He killed a very limited number of people. He created very few tragedies, all to his perfect enjoyment. And what is his place in history? By what names do the historians mention him? All the venomous epithets are showered upon him. Pages are blackened with invective diatribes condemning Nero, the tyrant, the heartless, the wicked. One Changezkhan sacrificed a few thousand lives to seek pleasure in it and we hate the very name. Then how are you going to justify your almighty, eternal Nero, who has been, and is still causing numberless tragedies every day, every hour and every minute? How do you think to support his misdoings, which surpass those of Changez every single moment? I say why did he create this world—a veritable hell, a place of constant and bitter unrest? Why did the Almighty create man when he had the power not to do it? What is the justification for all this? Do you say to award the innocent sufferers hereafter and to punish the wrong-doers as well? Well, well: How far shall you justify a man who may dare to inflict wounds upon your body to apply a very sort and soothing ointment upon it afterwards? How far the supporters and organisers of the Gladiator Institution were justified in throwing men before the half-starved furious lions to be cared for well looked after if they could survive and could manage to escape death by the wild beasts? That is why I ask. Why did the conscious supreme being created this world and man in it? To seek pleasure? Where then is the difference between him and Nero?

You Mohammedans and Christians: Hindu Philosophy shall still linger on to offer another argument. I ask your what is your answer to the above-mentioned question? You don't believe in previous birth. Like Hindus you cannot advance the argument of previous misdoings of the apparently quite innocent sufferers? I ask you why did the omnipotent labour for six days to create the world through word and each day to say—that all was well call him today. Show him the past history. Make him study the present situation. Let us see if he dares to say, "All is well".

From dungeons of prisons, from the stores of starvation consuming millions upon millions of human being in slums and huts, from the exploited labourers, patiently of say apathetically watching the procedure of their blood being sucked by the Capitalist vampires, and the waste of human energy that will make a man with the least common sense shiver with horror, and from the preference of throwing the surplus of production in oceans rather then to distribute amongst the needy producers—to the places of kings built upon the foundation laid with human bonus.....let him see all this and let him say "All is well". Why and wherefore? That is my question. You are silent. All right then, I proceed.

Well, you Hindus, you say all the present sufferers belong to the class of sinners of the previous births. Good. You say the present oppressors were saintly people in their previous births, hence they enjoy power. Let me admit that your ancestors were very shrewd people, they tried to find out theories strong enough to hammer down all the efforts of reason and disbelief. But let us analyse how far this argument can really stand.

From the point of view of the most famous jurists punishment can be justified only from three or four ends to meet which it is inflicted upon the wrong doer. They are retributive, reformative and deterrent. The retributive theory is now being condemned by all the advanced thinkers. Deterrent theory is also following the same fate. Reformative theory is the only one which is essential, and indispensable for human progress. It aims at returning the offender as a most competent and a peace-loving citizen to the society. But what is the nature of punishment inflicted by god upon men even if we suppose them to be offenders. You say he sends them to be born as a cow, a cat, a tree, a herb or a beast. You enumerate these punishments to be 84 lakh. I ask you what is its reformative effect upon man? How many men have met you who say that they were born as a donkey in previous birth for having committed any sin? None. Don't quote your Puranas. I have no scope to touch your mythologies. Moreover do you know that the greatest sin in this world is to be poor. Poverty is a sin, it is a punishment. I ask you how far would you appreciate a criminologist, a jurist or a legislator who proposes such measures of punishment which shall inevitably force man to commit more offences? Had not your God thought of this or he also had to learn these things by experience, but at the cost of untold sufferings to be borne by humanity? What do you think shall be the fate of a man who has been born in a poor and illiterate family of, say, a *chamar* or a sweeper. He is poor, hence he cannot study. He is hated and shunned by his fellow human beings who think themselves to be his superiors having been born in, say, a higher caste. His ignorance, his poverty and the treatment meted out to him shall harden his heart towards society. Suppose he commits a sin, who shall bear the consequences? God, he or the learned ones of the society? What about the punishment of those people who were deliberately kept ignorant by the haughty and egotist Brahmans and who had to pay the penalty by bearing the steam of being led (not lead) in their ears for having heard a few sentences of your Sacred Books of learning—the Vedas? If they committed any offence—who was to be responsible for them and who was to bear the brunt? My dear friends. These theories are the inventions of the privileged ones. They justify their usurped power, riches and superiority by the help of these theories. Yes: it was perhaps Upton Sinclair, that wrote at some place, that just make a man a believer in immorality and then rob him of all his riches and possessions. He shall help you even in that ungrudgingly. The coalition amongst the religious preachers and possessors of power brought forth jails, gallows, knouts and these theories.

I ask why your omnipotent God, does not stop every man when he is committing any sin or offence? He can do it quite easily. Why did he not kill war lords or kill the fury of war in them and thus avoid the catastrophe hurled down on the head of humanity by the Great War? Why does he not just produce a certain sentiment in the mind of the British people to liberate India? Why does he not infuse the althuistic enthusiasm in the hearts of all capitalists to forego their rights of personal possessions of means of production and thus redeem the whole labouring community—nay the whole human society from the bondage of Capitalism. You want to reason out the practicability of socialist theory. I leave it for your Almighty to enforce it. People recognise the merits of socialism in as much as the general welfare is concerned. They oppose it under the pretext of its being impracticable. Let the Almighty step in and arrange everything in an orderly fashion. Now don't try to advance round about arguments, they are out of order. Let me tell you, British rule is here not because God wills it but because they possess power and we do not dare to oppose them. Not that it is with the help of God that they are keeping us under their subjection but it is with the help of guns, and rifles, bombs and bullets, police and militia and our apathy that they are successfully committing the most deplorable sin against society—the outrageous exploitation of one nation by another. Where is god? What is he doing? Is he enjoing all these woes of human race? A Nero; A change (Changez): down with him:

Do you ask me how I explain the origin of this world and origin of man? All right I tell you, Charles Darwin has tried to throw some light on the subject. Study him. Read Soham Swami's "Commonsense". It shall answer your question to some extent. This is a phenomenon of nature. The accidental mixture of different substances in the shape of nebulace produced this earth. When? Consult history. The same process produced animals and in the long run man. Read Darwin's 'Origin of Species'. And all the later progress is due to man's constant conflict with nature and his efforts to override it. This is the briefest possible explanation of this phenomenon.

Your other argument may be just to ask why a child is born blind or lame if not due to his deeds committed in the previous birth? This problem has been explained a way by biologists as more biological phenomenon. According to them the whole burden rests upon the shoulders of the parents who may be conscious or ignorant of their own deeds led to mutilation of the child previous to its birth.

Naturally you may ask another question—though it is quite childish in essence. If no God existed, how did the people come to believe him? My answer is clear and brief. As they came to believe in ghosts, and evil spirits; the only difference is that belief in God is almost universal and the philosophy well developed. Unlike certain of the radicals I would not attribute its origin to the ingenuity of the exploiters who wanted to keep the people under their subjection by preaching the existence of a supreme being and then claming an authority and sanction from him for their privileged positions. Though I do not differ with them on the essential point that all faiths, religions, creed and such other institutions became in turn the mere supporters of the tyrannical and exploiting institutions, men and classes. Rebellion against king is always a sin according to every religion.

As regards the origin of God, my own idea is that having realised the limitations of man, his weaknesses and shortcoming having been taken into consideration, God was brought into imaginary existence to encourage man to face boldly all the trying circumstances, to meet all dangers manfully and to check and restrain his outbursts in prosperity and affluence. God both with his private laws and parental generasity was imagined and painted in greater details. He was to serve as a deterrent factor when his fury and private laws were discussed so that man may not become a danger to society. He was to serve as a father, mother, sister and brother, friend and helpers when his parental qualifications were to be explained. So that when man be in great distress having been betrayed and deserted by all friends he may find consolation in the idea that an ever true friend was still there to help him, to support him and that he was Almighty and could to anything. Really that was useful to the society in the primitive age. The idea of God is helpful to men in distress.

Society has to fight out this belief as well as was fought the idol worship and the narrow conception of religion. Similarly, when men tries to stand on his own legs, and becomes a realist he shall have to throw the faith aside, and to face manfully all the distress, trouble, in which the circumstances may throw him. That is exactly my state of affairs. It is not my vanity, my friends. It is my mode of thinking that has made me an atheist. I don't know whether in my case belief in God and offering of daily prayers which I consider to be most selfish and degraded act on the part of man, whether these prayers can prove to be helpful or they shall make my case worse still. I have read of atheists facing all troubles quite boldly, so I am trying to stand like a man with an erect head to the last; even on the gallows.

Let us see how I carry on: one friend asked me to pray. When informed of my atheism, he said, "During your last days you will begin to believe". I said, No, dear sir, it shall not be; I will think that to be an act of degradation and demoralisation on my part. For selfish motives I am not going to pray. Readers and friends, "is this vanity"? If it is, I stand for it.

Durga Das Khanna reminisced thus about the mental make-up and working of mind of Sardar Bhagat Singh...Bhagat Singh was one of the finest characters I have come across in my life. He was an intellectual who had studied various systems of social order that had prevailed in the world from time to time and had made up his mind as to what the freedom movement in this country should aspire to achieve. It was a treat to engage in a dialogue with him right from the first meeting. I found that he had very clear views on life both as it was under British rule and as to what it should be in free India. Often, he pointed out that it was the common man who was worst hit by British rule.

I remember, when Bhagat Singh would refer to some of the brutalities committed by the British, tears tolled down his cheeks.... There were several other occasions when we discussed the shame of continuing to be ruled by a handful of foreigners and submit to the economic exploitation of our people by them. We would fight for a social system which would not allow any exploitation of man by man...We decided to give socio-economic content also to the concept of freedom which suited the genius of our people and the conditions prevailing here generally.[2]

Bhagat Singh did not believe in individual terrorism as such. He was of the opinion that if they were going to kill people merely because they were English or their henchmen, it would serve no useful purpose. But he was of the view that it might become obligatory for them to do so in order to counteract British repression and terrorism. They might be compelled to resort to it. In that the case, he opined, 'We should meet force with force'.

He made this clear in his statement in connection with the Assembly Bomb Case. What was intended was to make the deaf hear. He indeed had no intention of killing any one in the Assembly. He only threw live bombs on empty benches and no wanton spilling of blood was intended with this kind of action.

Bhagat Singh, Sukhdev, Rajguru and their associates seemed to have been very clear in their minds that it was an armed insurrection on a mass scale for which they had to prepare the country to fight with full strength against the British Raj. They thus wanted to take a realistic view of things and considered it inadvisable to insist on non-violence of Mahatma Gandhi's connection at all times and in all circumstances. They, therefore, were not happy the way the withdraw the Non-co-operation Movements on the eruption of violence by some Congress volunteers at Chauri Chaura in 1922. This was, according to them, a betrayal of the people who had been assured that the non-violent *satyagraha* was bound to usher in *swaraj* within a year...Bhagat Singh pooh-poohed the idea of non-violence as the sole weapon in the country's armoury. But with Gandhi, it was a matter of creed and a faith in which he had firm belief and practised it in his political movements.

Jai Dev Gupta reminisced thus :

'Bhagat Singh was impressed very much by Gandhi's mass awakening. He, however, disagreed with the means of non-violence. He believed that independence could never be won by folding hands. It had to be wrested from unwilling hands. The whole British Empire was based on India's slavery. So how the British could leave it by Gandhian method of negotiation. No freedom is worthwhile unless millions make supreme sacrifice for it'.[3]

He seemed to be a determined man who was destined to do some thing great. He did not speak about the secret party which he had formed.... He was a very different man. He was such a person that if he wanted his right hand to do something, he would not tell the left hand, what the right hand was doing. And those people who were not concerned with their affairs, he would not utter a word even, whatever intimacy might be there...Outwardly, he looked like an ordinary youth. In jail, I found him an absolutely changed man. It seemed that he was a seer, a prophet having a halo round his face. He received us standing straight and casting a kind look at all of us. His voice was clear and showed no seemed when he spoke to us after such long time[4].

Bhagat Singh was fully convinced that the land belonged to the tiller of the soil and not to the actual owner. In this regard, he was greatly influenced by the well-known book, Resurrection by Leo Tolstoy who was a big landlord himself. He distributed all his land amongst the peasantry who tilled the land. Greatly affected by this kind of model of land allotment and its distribution amongst the deprived and landless class. Bhagat Singh gave the idea that the land owned by his father must be distributed among the tillers. He very well understood their economic plight and the standard of living which in most cases was below the line of poverty and want. One day he talked to his father about this kind of decision that the tillers were real masters and they were exploiting the hard labour of these people. Their condition, he explained, was pitiable since generations. His father listened to his son patiently, but he got angry with him and asked him who would give him the necessaries of life for the members of his family if land was given away to the cultivators. Thus, the noble and grand idea could not materialise.

Bhagat Singh did not believe in the efficacy of any kind of appeal to the British authorities. He well understood that this in the political organisation of which he was a member. His important letter addressed to his comrades was smuggled out of jail and was published in the issue of the *Punjab Kesari* on 2 February, 1931. Curiously enough, Bhagat Singh has made two references to Mahatma Gandhi and levelled criticism of his method and approach to win independence for India.

Bhagat Singh wrote : I would like to say something on the object and means of our party. It is named ' Socialist Republican', its object is to establish a socialist society. The difference between the Congress and our party is that the Congress after the power has passed from the hands of the British to the hands of the Indians, will rest on its oars, but our object is to bring power to one and all, who are committed to socialism. For this the toiling masses have to be mobilized, because for them it won't matter much if Lord Reading is replaced by Sir Tej Bahadur Sapru or Purshottamdass Thakurdas. Our Party means all this by complete independence. Even during the Lahore Congress (where the Congress ceremonially passed the resolution of compete independence) the Mahatma said: "We have not banged and bolted the door of compromise, it is still open". This means that he was aware of the fact that this type of struggle could end only in some sort of compromise. His aim was a half-hearted advocacy of a compromise. It is this half-heartedness that we abhor".

Bhagat Singh goes on : "To youths I say, they should enlist as workers in this cause, as for leaders we have them galore. Our Party does not need leaders. If you are a wordly man, a family man, do not come to us. However, if you are sympathetic to our cause, help us in other ways. Only strictly disciplined people can take a movement forward. It is not necessary, for the party to work in secret for these objectives. We may propagate our ideas everywhere through leaflets, pamphlets, booklets, small libraries, lectures, private conversations".

Bhagat Singh wanted that his party should have a military wing. "Let me make myself clear. It is said that I am a terrorist, but in reality, I have all along been a revolutionary with definite ideals and ideology. I may be blamed as they as they blame Ramprasad Bismal that the condemned cell wrought a change in his ideology, but this is not true. I am the same man as I used to be, and have the same ideas. It is my considered opinion that bombs cannot serve our purpose. This is proved by the history of the Hindustan Socialists Republican Association. Throwing bombs is not only useless, but is often harmful as well. They are to be used on certain occasions only. Our chief aim should be to mobilise the toiling masses. The military wing should collect material for war for use on special occasions."

Bhagat Singh concluded his letter thus: "Finally, I would like to appeal to the youth to work feryantly for the established of a socialist republic. If they carry on the struggle relentlessly, then they can attain the objectives, 'not within a year' but after heavy sacrifices and passing through very grueling trials".

Bhagat Singh had much love and respect for his comrades. Indeed, he sincerely believed in the effectiveness of revolutionary methods and could sacrifice any thing dear–even his life for the sake of his motherland. At the time of hanging, he is said to have remarked to the British Deputy Commissioner who as a rule was a witness to these executions, 'Well, Mr. Magistrate, you are fortunate to be able today to see how Indian revolutionaries can embrace death with pleasure for the sake of their supreme ideal.'

The political ideology of Bhagat Singh is based on the fundamental principles of bravery, fearlessness and firm determination. The element of fear or cowardice was never shown. It is quite clear soon after the murder of Saunders. A suggestion was made that Sardar Bhagat Singh and his associates in the murder should escape to some foreign land so that they could not be intercepted. This kind of advice was never acceptable to him. He wished to live in India and carry on the unfinished task.

An other example of his fearlessness was shown at the time when he threw a bomb in the Central Legislative Assembly. He could escape but he did not. He knew that the punishment under the British region would be very severe. And for all this, he was fully prepared to suffer, as the cause of the country was ever dear to him.

Another important writing of Bhagat Singh is 'An Introduction to the Dreamland' a poetical work written by his 'noble friend', Lala Ram Saran Das, a revolutionary who was sentenced to transportation for life in 1915. 'Writing more like a poet than a political-philosophical commentator, Bhagat Singh first establishes his own generations' continuity with the old revolutionaries from whom it imbibed the spirit of nationalism, love of the people and the capacity to sacrifice. He then brings out his philosophical, political and ideological differences with them'[5].

My noble friend, Lala Ram Saran Das, has asked me to write an introduction to his poetical work, 'The Dreamland'. I am neither a poet nor a literature, neither am I a journalist nor a critic. Hence, by no stretch of imagination can I find the justification of the demand. But the circumstances in which I am placed do not afford any opportunity of discussing the question with the author arguing back and forth, and thereby do not leave me any alternative but to comply with the desire of my friend.

As I am not a poet I am not going to discuss it from that point of view. I have absolutely no knowledge of meter, and do not even know whether judged from material standard it would prove correct. Not being a literateur I am not going to discuss it with a view of assigning to it its right place in the national literature.

I being a political worker can at the utmost discuss it only from that point of view. But here also one factor is making my work practically impossible or at least very difficult. As a rule the introduction is always written by a man who is at one with the author on the contents of the work. But, here the case is quite different. I do not see eye to eye with my friend on all the matters. He was aware of the fact that I differed from him on many vital points. Therefore, my writing is not going to be and introduction at all. It can at the utmost amount to a criticism, and its place will be at the end and not in the beginning of the book.

In the political field 'The Dreamland' occupies a very important place. In the prevailing circumstances it is filling up a very important gap in the movement. As a matter of fact all the political movements of our country that have hitherto played any important role in our modern history had been lacking the ideal at the achievement of which they aimed. Revolutionary movement is no exception. In spite of all my efforts, I could not find any revolutionary party that had clear ideas as to what they were fighting for, with the exception. Of the Ghadar Party which having been inspired by the USA form of government clearly stated that they wanted to replace the existing government by a Republican form of government. All other parties consisted of men who had but one idea, i.e. to fight against the alien rulers. That idea is quite laudable but cannot be termed a revolutionary idea. We must make it clear that revolution does not merely mean an upheaval or a sanguinary strife. Revolution necessarily implies the programme of systematic reconstruction of society on new and better adapted basis, after complete destruction of the existing state of affairs (i.e., regime).

In the political field the liberals wanted some reform under the present government, while the extremists demanded a bit more, and were prepared to employ radical means for the same purpose. Amongst the revolutionaries they had always been in favour of extreme methods with one idea, i.e., of overthrowing the foreign domination. No doubt, there had been who were in favour of extorting some reforms through those means. All these movements cannot rightly be designated as revolutionary movements.

But, Lala Ram Saran Das is the first revolutionary recruited formally in the Punjab by a Bengali absconder in 1908. Since then he had been in touch with the revolutionary movements and finally joined the Ghadar Party but retaining his old ideas that those people held about the ideal of their movement. It has another interesting fact to add to its beauty and value. Lala Ram Saran Das was sentenced to death in 1915, and the sentence was later on commuted to life transportation. Today sitting in the condemned cells myself, I can let the readers know as authoritatively that the life imprisonment is comparatively a far harder lot than that of death. Lala Ram Saran Das had actually to undergo fourteen years of imprisonment. It was in some southern jail that he wrote this poetry. The then psychology and mental struggle of the author has stamped its impressions upon the poetry and makes it all the more beautiful and interesting. He had been strugging hard against some depressing mood before he had decided to write it. In the days when many of his comrades had been let off on undertakings and the temptation had been very strong for everyone and for him, too, and when the sweet and painful memories of wife and children had added more to the longing for liberty, he had to struggle hard against the demoralising effect of these things, and had directed attention to this work. Hence, we find the sudden outburst in the opening paragraph:

> *"Wife, children, friends that me surround*
> *Were poisonous snakes all round".*

He discusses philosophy in the beginning. This philosophy is the backbone of all the revolutionary movements of Bengal as well as of the Punjab. I differ from him on this point very widely. His interpretation of the universe is teleological and metaphysical; while I am a materialist and my interpretation of the phenomenon would be casual. Nevertheless, it is by no means out of place or out of date. The general ideas that are prevailing in our country are more in accordance with those expressed by him. To fight that depressing mood he resorted to prayers as is evident that the whole of the beginning of the book is devoted to god. His praise, his definition, belief in god is the outcome of mysticism, which is the natural consequence of depression. This world is 'Maya' or 'Mithya', dream or a fiction, is clear mysticism, which has been originated and developed by Hindu sages of old ages, such as Shankaracharya and others. But in the materialist philosophy this mode of thinking has got absolutely no place. But this mysticism of the author is by no means ignoble or deplorable. It has its own beauty and charm. The ideas are encouraging just look:

"Be a foundation-stone obscure,
And on thy breast cheerfully bear
The architecture vast and huge,
In suffering find true refuge.
Envy not the plastered top-stone,
On which all wordly praise is thrown." etc. etc.

From my personal experience I can safely assert that in the secret work, when a man constantly leads a risky life, 'without hope and without fear'. 'Always prepared to die unknown, unhonoured and unsung', then, he cannot but fight the personal temptations and desires by this sort mysticism which is by no means demoralising. The next thing he deals with is the mentality of revolutionary. Lala Ram Saran Das was the member of the revolutionary party, which was held responsible for many a violent deed. But this by no means proves that revolutionaries are blood-thirsty monsters, seeking pleasure in destruction.

Read :—

"If need be, outwardly be wild,
But in thy heart be always mild
Hiss if need be, but do not bite,
Love in thy heart and outside fight. etc., etc.

Destruction is not only essential but indispensable for construction. The revolutionaries have to adopt it as a necessary item of their programme, and the philosophy of violence and non-violence is beautifully described in the above lines. Lenin said to Gorky once that he could not hear music which upset his whole nervous system and used to feel a desire to pat the heads of the artists. "But", added he, 'This is not the time to pat the heads. The hands descend now to smash the skulls, though our ultimate aim is the elimination of all sorts of violence." This is truly how the revolutionaries feel when they have to resort to violent means as a terrible necessity.

Next the author deals with the problem concerning the various conflicting religious. He tries to conciliate them just as all the nationalists try to do. His method of dealing with the question is lengthy and round about, though on my part I would have dismissed it with one sentence of Karl Marx that "Religion is opium for the masses."

Lastly comes the most important part of his poetry where he deals with the future society which we all long to create. But I like to clear one thing at the very outset. "The Dreamland" is a veritable utopia. The author has very candidly admitted it in the title. He does not pretend to have written a scientific thesis on the subject. The title 'Dreamland' makes it clear enough. But utopias play undoubtedly a very important role in social progress. Without St. Simon, Fourier and Robert Owen and their theories there would have been no scientific Marxian socialism. Lala Ram Saran Das's utopia occupies the same place when our work will realise the importance of systematising the philosophy of their movement and of framing a scientific outlook of the movement, then this book will be very useful to them.

I have marked that the mode of expression is crude one. The ideas of the existing society have in no way left him untouched while dealing with his utopia.

"Giving of alms to those who need".

In the future society i.e., the Communist society that we want to build, we are not going to establish charitable institutions, but there shall be no needy and poor, and no alms giving and alms-taking. In spite of this discrepancy the question has been dealt with in a very beautiful way.

The general outline discussed by him is very the same as that of the scientific socialism. But there are things which one has to oppose or contradict or to be more precise, to amend. For instance, in a footnote under stanza 427, he writes that public servants have to work in farms, or say, factories for four hours daily to earn their living. But this is again utopian and impracticable. It is rather the outcome of repulsion of the existing order where the public servants are paid unduly very high. As a matter of fact the Bolshevists even had to recognise that mental work also is as productive a labour as the manual labour. And in the future society when the relation of various elements shall be adjusted on the basis of equality, the producers as well as the distributors shall be considered equally important. You cannot expect a sailor to stop his ship and land every twenty-four hours to do his four hours daily labour to earn his livelihood; or a scientist to leave his laboratory and his experiment (work) to do his quota in the field. Both of are doing very productive labour. The only difference that the socialist society experts is that the mental workers shall no longer be regarded superior to the manual workers.

Lala Ram Saran Das's idea about free education is really worth considering, and the socialist government has adopted some what the same course in Russia.

His discussion about crime is really the most advanced school of thought. Crime is the most serious social problem which needs a very tactful treatment. He has been in jail for the better part of his life. He has got the practical experience. At one place he employs the typical jail terms, 'the light labour, the medium labour and the hard labour,' etc. Like all other socialists he suggests that instead of retribution, i.e., retaliation, the reformative theory should form the basis of punishment. Not to punish but to reclaim should be the guiding principle of the administration of justice. Jails should be reformatories and not veritable hells. In this connection the readers should study the Russian prison system.

While dealing with Militia he discusses war as well. In my opinion war as an institution shall only occupy a few pages in the encyclopaedia then, and war materials shall adorn the galleries in the museums, because in that society there shall be no conflicting or diverse interests that cause war.

At the almost we can say that war shall have to be retained as an institution for the transitional period. We can easily understand if we take the example of the present day Russia. There is the dictatorship of the proletariate at present. They want to establish a socialist society. Meanwhile, they have to maintain an army to defend themselves against the capitalist society. But the war-aims would be different. Imperialist designs shall no more actuate our dreamland, people to wage wars. There shall be no more war trophies. The revolutionary armies shall march to other lands not to rule or loot the people, but to pull the parasitic rulers down from their thrones and stop their bloodsucking exploitation and thus to liberate the toiling masses. But there shall not be the primitive national or racial hatred to goad our men to fight.

World federation is the most popular and immediate object of all the free thinking people, and the author has well dilated on the subject, and his criticism of the so-called League of Nations is beautiful.

In a footnote under stanza 571 (572) the author touches though briefly the question of methods. He says, "Such a kingdom cannot be brought about by physical violent revolutions. It cannot be forced upon society from without. It must grow from within... This can be brought about by the gradual process of evolution, by educating the masses on the lines mentioned above", etc. This statement does not in itself contain any discrepancy. It is quite correct; but having not been fully explained, is liable to create some misunderstanding or worse still a confusion. Does it mean that Lala Ram Saran Das has realised the futility of the cult of force? Has he become an orthodox believer in non-violence? No, it does not mean that.

Let me explain what the above quoted statement amounts to. The revolutionaries know better than anybody else that the socialist society cannot be brought about by violent means, but that it should grow and evolve from within. The author suggests education as the only weapon to be employed. But, every body can easily realise that the present government here or, as a matter of fact, all the capitalist governments are not only not going to help any such effort, but on the contrary suppress it mercilessly. What will his 'evolution' achieve? We, the revolutionaries are striving to capture power in out hands, and to organise a revolutionary government which should employ all its resources for mass education, as is being done in Russia today.

After capturing power, peaceful methods shall be employed for constructive work, force shall be employed to crush the obstacles. If that is what the author means, then we are at one. And I am confident that it is exactly this what he means.

I have discussed the book at great length. I have rather criticised it. But, I am not going to ask any alteration in it, because this has got its historical value. These were the ideas of 1914-15 revolutionaries.

I strongly recommend this book to young men in particular, but with a warning. Please do not read it to follow blindly and take for granted what is written in it. Read it, criticise it, think over it, try to formulale your own ideas with its help.

Bahgat Singh's revolutionaries ideas were always clearly articulated and they were undoubtedly brilliantly expounded at various levels. Whether he talked to a colleague, wrote something, gave a statement, corresponded with his relatives or government officials and last but not the least, planned to perform any kind of political action, he had full clarity in his mind and this is the reason that his performance at all levels was unquestionably meticulous in its nature. He indeed took particular care to be clear and distinct in his exposition for he was fully aware that the youths working for revolutionary task had 'all along been either deliberately or due to sheer ignorance, misrepresented and misunderstood'. He in fact had the programme of telling the people about the specific model of his approach to the complex political, social and economic problems facing the society.

In fact, the basic ideological formulations of Bhagat Singh were made in the early period of his incarceration on the basis of his earlier reading and thinking and he had made a great deal of progress in this respect in the pre-1929 period. Moreover, he had read Karl Marx's Capital in addition to other Marxist, socialist and revolutionary literature. This is not to deny that continuous development occurred in the thinking of the revolutionaries due to fresh experiences, study or discussion. But while those who were in jail accomplished all this inside the jail, others who escaped arrest did so outside[6].

In the Manifesto of the HSRA, the definition of the word 'revolution' has been clarified. This ideas contained in this kind of model clearly depict a phenomenon which was a guideline for those who volunteered to function for this political philosophy in order to bring a revolution. Upheavals have always been a terror to holders of power and privilege. (But) Revolution is a phenomenon which nature loves and without which there can be no progress either in nature or in human affairs. Revolution is not a philosophy of despair or a creed of desperadoes. Revolution may be anti-God but is certainly not anti-man. It is a vital, living force which is indicative of eternal conflict between the Old and the New. There is no concord, no symphony, no rhythm without Revolution. 'The music of the spheres' of which poets have sung, would remain an unreality if a ceaseless Revolution were to be eliminated from the space. Revolution is Law, Revolution is Order and Revolution is the Truth.

It is an open secret about the political philosophy of the revolutionary youths that they were not bothered about disorder, chaos or anarchy, which might be a glaring phenomenon during the revolutionary upsurge. The Revolutionary,[7] a publication of the HRA made it quite clear, 'Chaos is necessary to the birth of a new star and the birth of life is accompanied by agony and pain'.

The goal of achieving the basis of a society of socialistic pattern was based on firm principles and determination. In fact, this kind of thinking was the result of consistent study of revolutionary literature. Bhagat Singh had deep linkage with the libraries equipped with revolutionary literature.

It is evident that he had greatly helped them in collection of books on revolutionary theme, viz., on Russia, Ireland and Italy. J.N. Sanyal has made as assessment of Bhagat Singh's intellectual capacity thus. 'Bhagat Singh was an extremely well-read man and his special sphere of study was socialism... Though socialism was his special subject, he had deeply studied the history of the Russian revolutionary movement from its beginning in the early 19th century to the October Revolution of 1917. It is generally believed that very few in India could be compared to him in the knowledge of this special subject. The economic experiments in Russia under the Bolshevik regime also greatly interested him'.[8]

Besides, life in jail was full of a busy schedule. The idea was not to waste the best moments of life in idle gossips and frivolous thinking. Bhagat Singh did utilise his time in accordance with a set programme which made him busy in using his pen for writing his *Autobiography, The Ideal of Socialism, The Door to Death and The Revolutionary Movement of India.* It is indeed a strange coincidence that all these manuscripts have been lost.

So far as the work of HSRA amongst the masses is concerned, it seems evident that it could not make much headway in this regard. It could not lead them in class struggles. The lack of support from the people greatly affected the organization both politically and economically. Under these circumstances any kind of concerted action became difficult. Throughout 1930 not a single dramatic action could be organised. All the carefully prepared plans of Chandrashekhar Azad came to nothing.

By the end of 1920 the dominant political party on the Indian scene was the Indian National Congress which functioned under the leadership of stalwarts like Mahatma Gandhi, Motilal Nehru, C. Rajagopalachari, J.M. Sen Gupta, Dr. Rajendra Prasad, Jawaharlal Nehru, Maulana Abul Kalam Azad and others. At the national scene the HSRA had given a parallel political programme against the Gandhian leadership, his technique and principles. Whereas the Congress could mobilise the masses in their two all-India movements and gained better stature along with the success in some ways, the HSRA could not influence the people beyond north India. More or less its activities were confined to a few prominent towns of the Punjab and the United Provinces. Yet, with all their great popularity in 1929, 1930 and 1931,they failed to provide an alternative leadership to Gandhi. Of course, they failed to achieve their aim of establishing revolutionary socialist hegemony over the national movement or to give it a revolutionary turn.

Bhagat Singh wrote in a message from the prison: "The peasants have to liberate themselves not only from foreign yoke but also from the yoke of landlords and capitalists." His message of 3 March, 1931 was even more explicit: the struggle in India would continue so long as "a handful of exploiters go on exploiting the labour of the common people for their own ends. It matters little whether these exploiters are purely British capitalists, or British and Indians in alliance, or ever purely Indians."

It may be noted that the revolutionary terrorists did not make a detailed class analysis of Indian society. There was no concrete analysis of the rural society; no discussion of the structure of Indian capitalism or its complex relationship with imperialism. They even failed to draw a clear distinction between the landlords, zamindars, and money-lenders and the industrial capitalists. It seems that to them capitalism was the epitome as well as the symbol of economic exploitation. What stands out, however, is their firm grasp of the class approach to society, their commitment to socialism, their anti-imperialism, and their recognition of the leading role of the working class. It was, therefore, not fortuitous that the overwhelming majority of the revolutionary terrorists turned to Marxism and Communism once their own movement reached a dead end.[9]

Basically, their failure can be expressed in a series of contradictions between their ideology and their work. While in theory they were committed to socialism, in practice they could not go beyond nationalism. While in theory they desired mass action and armed struggle, in practice they could not rise above terrorist or individual action. While in theory they wanted to base their movement on the masses—the peasants and workers in practice they could only appeal to the urban lower middle class or petty bourgeois youth. While in theory they wanted to create and lead a mass movement, in practice they remained a small band of heroic youth. While in theory their small organisation was to serve as a "foco", a cell around which would gather the rising revolutionary forces of the country, in practice they found it difficult and in the end impossible even to maintain the integrity of the original group itself.[10]

On the whole, the revolutionaries believed in the ideology of propagating their political creed and philosophy by means of consistent propaganda either by deed or by sacrifice, even of precious life, whenever a challenge of serious nature was to be faced. This kind of model in their thinking and practice resulted into early death of a few prominent revolutionaries who were either shot dead or sent to gallows under the existing British law. Others were arrested and convicted for various terms of imprisonments. 'One of their major mistakes lay in thinking that revolution could be initiated by a handful of young men in a period when the bourgeois nationalist leadership yet retained vigour enough to fight against imperialism though by non-revolutionary means.'[11]

While he was in Central Jail, Lahore, Bhagat Singh scribbled something from the writings of Plato, Aristotle, Socrates, Hobes, Marx, Mill, Engels, Mark Twain, Rabindranath Tagore, Rousseau and other renowned writers of the time in his personal diary, which is now available in the Nehru Memorial Museum and Library, New Delhi. The themes he covered in his beautiful handwriting are diversified viz., these are on freedom from poverty, orgin of the institution of family, savegery, development of civilisation, marriage as an institution and its deficiencies;

power of coercion; origin of the state; religion; benevolent despotism; British rule in India; liberty and its concept amongst English people; monarch and concept of monarchy; natural and civil rights; right of labour; anarchism; condition of labour class; morality; hunger; freedom; alms; liberty; free thought; oppression; martyrdom; charity; prison and the prisoner; death; child labour; capitalism; social institutions; revolution and classes; democracy; reforms; aims of scocialism; alms of world revolution; man and machinery; imperialism; dictatorship; bourgeois democracy; concept of leadership; arbitrariness; political party; aims of Communists; tacties and strategy; Marxism vs Socialism; law of justice; kinds of law; political crimes and punishments; foreign subjection; life and education; truth, crime and criminals; production and distribution; theory of Divine Right of Kings; French Revolution; Constitution of free India; untouchable; India and China; rural and urban problems; Arya Samaj and last but not the least various kinds of statistics about India.[12]

Although there is no independent comment of Bhagat Singh on these writings, yet it clearly indicates the interest he had taken in the writings of these eminent philosophers, thinkers and writers. He indeed scribbled only those ideas, which he thought would be applicable to the society he had in mind. It also indicates his cherished desire to value such ideas and put them into practice in a kind of set-up which would be indigenous in every respect and in which he dignity of each and every human being would be maintained. This kind of model must build a state of his dream on a better social, cultural, political, economic and constitutional footing.

It is indeed a remarkable phenomenon to record that Bhagat Singh's morale, spirit and courage remained high till the last day of his life in the jail. He had no regrets for what he had done for the country. He was not to apologise for his acts. He even did not allow his father to engage a lawyer for him. He informed his father on 26 April, 1929 when he was lodged in Delhi jail: 'I have learnt that you came here and talked to somebody about engaging a lawyer...There is no need for a lawyer etc....' Not only that. Bhagat Singh and his associates openly boycotted the proceedings of the Tribunal in the Lahore Conspiracy case. They did not recognise it a proper court of law. Time and again, they were forcibly taken upto the main gate of the jail, but thereafter they did not budge even an inch to appear in the court. The police expressed its helplessness to drag them further. Indeed, this king of boldness and determination were rare in the history of the revolutionary movement in India.

Bhagat Singh sums up the philosophy of his life in a romantic poetic couplet.

Tuje zibha karne ki khushi,
Aur mujhe marne ka shauq,
Meri bhi marzi wohi hai,
Jo mere sayyad ki hai.[13]

REFERENCES

1. Bhagat Singh, *Why I Am An Atheist*, Delhi, 1979, p. 9ff.
2. Transcript of Interview with Durga Das Khanna, N.M.M.L.
3. Transcript of Interview with Jai Dev Gupta, *op. cit.*
4. *Ibid.*
5. See *Introduction* by Bipan Chandra in *Why I Am An Atheist*, Delhi, 1979, p. 7.
6. Bipan Chandra, *op. cit.*, pp. 228-29.
7. It was published in January 1925.
8. J.N. Sanyal, *Sardar Bhagat Singh*, Lahore, 1931, p. 15.
9. Bipan Chandra, *op. cit.*, p. 237.
10. *Ibid.*
11. *Ibid.*, p. 245.
12. See Bhagat Singh's Diary in Nehru Memorial Museum and Library, New Delhi.
13. See Bhagat Singh's Papers in Nehru Memorial Museum and Library, New Delhi.

3 Naujawan Bharat Sabha

I

The part played by the young revolutionaries in 1920s is most significant and remarkable as this period covers a most crucial phase of our freedom struggle. The revolutionary spirits, fervour as well as their political ideology received impetus and encouragement from the doings and writings of earlier heroes and the historic cases, which came to light as a result of early revolutionary activities. Whereas the influence of Rash Behari Bose and Shachindranath Sanyal was immense on them, the Hardinge Bomb Case, the Ghadr Movement, the the Mainpuri Conspiracy . The First Lahore Conspiracy Case and other political events had most significant impact on the working of minds of the young revolutionariers.

The other important factor which had greatly effected their thinking was the inauguration of the first Non-cooperation Movement launched under the leadership of Mahatma Gandhi. In this kind of non-voilent satyagraha, numerous youngmen like Bhagat Singh, Sukhdev, Jatin Das, Chandrashekhar Azad, Bhagwati Charan Vohra, Yashpal, Jogesh Chandra Chatterjee and Dr. Gaya Prasad participated along with many other satyagrahis. They left their homes, schools and colleges and courted arrests at the call of Gandhi. But the sudden withdrawal of movement on the account of a gruesome tragedy at Chauri Chaura and perpetration of violence at other places made these youngmen very angry and dissatisfied with the kind of approach Gandhi had in mind. Their sense of gloom was heightened by the replacement of Hindu-Muslim unity forged in common struggle by an orgy of communal riots and an atmosphere poisoned by mutual communal hatred. These idealist youth could not see anything wrong with Chauri Chaura. Nor could they appreciate a conception of political and morality which would fell a powerful popular movement with a single blow. Nor were they satisfied with the two substitutes that the national leadership offered them: parliamentary politics of the Swarajists of the so-called constructive programme of the No-changers.... Their rejection of Gandhism made them search for altarnatives. This search led them to socialism on the one hand and revolutionary terrorism on the other. They embraced both, as had been done half a century earlier by the Revolutionary Russian Youth.[1]

In mid-twenties, there was so much revolutionary fervour amongst the youngmen that it indeed became essential for them to work under the banner of an organised and well-disciplined forum.

The Naujawan Bharat Sabha was formed in March 1926 at the suggestion of Dr. Satyapal to educate youngmen, especially the students community of the educational institutions located at Lahore. The programme of the sabha comprised debates on moral, literacy and social subjects; the popularisation of *swadeshi* goods, the inculcation of a sense of brotherhood, simple living and physical fitness and the stimulation of interest in Indian languages and civilisation.[2]

Jai Dev Gupta, an active worker of the Naujawan Bharat Sabha reminisced thus: 'Bhagat Singh did not believe in God or in any religion. Why? After studying history, we found that Christians carried out crusades, Muslims carried out *Jehads* only in the name of same God. But, because the other was not following the same faith, he must be killed. What was this? Was this God's order or what? He came to the conclusion that in order to remove the physical slavery, we must remove the mental slavery and it was the most effective weapon in the armoury of our rulers—the British. Whenever they liked to disturb the communal harmony for their own ends, they would incite different religious heads against each other and create communal frenzy on large scale. Those who ruled us were successful in implementing their policy of divide and rule. All clashes were there only in the name of God. So when this wall of God would be removed among communities, then those watertight compartments, artificially created, would crumble down and humanity would prevail all over. He replaced God by humanity and religion by service to humanity. So this must be taught to the people if we had to free them from the mental slavery.

This was one of the main planks of the Naujawan Bharat Sabha. And to practise this, we used to arrange community dinners, lunches in which all sorts of people would come Hindus, Muslims, Sikhs, *Chamars, Bhangis* and everybody would cook. They would have *Jhatka* meat for the Muslims and *Halal* for the Sikhs. In order to remove that feeling, these meals were freely arranged. Secondly, lectures were delivered by the persons against their own religion. A Muslim or a Hindu or an Arya Samajist would speak against his own religion to the audience. So that the hearers might have some idea about the reality of God. In order to remove physical slavery, removal of mental slavery was necessary. Consequently, Bhagat Singh bade goodbye to this creation and became an out and out atheist.

"....The platform of Naujawan Bharat Sabha was utilised to create hatred or some sort of ill-feeling against the British and prepared the country for final assault in due course...The story of Kartar Singh Sarabha's life was also propagated from that platform. His photographs were exhibited with projected slides. So the Naujawan Bharat Sabha, on the one hand, wanted to preach non-existence of God and removal of mental slavery, on the other, they wanted to enthuse nationalism by highlighting the heroic deeds and sacrifices of such revolutionaries. In this way, impressionable youths were screened out for secret revolutionary work."[3]

Thus, Naujawan Bharat Sabha was an open platform for discussion and expression of their opinion, anti-Raj in substance. Amonst them, suitable, reliable, sincere and trustworthy youngmen were entrusted to perform various kinds of jobs while maintaining strict secrecy and taking full care of their personal safety from the clutches of C.I.D. and other agencies of police operating to curb their work, arrest them and convict them in every possible way.

The rules and regulations of the Hindustan Republican Association were clearly enshrined in the from of a manifesto. Its object was to establish a Federal Republic of the United States of India for an organised and armed revolution. The final form of the constitution was to be framed and declared by the representatives of the people at the time when they would be in a position to enforce their decisions. The fundamental principle of the Republic was universal suffrage and the abolition of all systems which made any kind of exploitation of man by man possible.

The governing body of the Association was Central Council, which was composed of the representatives of all the provinces of India. All the decisions of this Council were to be arrived at by unanimous consent and it was vested with the absolute powers. The main functions of the Council were to supervise, adjust and coordinate the various kinds of activities in the different provinces. The Council was also required to direct charge of the work which was carried in the countries outside India.

In the provinces, this organisation took its roots on firm footing. A committee consisting of five persons represented five different departments of the Association in every province, which was required to regulate all the activities of the Association in the province. The decisions arrived at were to be by unanimous consent.

Every provincial organisation had the following departments. These were propaganda, collection of men, and collection of funds, collection and storage of arms and ammunition, and foreign connections. The propaganda was to be carried on in a systematic way and the media was by an open and a secret press; through public platform; through a system of organised *Kathas* and through magic lantern slides.

Funds were to be collected by means of voluntary subscription and occasionally force could be used for such a collection.

It was made incumbent to arm each and every member of the Association, but all such arms and ammunitions were to be stored at different centres and were to be used according to the direction and advice of the Provincial Committee only. The district organiser was required to start branches of the Association in every nook and corner of his district. And for this he was to keep himself in touch with different public bodies and institutions of the district.

Besides the district organisers were to see that the members of the Association were properly divided into separate groups and they maintained perfect secrecy of their activities in their respective areas. The district organiser was to be a tactful and an intelligent person to handle people of different temperament; he was to be well-conversant with the social, economic and political conditions of the people; he must be courageous, fearless, imbued with the spirit of self-sacrifice and, above all, he must have full faith in his mission.

The activities of the Association were both public and private. The aims of the Association were to start social organisation and learned bodies like clubs, libraries, sewa samities and the like; to start labour and peasant organisation and control the labourers in the different factories, the railways and in the coalfields; to start a weekly paper in every province, to propagate the idea of an independent Indian Republic and to publish booklets and pamphlets with a view to enlightening the public regarding the course of events and the current of thought as was prevalent in the countries outside India. Besides it was required to establish a secret press and through it publish such literature as could not easily be published openly; to circulate such literature; to collect funds; to send suitable men to foreign countries where they might get military or scientific training so that they might become military or scientific experts to take charge of armies and ammunition factories at the time of open rebellion; to impart arms and ammunition and also to manufacture them, as far as possible, in the country; to remain in close touch and to cooperate with the Indian revolutionaries outside India and to get the members of this Association enlisted into this army.

The membership was open only to those persons who could devote their whole time for the Association and to risk their lives for the sake of their country if necessary. No member of this Association was to become the member of any other organisation without the consent of the district organiser. Every member must try to avoid being suspected of revolutionary connections by the police or public. Members who were to betray must be punished with expulsion or death and the authority of punishment was to rest entirely with the Provincial Council.

Before enrolment as its member, the youngman was made to sign a pledge that he would place the interests of his country above those of his community. 'It soon became clear, however, that the social objects of the Sabha were only a cloak for the dissemination of revolutionary ideas.'

As its political activities expanded in the country-side, its workers and their activities became the centre of attraction for the uneducated simple village folk. They realised the unquestioned and unflinching sincerity of these youngmen for the cause of the country and the great and partriotic role they were destined to play in the near future.

The Sabha held the first provincial conference at Amritsar on 13 April, 1928 and attracted a huge gathering. It declared its aim in unequivocal terms that it was establish in India an Independent Socialist Republic of the workers and peasents by all possible means.

The founders of the Naujawan Bharat Sabha had firm faith and belief in the philosophy of communism and the inevitable class struggle of the peasants and workers against the Indian capatilists and also waging a revolutionary war against British imperialism. Thus, they had much sympathy and faith in the great and successful experiments being done in the Union of Soviet Socialist Republic of Russia. They read with immense interest the speeches and literature of Lenin, Trotsky and other Russian leaders.

To propagate the ideology and the programme of the Naujawan Bharat Sabha in an effective way amongst the uneducated masses and simple village folk, it was essential to have literature, which should be understood easily by one and all. It was, therefore, dicided to form a Tract Society which was to publish the aims and objects of the Sabha along with popular poems and songs against the British Raj. This task was entrusted to a dedicated, young and intelligent worker, Principal Chhabil Das who had the scholarly bent of mind. To make it popular and mass-based medium of political propaganda in numerous regions, the policy of Naujawan Bharat Sabha was to soil it at a very cheap price of two pice, which could be within the prevailing economic capacity of a common Indian. As these tracts contained articles on the economic and social status of an ordinary citizen under the British Raj, it gained a wide market for its circulation even in the remote areas of the Punjab, Haryana, Himachal, United Provinces, Delhi, Jammu and Kashmir and elsewhere. Its circulation rose to a few thousands in a very short period.

It is interesting to note that Principle Chhabil Das gave a fearless and daring expression his patriotic sentiments in one of the tracts.

Duniya se ghulami ka mein nam mita dunga
Ik bar zamane ko mein azad kara dunga
Jo log gharibon par karte hein sitam nahaq
Gar dam hai mera kayam gin gin ke saza dunga

Three important pamphlets were published by the Sabha. 'The Wealth of Nations' by Hardyal; 'India and the Next War' by Agnes Smedley and 'Bharat Mata Ka Darshan' by Principal Chhabil Das. All these writings were a stirring appeal to the youngmen of India who were urged to follow the example set by the youths of Ireland, Turkey, Japan and China in their struggle for independence for their respective countries. These writings also enumerated the economic and social ills and the exploitation under the British Raj which had made the people of India impoverished, backward in every respect, and uneducated at a mass scale. They also criticised the prevailing system of justice meted out to people of India. Thus, it was a direct appeal to the people and the youths of the country to follow the principles, aims and objects of Communism which might be put into practice by their dedication and sense of high degree of devotion and patriotism.

'The Naujawan Bharat Sabha did not confine its secularism to sloppy ambraces. It struck at the very root of communalism and untouchability by organising joint dinners of Hindus, Muslims and untouchables. To make such dinners cheap and feasible, the menu was confined to items like *Khichri*,[4] pilao of grams and curd. Sackcloth was spread on the ground to seat the guests. Earthen cups and earthen plates were used. The object was to bring people of all communities together and strike at such supertitions that created a gulf between man and man. Once a dinner was organised in which *Jhatka* and *Halal* meat were cooked together and Hindus, Muslims and Sikhs partook of it.... Principal Chhabil Das cooperated with this type of work. Among Muslim comrades were to be found Fazl, Mansur, Ahsan Ilahi and others.[5]

The Naujawan Bharat Sabha was reported to have revived at Amritsar and that a public meeting of the society was held on

7 July, 1930. This kind of revival of the Sabha resulted in the arrest of four leaders i.e. Shaban Dutt, Ram Parshad Shastri, Ghulam Nabi and Dr. Sant Ram Arora under section 17(2) of the Criminal Law Amendment Act. Besides, action was taken against Babu Singh, Kuljit Sehgal, Bishen Dass and Sunder Dass—all active members of the Sabha at Lahore. They were, however, released on bail.[6]

It was also reported that meetings of the Naujawan Bharat Sabha were arraged at Amritsar on 19th, 21th, 27th and 29th, July, 1930.

On 27th July, when a meeting of the Naujawan Bharat Sabha, Hissar was been, it was announced that Sabha had been re-organised. On this occasion, several persons who took part in the deliberations were arrested under Section 17(2) of the Criminal Law Amendment Act.[7]

The Sabha in Amritsar and its allied bodies had been most active during August1930, when its members organised a meeting which was dispersed by the police and five persons were arrested. Their other meetings held on 15th and 17th of the same month, were interfered with by the police, and its members and presidents were arrested.

The Naujawan Bharat Sabha at Amritsar have recently become openly defiant. On September 4, a meeting was held at which the President and the speakers after a few hurried speeches jumped up from the stage and disappeared in the darkness, thus preventing the police from arresting them. Stones and brickbats were thrown at the police. As the mob became more and more excited, it was dispersed by the police. On the 5th September another, meeting was held at which 4 arrests were made... The Amritsar police raided the Jallianwala Bagh on the night between the 3rd and 4th September] 1930. They demolished all the huts and took away all the property belonging to the Sabha and other lawful organisation.[8]

Principal Chhabil Das reminisced,...Naujawan Bharat Sabha encompassed two different trends of thought, because during those days, India used to get light either from Russia and Russian Revolution of Lenin or from Ireland-De Valera and Sinn Fein movement. So, naturally, Naujawan Bharat Sabha also ideologically was split into two factions: the emphasis of one was on Irish revolution and the methods adopted by those people that was collecting arms, throwing bombs. The other section was like the Russians and wanted to create class consciouness amongst the masses, rural people, peasantry and factory workers.[9]

From September 1930 onwards a number of prominent members of Naujawan Bharat Sabha toured various parts of the Punjab and delivered their speeches against the misrule of the British Raj. These were mainly in connection with the first anniversary of Jatin Dass who breathed his last in the Lahore jail.[10]

Master Laxmi Chand of Ambala City delivered such a speech at Shahabad in Karnal district on 16 September. The tyrannous Government has applied section 124-A, Indian Penal Code and 144, Criminal Procedure Code, so that we may not be able to talk in a free manner. Besides in other countries such as England, France, Germany, etc. government cannot impose taxes without the consent of the public; but in India the principles are quite different. Indians earn while *shaitan*[11] and mean Britishers enjoy luxuries in their bungalows. How much injustice is being done. Do you like to live such a disgraceful life? If not, then why don't you join this religious war and struggle for it?.... Look! What plans these *saitans* have devised to ruin us. Don't you feel ashamed and do you not feel these tyrannies which are being exercised upon you.... Mother! If the men of Shahabad do not help their children and Mother India, you should join the warfare for the freedom of the country and for the safety of poor children. O ye men ! You should wear bangles and take their places.... Brethren ! It is not the time for sleeping. Make so many sacrifices so that these tryants may give you freedom....Bread is placed before you, till it is not eaten it will not satisfy your hunger. Likewise nothing can be gained by merely uttering *Bande Mataram*, Hindustan Azad, etc. unless something practical is done by making sacrifices–bodily, mentally and monetary.... Gentlemen! This *Shaitan* Government came to India 325 years back as traders and have now become the owner of India. By the exercise of the principle of divide and conquer, they now claim to be our sovereign. This Government is so. You might remember the treaties which they (tyrants) made with Maharaja Ranjit Singh, Sher-i-Punjab and that after death how through deception and fraud the ruined the Punjab and got possession of it having no regard for their agreements and treaties....Wake up and make sacrifices so that this tyrannous government may be obliged to grant you freedom. You will get no other golden chance like the present one. If you not come to the front now your coming progeny will abuse and hate you.[12]

The members of the Sabha who at no time exceeded about 30 in number held several public meetings during the summer of 1926. In September 1926, Kidar Nath Sehgal and others issued a pamphlet on behalf of the Naujawan Bharat Sabha entitled 'An Appeal To The Young Punjab' attacking Lala Lajpat Rai as a traitor.[13] The pamphlet concluded with an appeal to young patriots to sacrifice themselves at the call of the Mother and exclaiming 'Victory to the Mother;' 'Martyrdom to the Patriot'.

The attcak on Lala Lajpat Rai was the beginning of the end of Sabha. Meetings continued to be held but less frequently, and it was obvious that the attack on Lajpat Rai had divided the members. In March 1927, Dr. Bhupendra Nath Datta, a well known Bengali revolutionary, lectured on the youth movement in the west. This meeting marked the close of the Sabha's activities for a year, and it was not until March 1928, that it was again heard of.[14] On 28th March, S.A. Dange and Phillip Spartt of the British Communist Party spoke at a meeting organised by the Naujawan Bharat Sabha on the meaning of Indian Independence.[15]

During the Punjab Political Conference at Amritsar in April 1928, a Young Mens' Conference was also help and was presided over by Kider Nath Sehgal, who delivered a most objectionable presidential address. A number of seditious and subversive resolutions were passed including *inter alia* resolution appreciating the sacrifices of certain convicts hanged in the Kakori Train Dacoity Case, advising youngmen to prevent the people from taking any part in a war of the future and appealing to the country to start a regular agitaion for the repeal of the Arms Act. At the same time great stress was laid on the necessity for the subjection of religion to politics in the cause of nationalism. A resolution proposing that no youngmen who desired the complete independence of his country should become a member of any politico-communal organisation was, however, opposed by several Muslims and had to be shelved. During the conference, it was decided to organise the youths of the Punjab in a central body called the Naujawan Bharat Sabha with headquarters at Amritsar and branches in every district and to associates the Sabha with the Kirti group of Amritsar. Thus, it is evident that the proceedings of the conference were generally directed towards the inculcation of a spirit of violence amongst the youths of the country.[16]

This conference infused new life into the Naujawan Bharat Sabha and encouraged it to take part in subsequent phases of anti-government agitation. In conjunction with the group of agitators, which at that time controlled the activities of the Congress and the Kirti parties, the Sabha was to stir up agrarian agitation over the failure of the wheat harvest. In this connection, a meeting was held on 23 May at village Jahman in the Lahore district to discuss the failure of the crops and was attended by prominent extremists such as Satyapal, Kidar Nath Sehgal and M.A. Majid. While advertised as a Congress meeting, there was reason to believe that it was in reality inspired by the Naujawan Bharat Sabha. The attempt to stir up agrarian agitation was, however, 'killed' by the large remissions of land revenue sanctioned by the government.

The Sabha's next move was to start a tract society for the dissemination of national literature. This society published three 'objectionable' pamphlets, strongly impregnated with Bolshevik and Communist doctrines, entitled '*The Wealth of Nation,* by Hardyal; '*India and the Next War,* by Agnes Smedly and '*Bharat Mata Ka Darshan,* by Chhabil Das. In June, it seized the occasion of a students' week, organised by the Lahore Student's Union, to publish and distribute another objectionable pamphlet *Naujawanon se do Baten*. (A Few Words to the Young Men). This pamphlet urged the youngmen of India to follow the example set by the youngmen of Ireland, Turkey, Japan and China in their struggle for independence, accused the British government of exploiting India and of keeping the inhabitants impoverished and uneducated, stated that the administration of justice in India was tainted by racial considerations, and that the state of slavery in which India was held had calamitous results on neighbouring countries, and urged the youngmen of India to study such movements as Communism and Bolshevism, the lives of political martyrs, the doctrines of freedom and equality, democracy and self-determination which alone could bring self-government and economic freedom. These pamphlets represented the Sabha's attempt to capture the Lahore Student's Union. It made an attempt actually to control the organisation of the union, being content to allow the effect of its propaganda divert the activities of the students, union into channels which would run parallel to its own.

In June the Naujawan Bharat Sabha supported the Congress in its campaign of agitation over the Bardoli reassessment, and held meetings to spread the belief that the satyagraha campaign in Bardoli was an economic protest against the high-handed policy of the Bombay government, and to hold up the movement as one worthy of imitation.

In July 1928, Kidar Nath Sehgal, president of the provincial Naujawan Bharat Sabha issued a long statement to the press regarding the future programme of the Sabha in the course of which he wrote that in order to organize the youngmen throughout the Punjab, the Sabha had decided to have branches in all villages, towns and districts of the province. He expressed the hope that the provincial workers would find it easy to reach the villages and towns if the branches of the Sabha were established at the headquarters of the districts of the province. He added the prompt help would be much appreciated as the *Sabha* wanted to build up a strong organisation before the Simon Commission came to India again.

In July, the bond between the Kirti party and the Naujawan Bharat Sabha was strengthened by the election of Sohan Singh Josh, the leader of the Kirti party, as president of the Amritsar branch of the Sabha. The alliance of these two organisations resulted in their joint celebration, aided by Congress extremists, of the 'Friends of Russia Week', early in August when resolutions were passed stating that Indians would render no assistance to the British government in any future war, proclaiming that they had no enmity with Russia, and that they were in full sympathy with the anti-imperialistic policy of Russia. The theme of the speeches was that England's engagement in war with Russia would be India's opportunity to free herself from foreign rule, while the argument was developed that the destruction of capitalism and the government of the country by labourers and peasants were the only road to freedom and prosperity.

The Naujawan Bharat Sabha took prominent part in spreading propaganda for the workers and peasants' conference at Lyallpur at the end of September. In the absence of S.A. Dange, Chhabil Das was elected president and Ram Chandra as chairman of the reception committee. Ram Chandra delivered a discourse on Communism coupled with laudatory references to revolutionaries and denouncement of imperialism, capitalism and the present system of society. He further recommended the nationalisation of wealth, a social revolution, the organisation of workers and peasants to resist exploitation by capitalism and made specific demands for the assessment of the land revenue on the principles of the Income-tax Act, the unrestricted Indianisation of the army and the withdrawal of the British army from India.

An other prominent worker and general secretary of the Punjab Naujawan Bahrat Sabha gave vent to his patriotic feelings in the Jallianwala Bagh, Amritsar. The audience was advised thus: I learn with much regret that the police visited the camp of the Naujawan Bharat Sabha twice today[17] to arrest us, but I am very sorry to say that both the President and I had gone out. When we arrived here, we learnt of the fact. Our hearts were greatly shocked at the fact that the police had to return unsuccessful. I request the police brethren that if they have got with them warrants for our arrest, they may inform us that fact in writing through a chit. We are prepared to come at the end of the meeting. They should not create disturbance at the meeting so that the public may not be put to trouble. I tell the policemen again that they should remember that if they create disturbance at the meeting, youngmen whose hearts have been shocked at the sentence of death passed on Bhagat Singh will get excited. They should not say afterwards that they were ignorant of this fact. O Youngmen! You have arrived at no decision regarding Bhagat Singh so far during these 24 hours, and have sent no reply to the Naujawan Bharat Sabha. Will our Bhagat Singh, Rajguru and Sukhdev separate from us in this way? O Youngmen! If the existing savage government made those three gems to the gailows, will you be able to show your face to the world?....... O Youngmen! Make sacrifices in thousands and hang at the gollows in thousands, but save dear Bhagat Singh ... He is a gem whose uncle Sardar Ajit Singh is at present wandering about in Persia like nomads. If there is any love for Bhagat Singh in your hearts, sacrifice yourselves like a moth over the lamp of freedom and tell the government that it should release Bhagat Singh, in return for which we are prepared to give thousands of lives...Today orders were passed that they would be executed on the 27th October.[18]

O Youngmen ! Leave schools and colleges. Leave your parents. Come into the field of action like Bhagat Singh...(There were shouts of Bhagat Singh *zindabad*, Sukhdev *zindabad* and Rajguru *zindabad*).

The Naujawan Bharat Sabha still exits. This tyrannical government has declared all the societies as unlawful but they must remember that the roots of the Naujawan Bharat Sabha have reached the northern most regions and they cannot be destroyed. Its name will endure as long as the world lasts...If you want to see Bhagat Singh alive and if you want to see Rajguru alive you should plunge into the field of action. On that side Bhagat Singh, Rajguru and Sukhdev have been sentenced to death and on this side you are sitting at your homes. Let us ask those in whose hearts abides the picture of Bhagat Singh...Ask that old Sardar Kishan Singh what were his feelings at the time when he heard of the sentence of death passed upon Bhagat Singh. Just enquire from the father and mother of Bhagat Singh what thoughts passed their hearts when they heard of the sentence of death passed against Bhagat Singh. O Youngmen! Making yourself extinct at the tide of liberty you should tell the parents of this brother that Bhagat Singh is not dead and that we are at all times ready to die for Bhagat Singh.

Without saying anything further I request you to observe complete *hartal* in the city tomorrow. I make to those confectioners, green-grocers and fruit-sellers the submission that tomorrow if they open any shop or expose any goods for sale, they must remember that the Naujawan Bharat Sabha will not be responsible if they suffer any loss. Tomorrow, at Amritsar, neither any hawker should sell his stuffs nor should any goods be sold at any shop. The *Mohalla* people will tell persons living in their *Mohalla* not to open their shop. If anyone will open his shop he will have to suffer the consequences. Our volunteers will have their goods thrown into drains....I request my brethren–

the *tongas*, but if they ply them on one should take a trip in them...I request these students brethren not to attend schools and colleges tomorrow at all and observe a complete *hartal*.[19]

Yet another prominent worker and president of the Punjab Naujawan Bharat Sabha delivered an emotional speech on this occasion.[20]

....'I now ask this Government. O Government people! Just tell me where is your peace today? To what extent will youngman remain sitting in your presence after keeping their strength under restraint? Listen! Listen again! The youngmen today make the announcement. On the execution of Bhagat Singh or on the execution of Sukhdev or Rajguru, it will become known to you that not one but thousands will become Bhagat Singh and I will be the first person to be executed on the gallows... Execute me on the gallows. I am prepared to be executed'.

'We wish to arouse your independent views and feelings which have been suppressed owing to your living in slavery... If there is regard in your heart, take a vow here today that you will never live as slaves in this would. Those men are also like you who are to ascend the gallows'.

'I know Sardar Kishan Singh whose beard has turned white. I know his mother and brethren who are yet of tender years. There is no one to earn a living for them. There was Bhagat Singh alone to earn a living for them.... O Youngmen ! You have organised the Naujawan Bharat Sabha in my absence. On the day of Bhagat Singh's execution, the British government will, I hope, confine me within four walls and will put fetters round my feet which I shall gladly accept. You who will take my place! Keep in view my honour. God who knows of this fact will be with you.'[21]

The provincial government as well as the government of India noted with much concern the objectionable and dangerous speeches by various leaders. H.G. Haig, the Home Secretary, also expressed much concern over the whole episode at Amritsar.[22] 'I think we ought to address the Punjab Government with regard to the proceedings of this session of the Naujawan Bharat Sabha and ask what measures they have contemplated to deal with what appears to be highly seditious and inflammatory propaganda disseminated by this association. We should refer to the correspondence on our life regarding the Secretary of State suggestion that the Naujawan Bharat Sabha should be proclaimed an unlawful association under Part ii of the Criminal Law Amendment Act. If the action under Part ii of the Criminal Amendment Act is either not feasible or not desirable do they comtemplate prosecuting some of the more important speaker. J.C. Crerar stated, 'I agree. There are signs that this movement if unchecked may develop seriously.'[23]

The Punjab government felt that the Sabha interfered with the maintenance of law and order and constituted a danger to public peace, and, therefore, declared it to be an unlawful organisation. On 23 June, 1930 the office of the Sabha was searched and a list of members and other material were recovered.[24]

By 1928, the activities of the Sabha had crossed the borders of the Punjab, and at this point of time Bhagat Singh made himself very busy in maintaining deep linkages with other revolutionaries working in the United Provinces. He and his associates like Sukhdev and Bhagwati Charan Vohra enrolled themselves as prominent members of a revolutionary organisation of U.P., namly, Hindustan Republican Association. It was formed in 1924 under the leadership of Shachindranath Sanyal, Jogesh Chandra Chatterjee and Ram Prasad Bismal.

An important meeting of young revolutionaries was held at Ferozeshah Kotla grounds in Delhi on 9-10 September, 1928 when after discussions and serious deliberations, the party was renamed as Hindustan Socialist Republican Association. So Bhagat Singh, after, 1928, was very active under the direction and mandate of the HSRA.[25]

The Sabha, meanwhile, published the *Independent India Tract Series* and it highlighted the important of peasants and workers. In another leaflet, 'Worst Sin in the World is Poverty' youngmen were exhorted to eradicate poverty, root and branch, to make an equitable distribution of wealth amongst one and all and also devise means for advancing opportunity for sharing power in perfect equality amongst the members of the society.[26]

This kind of model had much impact on the thinking of the students, workers and peasants of north India. The Lahore Students' Union become almost part and parcel of the Sabha and its political activities had deep linkage with it. In various centers of the Punjab, youth leagues and students' union, with revolutionary fervour, were established. The D.A.V. College, Lahore, one of the premier institutions in north India had become a prominent centre for the revolutionaries' activities and the government showed its disinterestedness in recruiting young educated lot to government service.[27] Even the Governor of the Punjab warned the school managements to the fact that their grants would be stopped if they failed to curb the revolutionary activities of their students. Besides, the teachers working in these institutions were threatened with dire consequences, if they extended any kind of political support to their students.[28]

But this kind of approach on the part of the government did not bear any beneficial results. The atmosphere everywhere was mingled with patriotic fervour and the youths were not at all hesitant to participate in any political activity, which had anti-Raj stance.

II

Chandrashekhar Azad

Bhagat Singh enjoyed the company of great personalities and learnt a lot from them and conceded a lot to them in return as he himself was no less. The revolutionaries who were accused in the Kakori Conspiracy Case, but who were evading the police namely Ashfaqulla and Bakshi were arrested after a few months and were implicated together in a supplementary case. Chandrashekhar Azad could not be arrested till the very end. He hailed from Bhabhra, Madhya Pradesh and had come to Benares to learn Sanskrit. Sanskrit students are generally conservative, but when the call for non-cooperation was given in 1921, it was the Sanskrit students of Benares who led the trail. Chandrashekhar Azad was one of them. In the 1921 movement he was punished 15 stripes. At every stroke of stripe he said, "Mahatma Gandhi Ki Jai". This made him overnight the idol of the nation. His photo was published in the prestigious *Maryada* (Hindi monthly) edited by Sampurnanand. He was subsequently disillusioned with Gandhi and joined hands with the revolutionaries. He worked assiduously and turned to be a prominent figure in ever sphere of revolutionary work. His was a restless soul. He was so devoted to his work and so vagarant that he was nicknamed 'quicksilver' by Ramprasad Bismil.

When he saw that after the train hold-up at Kakori, police vigilance had beefed up, he quietly disppeared from the scene. When after the Kakori round up, the revolutionaries again began to reorganise, Azad came forward.

He had an open mind and although he had worked under Shachindranath Sanyal and Ramprasd Bismil, conservatives among revolutionaries, he could foresee the strom that was brewing. Although a fighter all his life, there was an inner tranquility about the man and he did not turn about from new ideas. When he met people like Bhagat Singh, Sukhdev, Bejoykumar Sinha who had become Marxists, he had no difficulty in complying with them. There was no communication gap. For him learning was a process of growth. From a recalcitrant Gandhite, he had become an ardent revolutionary.

He was a man of courage, character and penetrating mental powers. His bone-deep honesty overshadowed his rugged, pock marked face. The party intellectuals felt that here was psyche that was at peace with itself despite the fact that there was a price on his head. The relationship between Bhagat Singh and him became fervent and trusting one. With the modesty of truly great men Bhagat Singh and the intellectuals of the party gave credence to Azad's superiority.

Thus, Bhagat Singh and Azad, this incomparable twin were like one personality. Neither them felt that the other was working under the wing or shadow of the other. Their minds were so similar that there was hardly any need for them to talk a great deal.

Dr. Mahore writes: "The secret of Azad's success did not lie so much in his heroism as in his capacity to establish soulful rapport immediately with all and sundry he met. He did not confine himself to touching political cords, he touched the more delicate human cords. Hefty, rather short, of brownish colour with pock marked rugged face, this exterior was amply compensated by nature by a bestowal on him of a beauty reflecting inner tranquility. To know him was to adore him."

As long as the Kakori conspiracy case was raging on, Azad was kept in leash for if he did anything, the judge would spew his vengeance on the accused. Manindranath Banerjee was forbidden by the leadership from becoming a live wire on the same ground. But when by December 1927 Bismil and 3 others were hanged, that excuse no longer held and Azad came out of his long hibernation.

Bhagat Singh was already active. A band of bond youths now inseparable from him had gathered round him. When Azad and Bhagat Singh were girding up their lions to take a huge leap into history, Manindranath Banerjee, a youth from Benares lugged two bullets into Jatin Banerjee, D.S.P., police saying 'Here are your thirty pieces of silver for getting Lahiri hanged.'

The weapon used by Manindra could not be recovered although Manindra was arrested on the spot. This weakened the court case and he could only be sentenced to 10 years R.I. Later on Manindra Banerjee died under very tragic circumstance on the 20 of June, 1934, in Fatehgarh Central Prison.

The union of Bhagat Singh and Azad was great event in the revolutionary movement. Thus, burgeoned a relationship, which executed wonders. There had never been a time when both did not achieve rapport stimulating and enjoying each other's heroism.

Up to this time Bhagat Singh had been more or less bookish type of revolutionary. Azad contrastingly was a seasoned and hardened revolutionary. He had seen action, was an expert in hold-ups. He had participated in at least a dozen of them. He had not wasted his period of hibernation. He had become a crack shot and a good driver. He had become expert in giving the police spies the slip. He had many narrow escapes.

Again we shall quote Dr. Mahore: "Once while living on the bank of the Satar in Jhansi he was returning to Jhansi along with another *sadhu*. Two constables interrupted him and asked him to accompany them to the police station. Probably the story of the price on Azad's head had reached them and they were suspecting and apprehending everybody. They shot the question—'Tell us if you be Azad'.

Immediately he came out with a story punning on the word *Azad* (independent). Baring his teeth like a fool, in a drawl that was natural to *sadhus* he said, 'Er...of course I am Azad, independence being our very nature. We pray to the monkey God

Hanuman and lead a life without worries er... 'But the policemen were adamant. Azad gently threatened, If we are late, the God Hanuman er... would also be late, and you know er... 'The constables were not impressed, they still insisted. At this, as became a holy man, he lost his temper and admonished,'For you, may be, the inspector be important, but I will only obey the monkey God'."

Saying this he walked away. Dr. Mahore writes: "It was fortunate for the constables that this stance convinced them that he was really a holy man, otherwise it would have been their last day."

"A murder occurred in the vicinity of the hideout. The police suspecting that burglars were hiding in nearby jungle were very active in that area. Azad was quite safe as Harishankar, the brother of village chief. But now the police asked him about his antecedents, it which Azad said, 'Er...the *Sadhu* is homeless. You shouldn't aks a *Sadhu* about his antecedents, because this militates against his vow".

"For a while, everything cooled down,but he anticipated that another wave, and he would be washed away. His drawl and his quaint mannerisms would not save him. He realised it was time to change his jungle hide-out. Master Rudranarayan, a photographer of Jhansi lodged with one Ramanand, motor driver. Here he lived as the younger brother of the driver and started working in a motor company.

Both Azad and Bhagat Singh needed each other, fulfilled each other. Without Azad, Bhagat Singh could not become what he was nor could Azad attain the eminence that he achieved.

Yashpal in a couple of paragraphs brings out the essence of Azad's leadership—

"Azad is reputed to be a dare devil. As an individual he was certainly a dare devil, but he was leading some action, he was very calculative and cautions. Every step that he took was measured. He did not lose sight of the objective. No risk no game this he knew well, but the question was would he win after the risk? On such occasions he was not emotional, he was all mathematics. On the day he went to rescue Bhagat Singh from the gate of borstal prison, I was spoiling for fight, my hands were itching Azad understood my condition and growled—'Stop.' After ten minutes I understood that he was right. Had I been allowed to follow my inveterate itch, some six or seven casualties would have occured which would have included Bhagat Singh and Dutt. It was owing to this sterling quailty that he became the unquestioned commander-in-chief of the party."

Bhagavaticharan Vohra

Among Bhagat Singh's eminent companions Vohra should be rated only second to Azad. It occurred to an important outsider like Muzaffar Ahmed that Bhagat Singh was working under Vohra. Ahmed was not very much off the mark. Bhagat Singh is known as the leader of *Naujawan Bharat Sabha,* but Yashpal disclosed that it was under their twin leadership that the Sabha marched from victory to victory. Vohra had held the key post of publicity secretery.

This proves that in the eyes of the comrades, Vohra was effective in doing work of mass contact. Vohra's predecessors had come from Gujarat. His father was a railway official, whose work was rated so high to honour him with the title *Rai Sahib.* Bhagavaticharan's grandfather used to do *kitabet* (copying of lithography). It is said he used to do that much to earn one rupee each day. After that, he would stop all work. In 1925 'The revolutionary was distributed secretly through the length and breath of India. A copy of the leaflet came to Prof. Jaychandra, but they were stacked in Bhagvaticharan's home because he till then was considered a safe layman in the eyes of the police.

Bhagavaticharan Vohra was married very early. Durga, his wife, was devoted to him and became a revolutionary knowing fully well that the path was one that bristled with thorns. When she first married, she had not pretentions to learning, but gradually she qualified all the examinations, working at the same time in the party. Bhagavaticharan's life culminated with an accident

Rajguru

Rajguru and Sukhdev were hanged along with Bhagat Singh. Born in Poona 1909, Rajguru lost his father at the age of 6. He was looked after by his elder brother.

Rajguru was asset to the revolutionary party. He was always the leader in taking risks. When the blue-print for forcibly rescuing Jogesh Chatterjee from jail was prepared, Rajguru was not included in the plans. When he was apprised of it he almost forced the leaders to include him. Again when a decision was reached to avenge the death of Lala Lajpat Rai, Rajguru insisted that he should do the shooting. He offered to step inside the police headquarters, Lahore, and shoot the British police chief. Azad had reconnoitred the terrain thoroughly, so he thought Rajguru's offer too reckless.

He had formed a plan and stuck to it. It was an integrated plan and nothing was left to chance. When it was decided that Bhagat Singh should go alongwith another revolutionary and drop bombs in the Central Assembly and Bhagat Singh went for B.K. Dutta as his companion, Rajguru protested. Rajguru wanted to take the place of Bhagat Singh and when he was told that the latter was chosen because, if apprehended, he could utter the right statement regarding socialism being the goal of the party, Rajguru insisted on replacing Dutt.

According to Dr. Mahore: "Rajguru remarked to Azad—'Was it necessary to give the statement in English? If so, I shall learn the whole damned thing by throat and deliver it, I assure you, without a single mistake. I learned the whole of Sanskrit grammar by rote, so a few pages of the statement is nothing to me.' 'When he pleaded his case very hard, Azad gave him a chit and sent him to Bhagat Singh to take him along in place of Dutt. But Bhagat Singh was adamant. Then Rajguru returned saying, 'By myself I can work wonders'." May be one could say that this was not a very healthy streak in him, as apparent in all this, but his was a dedicated and a very restless soul.

He had the reputation of sleeping very soundly and also falling asleep at awkward times. Once he and Bhagat Singh were travelling together. The train was to arrive at the station at 2 a.m. Bhagat Singh had not slept some nights, so he asked Rajguru keep awake and wake him up at one-thirty. Bhagat Singh woke up at the stroke of three and found Rajguru missing. This intrigued him. Ultimately he found the latter happily coiled and sleeping in a corner.

Once Azad, Rajguru and Dr. Mahore were travelling from Kanpur to Jhansi. They were cleverly dressed in dirty clothes to pass off as working class people. When the train entered the hilly area of Bundelkhand, Rajguru burst out –'This terrain is good for Shivaji type of guerilla warfare …' This outburst chilled Azad to his bones. This could expose their identity to the other passengers. Azad immediately snapped— 'Sonny, forget that nonsense about Shivaji or whoever he is and you my wife's brother better sing that *Jab qua fas se lash nikli bulbule nashad ki'*, and gave him a kick. Rajguru realised his mistake.

In the case of the murder of Saunders, it was his first bullet that did the job. People praised him but he remorsefully answered—'I had put my sight on his chest and the bullet hit him on the head'. Later on Dr. Mahore discovered that Rajguru's marks-manship was not to be blamed but the bullet was a bit different. It had been forcibly fitted into the pistol.

Once Bhagat Singh, Rajguru and Shiv Verma were sleeping in a room. Shiv Verma woke up with an awkward feeling at a hissing sound. He pulled out his torch and found that a snake with its hood spread out was hissing some 2 feet from Rajguru. Verma woke Bhagat Singh up and dragged Rajguru by his feet warning him about the snake. Rajguru turned on his side and said, 'Don't disturb me', and napped again. By that time the snake, disturbed by the torch had left.

Shiv Verma has related another story about him. Verma and Rajguru were to board a train at Gorakhpur, but there was still a lot of time. So Verma went to meet a revolutionary friend Haldhar Bajpai and asked Rajguru to wait for him. Verma returned from his meeting on time for the train, but Rajguru was missing. So he boarded the train. Next day Rajguru reached the place and complained: 'How is it, you travelled without me?' He revealed that to spend time and toward the police off he had gone to enjoy a nap among the beggars at the railway station.

Rajguru had somewhere come across a beautiful calendar which he liked. He hung it on the wall inside the hide-out. When Azad came in he noticed the calendar with the picture of a beautiful nymphet. This seemed to Azad a breach of the revolutionary vow. He tore the calendar to pieces and threw then in the corner saying, If this is what the fellow is after, he should leave his pistols and go home. No rooms for double think here. When Rajguru came back, he noticed that his calendar was gone. People directed him to the torn pieces. Rajguru picked up the pieces and growled—'Who has done this?'

At this Azad snarled, 'It is I...'

'—Why did you tear this thing of beauty.'

'—Because it was beautiful.'

'—Would you then tear to pieces and break everything that is beautiful?'

'—Yes, I would ...'

'—Would you break the Taj-mahal?'

'—Yes I would if I could.'

All this was said in anger.

One hour after this Rajguru was still complaining, 'We set out to make this world more beautiful, and here we are out to destroy all beauty. This is nonsense.' This monologue of a tried comrade cooled Azad. He felt that he had overshot the mark and had been misunderstood. He said, 'Look, I didn't mean that I would break the Tajmahal. What I meant was that we have taken a vow and we should have all our sights on the target. I do not want that beauty should lead us astray.... just now.'

Sukhdev

Sukhdev was born at Lyallpur in 1907. His father passed away 3 month before he was born he was brought up by his father's brother, a grain merchant. His uncle was a freedom fighter. Sukhdev esteemed him for this. Sukhdev was a weak child . In reality all the members of his family were like that. He used to make mockery of this weakness—'My father had 8 brothers and sisters. One of them was gobbled by mice.'

By nature Sukhdev was outspoken and independent. His dress and living style verged on the border of eccentricity. He was nicknamed *ganwar* (rugged, rustic). For a long time he and Bhagat Singh were at par and comrades could not decide which one of them would take the leadership.

Even Shiv Verma says, 'It seemed to me that Sukhdev was a greater organises.' Sukhdev was a man who gave thought to detail, whereas Bhagat Singh was a man of vision ignoring small things. Shiv Verma disliked Bhagat Singh's 'self-centredness'. "Bhagat Singh," he says, cared for his own liked and dislikes, "his won food and clothes so much that he ignored the needs of others. Sukhdev was just the opposite. He thought more for other and less of himself."

Sukhdev showed a great affinity of flowers specially the jasmine. Once Shiv Verma and Sukhdev were strolling in front of a temple, where garlands were on sale. Sukhdev was attracted by the jasmine garlands. He immedietely bought two, one he wore round his own neck, the other he offered Verma, who twined it round his hand. Sukhdev insisted that Verma should wear it round his neck properly. But Verma refused. He snatched the garland from Verma's hand, twined it round his own and playing with it, barked out – 'If you don't love the fragrance of flowers, go and smell sometimes else....' In reality, all revolutionaries adored beauty but they forcibly restrained themselves to focus more on their objective.

The important of Sukhdev as a revolutionary is evident from the fact that although he was not actually involved in the murder of Saunders, he was sentenced to death. He, however, behaved sometimes very quizzically.

Once during a long hunger-strike he broke it and later again rejoined it. After arrest he made a confession, then denied. He confessed, not out of fear or a weakness of the mind, but out of eccentricity and pride that without him the country would not be emancipated, and that the earth would fail to rotate on her axis. Ideologically he was very clean as is evident from the letter which he wrote to Gandhi:

"The goal of revolutionaries is to establish a socialist republic. In this there is no room for compromise. You have been labouring under the idea that we believe in outright destruction. Nothing can be further from the truth. The truth is that we weigh every step that take, alone with the environment and we are fully alive to our responsibilities. In spite of understanding the importance of our constructive responsibilities the present circumstances have forced us to concentrate on the destructive side... However, the day is not far when the masses under the leadership of revolutionaries would march toward the lofty goal of socialist republic".

Giving a personal opinion, he wrote in the course of this letter: "The three revolutionaries condemned to death, have accidentally become very famous, but they do not constitute the revolutionary movement. Indeed, the country would gain more, if they are hanged."

Jatindranath Das

Jatin Das was in no sense a junior partner of Bhagat Singh. Das is the representative of another glorious tradition of the revolutionaries in which death lays his icy hand very slowly, though all the time keeping an option of life open to the victim.

Revolutionaries are in general associated with violence, but death by hunger-strike is the noblest form of the non-violence. It is not necessary to esteem hunger–strike spiritually as Gandhi did although every time Gandhi went on fast, he did it with great show keeping his gun-powder of propaganda obscure. Bukharin interpreted hunger-strikes as an intense appeal to public opinion in which the man using this weapon stakes his own life. The first ever Indian freedom-fighter to sacrifice his life in this way was Ramrakha revolutionary who was imprisoned far away in the Andamans. He is completely forgotten. When he went to the Andamans, prisoners were not allowed to put on the sacred thread. To him it appeared to be a great humiliation he went on the hunger-strike and starved to death. That was in the second decade of gone century.

Revolutionaries, who appeared after Ramrakha, thought the sacred thread a cause not worth fighting for, indeed they would themselves burn the so-called sacred thread , as it is only a caste-mark but, all this does not mitigate the importance of Ramrakha as a pioneer freedom fighter.

Jatin Das was born in Calcutta in 1904 in a well-to-do family. The call of the non-cooperation movement was hot when he had just left school. He was plunged into the movement, was arrested and released after 4 days. He was re-arrested and this time he was sentenced to one month.

After release he was again found to be on the culpable side by the British law and was sentenced to 3 months R.I. He returned with his health broken. He joined a college later on, then came in contact with Shachindranath Sanyal and joined the revolutionary party. He rose to be one of its leaders when the Kakori group was inside jail and died on the 63rd day of his hunger-strike.

He was hailed as a national hero. In spite of this Gandhi kept quiet, and when he did speak he said that Das could die in such a manner because he was a supporter of non-violence. This was a competely false and a misleading statement. Das has been a leader of the party and had come to Benares and taken part in a hold-up. I do not believe in hierarchy among freedom fighters, but it is a fact of history that only revolutionary prisoners gave their lives in hunger-strikes. It is another important fact of history, that the present classification of prisoners, still in vogue in free-India, was the result of the supreme sacrifice of Jatin Das.

The Lahore case partially owes its phenomenal fame to the fact that is presented the various ways in which revolutionaries offered their lives. Bhagat Singh, Rajguru and Sukhdev were hanged; Jatin Das starved to death and Chandrashekhar Azad was killed in a gunfight.

B.K. Dutt

Batukeshwar Dutt sentenced to a life term became as famous as Bhagat Singh, Sukhdev and Rajguru who were hanged. Yet it is true of history that none of his associates, who have written about Bhagat Singh in detail, gave him much importance beyond this that he was chosen to be his associate in the Assembly Bomb affair. Dutt proved quite competent for the job he was selected for. He made an in depth study of Marxism in the Andamans, but it appears that later on he was swirled back into the vortex of some form of religion like many other Marxists.

At least he was better than those who wear their Marxism like an overcoat while on the platform, and discard it on entering their house and inside they behave like good Hindus or devoted Muslims.

Bejoykumar Sinha

Studios Rajkumar Sinha was convicted in the Kakori revolutionary conspiracy case. After his incarceration his younger brother, who was a successful journalist became more active. Suresh Bhattcharya was the lynchpin round which a galaxy of important revolutionaries gathered. The Sinha brothers and B.K. Dutt were the most unparalleled of them. Bejoy rose to be one of the party intellectuals. He wrote *In Andamans—the Indian Bastille* and other books.

Yashpal

Yashpal wrote his revolutionary memories *Simhavalokan* in 3 volumes. He, however, had no connection with either the Saunders murders or the Assembly bomb case. He rose to be a top Hindi novelist. His life is itself a novel with plenty of ups and downs.

Kamalnath Tiwari

Tiwari was not connected with any action, he was active in the organisation. In free India he remained a member of parliament for many years and was an important Congress leader. Apart from him, there were some other ex-revolutionaries, who became members of parliament, for instance, Vishnusharan Dublish, Jogesh Chatterjee, Damodar Swarup Seth and Prem Krishan Khanna of the Kakori case and a few others from Bengal, UP and MP, such as Bishwanath Roy, Tarakeshwar Pande, Rajdeo Singh, Arunachandra Guha.

It would be interesting to analyse how far they served the revolutionary cause inside the parliament and outside during their membership.

Shiv Verma

Among Bhagat Singh's companions there were many lesser luminaries like Shiv Verma. Verma wrote his memories in Hindi entitled *Sansmritiyan*. From a human and literacy point of view this is one the best memories written by a revolutionary on Bhagat Singh.

Women Revolutionaries

Some women also played a prominent part during this period. Durga, the wife of Bhagavaticharan, Sushila Prakashvati (later. Mrs. Yashpal) are quoted as important. One of interesting episodes of the revolutionary movement was that Yashpal was more inclined towards Prakashvati (not yet married) than the rules of the revolutionary party would allow.

Chandrashekhar Azad, the Supremo sentenced Yashpal to death for this breach of rules and Virbhadra Tiwari was entrusted with carrying out of the sentence. But Tiwari apprised Yashpal, who took to his heels. It was good that the sentence could not be carried out, because Hindi literature would have lost a giant. At the same time Azad was right, because he acted according to the established traditions of revolutionary movement, with firmness and with malice towards none.

These above, were some of the men women who shone as gems in Bhagat Singh's sky.

REFERENCES

1. Bipan Chandra, *Nationalism and Colonialism in Modern India*, New Delhi, 1979, pp. 224-25.
2. For details see Home Poll. File 492, 1930.
3. Transcript of interview with Jai Dev Gupta, *op. cit.*
4. Rice and lentil-cooked toghter with salt and spices.
5. Manmathnath Gupta, *Bhagat Singh and His Times*, Delhi, 1977 p. 106.
6. Home poll, File 173/VIII, 1930.
7. *Ibid.*
8. *Ibid.*
9. Transcript of interview with Chhabil Das, N.M.M.L.
10. Home Poll, File 173/VIII, 1930.
11. Mischief-monger.
12. *Ibid.*
13. Home Poll, File 173/VIII, 1930.
14. *Ibid.*
15. *Ibid.*
16. *Ibid.*
17. *Ibid.*
18. *Ibid.*
19. *Ibid.*
20. *Ibid.*
21. *Ibid.*
22. Home Poll, File 120, 1930.
23. *Ibid.*
24. *Ibid.*
25. See an analysis of the work of HSRA in the chapter on 'Political Ideology'.
26. Sukhdeo Raj, *Jab Jyoti Jagi*, Mirzapore, 1971, pp. 26 ff.
27. Home Poll, File 4/35/1931.
28. *Ibid.*

4 Simon Commission, Lajpat Rai's Death and Reaction

In accordance with the Act of 1919, a Royal Commission was to be appointed after ten years which was to report to parliament about administrative set up in India and to suggest changes for the smooth functioning of the administration. Such a step, therefore, was to be taken in 1929 when a high powered committee or commission was to be appointed. But in 1927, the Montagu-Chelmsford reforms had been in operation for the last only eight years and the statutory period as laid down in the act had not yet expired. It was indeed the fear of the probable adverse results of the general elections in 1929 in Great Britain which prompted the Conservative party, headed by Stanley Baldwin to think of accelerating the appointment of the statutory commission before the scheduled time. Lord Birkenhead informed Lord Irwin, 'We must not run the slightest risk of the delay in selection so much that an election might either interrupt our plan or even come soon enough to make it not wholly unreasonable to attempt some monkeying tricks without election. It is, of course, obvious that the mere antedating of the commission would deprive us of nothing valuable. We can play with time as we want.'[1]

The members of the Conservative Party also thought that a labour government, if it come into power after the elections in 1929,would be more helpful, sympathetic and considerate in opening a dialogue and ultimately acceding to the political demands of Indian leaders and that it might also go a step further in granting them such favourable concessions as would be compatible with the vested interests of Great Britain in India.

They, therefore, thought, that it would be a safe, right, useful and prudent measure to appoint the statutory commission forthwith and thus forestall the labour government.

There was another important factor which weighed heavily in the Viceroy of India as well as the Secretary of State. The Swaraj party led by prominent leaders like Pandit Motilal Nehru and C.R. Das expressed the sentiments of dissatisfaction and unhappiness at the working of the reforms of 1919. They expressed much criticism in their statement and utterances from time to time. The Swaraj Party had been pressing hard of more and more autonomy in the provinces and responsibility at the centre. The objective, therefore, of the Conservative government was to utilise the appointment of the statutory commission as a bargain-counter and to disintegrate the Swaraj Party.[2]

Although it was the future constitution of India which was to be subject of inquiry, discussion and decision, the personnel of the statutory commission was selected solely from the British community without any Indian representative on it. This kind of exclusion was greatly resented by all the patriotic elements in India.

Tej Bahadur Sapru opined, 'I cannot understand why this scheme could not have fitted in with adequate representation of Indians on the personnel of the commission. The fear of minority reports is as naïve as it is disingenious. Nor can I believe that government could not find in the whole of the country even three or four Indians who could inspire confidence generally. It can only mean a complete want of confidence in the judgment and capacity of Indians to serve on a commission which is to determine the future government of their country. The utmost that can be said in favour of this scheme is that they want to associate us with them at some stages only to the extent of representing our views, but they deny to us the right of participation in the responsibility of forming our constitution. I have no doubt that this commission, even though it be presided over by Simon, will inspire no confidence and will command no public support.'[3]

Pethick-Lawrence also warned the Conservative government with a storngly worded speech. 'India, viewed from the standpoint of population, is the most important part of the British empire, and with the future of India, in my opinion, is bound up not merely the destiny of the country, but of the British Empire. It is not only those who sit on these Benches who are concerned with and committed to self-government for this great part of our Empire. That is a part of policy which has been definitely set forward by the Government of this country and in all parts of the House of Commons. All parties are committed to a change in that direction. . . If either through lack of psychological imagination or of administrative capacity, we botch the business, no excuse will serve us. If in place of creating healthy self-government in India, we produce in that part of the British Empire a festering sore, it will infect the British Empire and make it very doubtful whether that Empire can exist, except utterly weakened and enervated in the future.'[4]

A major cause for the appointing any Indian as a member of the statutory commission was that the framers of the Act of 1919 had the intention to confine and limit its scope to only those persons who were members of parliament in England. But this was indeed not very much a fact but a pretext to ignore Indians' membership on the commission.[5] In fact, the terms of the Government of India Act of 1919 did not lay down arbitrarily that a purely parliament commission must examine the working of the reforms of constitution. There was no bar to the appointment of an outsider as a member of this kind of statutory commission if the British cabinet had the inclination to appoint one.

It is indeed a fact that even if the British government wanted to restrict the membership of the statutory commission to only the members of parliament, the easy availability of two prominent Indians in the British government was the relevent answer to the decision of the Consertvative government. There were two well-known Indian members at the time in the British Parliament: one was S.P. Sinha and other was Shapurji Saklatvala. In fact, S.P. Sinha had been closely connected with the various stages of the constitutional reforms in India and his inclusion as a member of the commission would have been of great consequence.[6]

This kind of arbitrary exclusion of Indians from the membership of the commission led C.Y. Chintamani to remark, 'The stamp of inferiority was fixed on the brow of Indians merely because they were not God's own Englishmen.'[7] Their exclusion from the commission left no doubt in their minds that there was not to be found in India a statesman of sufficient calibre to sit in conference with men of experience. Thus, the ardent desire of Indians to convince themselves that they were the equals of the British, and their almost pathetic *amourpropre* were deeply affronted by this further implication of their unworthiness.

The statutory commission was appointed at a time when the race feeling was in its full swing in the east. To ride roughshod over Indian sentiments and appoint a commission consisting of all Englishmen on a subject, politically and constitutionally effecting India, was destined to invite trouble.[8] Even a leader of the statute of Lord Birkenhead was given a warning and was briefed about its aftermath effects and was advised against adopting such a procedure. In fact, the all-British composition of the commisson was destined to be regarded as racially insulting.[9] When Edwerd Cadogan, a member of the commission, questioned Lord Birkenhead as to whether he anticipated any trouble in India from the exclusion of representative Indians from it, he replied optimistically that although, inevitably, there would be an outcry in certain quarters, he did not believ that it would endure in any case, and ultimately the commission should experience no difficulty on that account.[10]

Lord Birkenhead was, however, of opinion that there were numerous mutually hostile sections in India that it would not be feasible to choose Indians without offending some of them, and, therfore, it would be better to leave them out altogether, and let British representatives decide these important matters for them. According to Lord Halifax, one of the dangers that the Secretary of State foresaw from a mixed commission was that an 'unreal alliance' might be created between the Indian and the Labour representatives.[11] Obviously, Lord Birkenhead and the Viceroy were in agreement on the point that there was no need of appointing Indians on the commission as the advantages of having Indians were outweighed by the disadvantages. But, they, however, knew that a mixed commission, consisting of the British and Indians would command the largest degree of confidence in India, and that a commission without Indians would command no such confidence.[12]

Defending the appointment and composition of the statutory commision, Earl Winterton, Under Secretary a State for India, stated in the House of Commons. 'No Indian or European who knows India could for one moment suppose that two Indian gentelmen, of whatever position or intellectual attainments, could possibly represent all the various political, religious, racial and economic factors who go to make up British India.'[13]

C.F. Andrews who was instrumental in sponsoring the patriotic sentiments of Indians in their struggle for Swaraj criticised Lord Birkenhead's statement and called it a decision akin to that of 'a conqueror imposing his sway upon a conquered and subject people'. He criticised and condemned it as an undemocratic action as it was like 'a racial superior acting with arrogance towards a racial inferior.'[14]

Baldwin, however, adopted a hard line in this regard and raised a point in justifying the appointment of such a commission without any Indian member on it. In one of his most significant speeches on Indian policy, delivered at the annual Lord Mayor's banquet, he said, 'In including in the commission not merely no Indian but no Englishman who have been associated hitherto with the government or commerce of India, our sole desire, paradoxical as it may seem, was to give the real, responsible and instructed opinion among Indians the best chance of playing an effective and constructive part in devising a solution.'[15]

It is evident that no serious opposition was encountered in British Parliament to the apppointment of the statutory commission. All political parties were practically unanimous in their opinion that what the Prime Minister and the Secretary of State had done was the best under the circumstances. The few voices of the members of the opposition like those of Saklatwala and Colonel Wedgwood were lost amidst the general chorous of approval.

On November 7, 1927, the Secretary of State sent a 'private and personal' telegram to the Viceroy; 'Statutory Commission announcement 5 p.m. Indian time,Tuesday, November 8th will be suitable time of release in India.'[16] In obedience to the orders of the Secretary of State, the Viecory made an important announcement on November 8, 1927, in connection with the statutory commission.[17] The following persons were appointed as members of the statutory commission. Sir John Allsebrook Simon (Chairman), Viscount Burnham, Baron Strathcona, George Richard Lane-Fox, Edward Cecil George Cadogan, Vernon Hartshorn and Clement Richard Attlee. J. B. Bhore and S.F. Stewards were appointed secretaries of the commission.[18]

In fact, Baldwin and Birkenhead had lost no opportunity of explaining their policy before the British public. Every one of their public addresses in the weeks preceding the announcement of the appointment of the commission contained some reference to India. India' indeed, became for some time a more important issue in British politics than it had been for a long time past.

The reception to the appointment of the all-white statutory commission in India was extraordinary in its nature. It was considered a calculated affront to the Indian opinion, to the Indian intelligence as well as to the Indian self-respect. Under the circumstances, it was a difficult proposition to accord any kind of welcome to such a commission whose members were all Englishmen. Naturally, a lot of criticism and anger were shown by the people of India soon after the announcement of the commission. Indeed, India was in the midst of a political upheaval and not only whole procedure proposed by the government condemned by Indian leaders from the extreme left to right the extreme but there was a clear indication that if the proposal were persisted in, the government would have to reckon with a vigorous and wide spread boycott. Moderates and extremists, swarajists and nochangers, Congressmen and some of the loyalists—all stood shoulder to shoulder with one voice on the same platform. Meetings of protest were held in almost all the towns and cities, throughout the country, on order to record their emphatic protest against the commission. However, with the exception of the European Association, the Anglo-Indian press and a small section of the Muslims, headed by Muhammad Shafi, in the Punjab, all shades of opinion merged in a common unanimity and the whole of India stood as one against the personnel and the proposed methods and procedure of the commission.

The working committee of the Indian National Congress felt much dissatified and perturbed over the appointment of the Simon Commission. It hastened to pass the resolution which stated that the British government had constituted a statutory commission in defiance of the national will and rejected the national demand for a Round Table Conference to settle a Swaraj constitution for India. It called upon the people of India and appealed to all political parties to abstain from co-operation with the commission; either by giving evidence or by voting for, or serving on any committee connected therewith.[19]

Besides, the prominent leaders like Mahatma Gandhi, Pandit Motilal Nehru, C.R. Das, Jawaharlal Nehru, Tej Bahadur Sapru, Rajendra Prasad, C.H. Setalvad, Annie Besant, M.R. Jayakar, M.A. Jinnah, Sarojini Naidu, H.P. Mody, H.N Kunzru, C.Y. Chintamani , M.V. Joshi, Sivaswami Iyer, A. Rahim, M.A. Ansari, Saifud Din Kitchlew, Syed Mahmud and others openly advised their countrymen to abstain from helping the commission in any way. Thus, from north to south and west to east of India, persons of different calling, belonging to various political parties and holding divergent views and interest—all united to lodge a common protest againt the commission.The *'bona fides'* of the Conservative party in instituting the Simon Commission were strongly suspected and questioned and leaders of different political parties took no pains to conceal that the conservatives in parliament were adopting rushing tactics in Indian affairs lest they should lose their change in the next general elections.Thus, the popular resentment against the commission mirrored the common feelings that the future constitution of India should be framed by the people themselves.

During its second and final visit to India, the members of the Simon Commission visited Lahore besides other prominent towns and cities of India. Sensing trouble in the city, the District Magistrate issued the following order.

Whereas it appears to be necessary in the interests of good order to regulate the holding of procession within the limits of Lahore Municipality on October 30, 1928, I hereby direct that the public shall abstain from organising or joining any procession which has not been permitted by Senior Superintendent of Police, Lahore, within the limits of the said Municipality on that day.

Whereas it is necessary in the interests of good order to control assembing of crowds in the vicinity of railway station of Lahore Junction, on Express and Egerton Road, and the roads adjacent thereto, I hereby direct the public that they shall not assemble within the precincts of the railway station or on the roads above-mentioned except at such places as the Superintendent of Police may permit.[20]

The Hindustan Socialist Republican Association in its meeting convened at the Kotla Feroze Shah in Delhi had decided unanimously to participate in every kind of boycott decided and arranged against the Simon Commission. In this regard, Bhagat Singh decided to participate in the protest procession to be led by Lala Lajpat Rai on the eve of the arrival of the Simon Commission in Lahore.

Jai Dev Gupta reminisced thus : We were living at that time in Shahenshahi Kutiya in Sutar Mandi Bazar. Bhagat Singh and I pasted posters whole night. Also Sukhdev and others pasted them throughout the city. In the morning, Sukhdev and I returned to Shahenshahi Kutiya and Bhagat Singh stayed at Perri Mahal with Vidya Sagar. Shortly after we returned, the police came to our place and arrested Sukhdev. . . . It is known that Bhagat Singh accompanied the procession. But so for as I remember, he saved himself from the arrest and did not come out. But earlier he arranged everything with Bhagwati Charan and Yashpal who went to Lala Lajpat Rai, and exhorted him to lead the procession. Because, on that day, except Lala Lajpat Rai, no other leader of national status was available to demonstrate against that Commission. The idea was to put equal weight from their side also; so no ordinary person or hireling should lead the procession, but by a responsible leader like Lala Lajpat Rai who was respected all over the country. At first, Lala Lajpat Rai didn't agree, but when he was told that persons of all shades and opinions, from parties like Hindu Mahasabha, Naujawan Bharat Sabha and Congress would be in the procession, he agreed.[21]

To express their resentment, anger and dissatisfaction against the Simon Commission, a largely attended public meeting of the citizens of Lahore was held in the evening of 29 October in the municipal gardens outside the Mochi Gate under the presidentship of a prominent leader, Sheikh Siraj-ud-din Paracha. Besides, a number of well-known leaders from outside Lahore, including Lala Bodh Raj of Mulatan, Raizada Hans Raj of Jalandhar, Syed Ataullah Bokhari, Lala Duni Chand of Ambala and others attended.

Lala Bodh Raj exhorted the people of the Punjab to offer a united front and a resolute will to boycott the commission, Sardar Kharak Singh spoke about the attainment of *swaraj* and advised the audience to work hard for its achievement. He futher stated that the appointment of the all-white commission was the greater insult that the Tory government of England could offer to India.[22]

The Simon Commission arrived at Lahore on 30 October, 1928. Enthusiastic scenes were witnessed in the town on that very day. A huge procession was arranged and it was attended by prominent leaders like Lala Lajpat Rai, Sardar Mangal Singh, Dr. Mohammad Alam, Sardul Singh Caveeshar, Lala Duni Chand, Lala Bodh Raj, Raizada Hans Raj, Dr. Gopi Chand Bhargava, Maulana Zafar Ali and Abdul Qadir Kasuri. Several thousands of followers carried black flags with the inscription, 'Simon go back', started at about 1 p.m. from the municipal gardens towards the railway station. It was quite peaceful and non-violent when it passed through Circular Road via Lunda Bazar and halted at the Mool Chand Temple road, a place about two hundred yards from the main gate to the railway station it was confronted with barbed wires strong wooden posts barricading the way to the railway station. In the first row near the barbed wires stood Lala Lajpat Rai, Maulana Zafar Ali and other leaders. While all of them were perfectly non-violent, some policemen under the direction and orders of J.A. Scott, Senior Superintendent of Police, used their *lathis* on the first row of the procession which included Lala Lajpat Rai. One of them struck him hard in the chest which proved fatal after a few weeks.[23]

Durga Das Khanna, one of the active political workers of the time and a participant in the procession led by Lala Lajpat Rai against the Simon Commission at Lahore reminisced thus, then came the visit of the Simon Commission to Lahore. On that occasion Lalaji had to lead a big procession which was to demonstrate against the commission at the railway station quietly, I also participated in that procession and was very near to Lalaji. The procession was not allowed to reach the railway station premises and was stopped at a distance from the station. When loud shouts began to be raised by the processionists, at the time the members of the commission came to the railway porch to board their cars, a police officer, probably Scott Senior Superintendent to Police, Lahore, took it into his head to teach a lesson to the processionists and ordered a wild *lathi* charge. He himself, in my presence, hurled cane blows at Lalaji's chest. Lalaji, however, did not allow the situation to become confused. He ordered that the processionists would disperse peacefully and not to be led astray by the police.

The injuries received by Lalaji in the chest besides having physical effect caused a deep psychological unrest in his mind. He wondered if a man of his stature could be so brutally and casually treated, what would be the fate of lesser people. As a result of the injuries received and the mental shock they gave him, Lalaji died on 17 November, 1928. . . .[24]

In a public meeting at Lahore, Lala Lajpat Rai condemned police officers' action which was illegal and brutal. He stated, we were absolutely peaceful, and gave no provocation to the police to attack us. But quite unprovoked, a police officer began to strike us with *lathis*. He had a knobbed *hunter* in his hand. He gave me two blows and two of his constables gave another two. One of these blows given to me was aimed at my heart, and very near my heart. I received a stroke which has caused a bruise sufficiently long and broad.

Similar blows were struck at Raizada Hans Raj whose hand was bleeding profusely even there at the spot. Dr. Satya Pal and Dr. Muhammad Alam received blows on their arms which are still paining and I can swear that none of these gentlemen did anything which deserved this cowardly treatment from the police.

Every blow that was hurled at us this afternoon was a nail in the coffin of the British Empire. . . . I wish to warn the government that if a violent revolution takes place in this country, the responsibility for bringing it about will fall on such officers as misbehaved themselves today. If the government and its officers continue to behave, as they did today, I would not wonder if the youngmen go out of our hands and do whatever they choose with the object of gaining the freedom of their country.[25]

Lala Lajpat Rai levelled trenchant criticism against the Simon Commission. 'If the government did not wish that the commission should see all those demonstrations, the best thing for them to do was to put bandages over their eyes and to take them to Government House.'[26]

Among other speakers in this meeting, the prominent were Dr. Muhammad Alam, Dr. Satya Pal, Dr. Gopi Chand Bhargava, Maulana Attaullah Shah Bokhari and Dr. Khan Chand Dev.[27]

Lala Lajpat Rai received a large number of telegrams from his numerous friends and leaders of India. Gandhi wired, 'Hearty congratulations. Wire details, assault and condition of health'.

Pandit Motilal Nehru wrote, 'returned last night. Just heard of the cowardly assault by official hooligans. Regard it as our first great victory. Blows aimed at you have really hit the bureaucracy, and I see it tottering before us. Trust Lahore will march undaunted from victory to victory, and the other places that the Simon Commission visits will follow Lahore's example. Hope your injuries are not serious. Please wire condition. Am ready to join you, necessary.'[28] Besides Gandhi wrote in Young India. '...Nor are we to think that the Punjab incident is to be the last of the barbarities committed during the pedency of the statutory commission. . . . The moral, therefore, I would have workers to draw from this incident is not to be depressed or taken aback by the assault, but to treat it as part of the game, we have to play to turn the irritation caused by the wanton assault into dynamic energy and husband it for future purposes.'[29] Jawaharlal Nehru stated, 'I am not surprised at what happened at Lahore, it was but to be expected. I am glad, Lahore has done well and I hope Lucknow would do better'.

In response to numerous messages received by Lajpat Rai, he expressed his sentiments thus. 'I am deeply touched by the numerous messages of congratulations and sympathy that I have received from my country-men all over India in relation to the recent incident of police attack on me. I cannot sufficiently thank the senders of these messages for their affectionate kindness and goodwill. I think the attack of the police has been on the whole a help to the national cause than otherwise. My first and foremost thanks are due to those who took on themselves the blows that were aimed at me, amongst them being Dr. Satya Pal, Dr. Gopi Chand Bhargava, Raizada Hans Raj, Dr. Alam and others. I accept Sardar Sardul Singh Caveesher's statement that the blows were really aimed at me and but for these gentlemen taking the blows on themselves would have been much more serious and perhaps fatal.'[30]

Raizada Hans Raj sought the intervention of the Governor of the Punjab and apprised him of the whole incident of *lathi* charge on Lala Lajpat Rai and the non-violent processionists. He promised full enquiry into the matter and the government appointed D.J. Boyd, Commissioner of Rawalpindi Division who was instructed to record the statement of any witness to make a relevant statement.[31] Lala Lajpat Rai, however, expressed much unhappiness over the attitude of the Punjab government and stated, 'We do not accept this enquiry and I have no intention of appearing before Mr. D.J. Boyd to give any 'relevant evidence'. If any enquiry is to be made, it must be an open enquiry by a commission consisting of two non-officials and one judicial officer. The members of police must be subjected to cross-examination if the falsity of their statements is to be exposed.'[32] Dr. Muhammad Alam said, 'We must boycott such a farcical enquiry'.[33]

In a comprehensive work on Lajpat Rai : *Life and Work*, Feroze Chand recorded thus about the police *lathi* charge on Lajpat Rai and the great endurance shown by him in this kind of ordeal and brutality.[34]

It is remarkable on the part of Lala Lajpat Rai that he received the blows of *lathis* like a man. He did not flee. He did not flinch. He did not budge. He did not permit his people to hit back. His lieutenants tried to surround him and to share the blows aimed at him. He still received the lion's share so that one of his doctors—Gopi Chand Bhargava who gauged the force of the blows not as a mere eye-witness but more intimately and more exactly as one of those who took on themselves some of the blows meant for the Chief kwondered how it was that he stoop up to it at all without collapsing on the spot.

Manfully he took the blows and shouted with a lion's roar at his assailant, asking for his name. More *lathi* blows were the only reply. Again he shouted and challenged the assaulter's manhood demanding his name once again. The challenge was lost on the unmanly, inhuman thing with the *lathi*. The brute automation just delivered more blows. He did not get the name—not at least from the unmanly thing itself. But his roar was effective in keeping the crowd firmly rooted where they stood—furious but perfectly under control.

After this, Lala Lajpat Rai attended to the usual daily routine though with not that vigour and energy. He attended a meeting of the A.I.C.C. on 3-4 November, 1928 in Delhi and participated in its deliberations. But he felt the strain too heavy to bear it and soon he left for Lahore.

Jawaharlal Nehru paid rich tributes to Lala Lajpat Rai and condemned the brutal *lathi* charge on non-violent procession at

Lahore[35]. ..... 'Lahore brought matters to a head and suddenly sent a thrill of indignation throughout the country. The anti-Simon commission demonstration there was headed by Lala Lajpat Rai, and as he stood by the road-side in front of the throusands of demonstrators he was assaulted and beaten on his chest with a baton by a young English police officer. There had been no attempt whatever on the part of the crowd, much less on the part of Lalaji, to indulge in any methods of violence. Even so, as he stood peacefully by, the and many of his companions were severely beaten by the police....Those were the days when we were not used to *lathi* chrges by the police; our sensitiveness had not been blunted by repeated brutality. To find that even the greatest of our leaders, the foremost and most popular man in the Punjab, could be so treated seemed little short of monstrous, and a dull anger spread all over the country, especially in north India. How helpless we were, how despicable when we could not even protect the honour of our chosen leaders'.

"The physical injury to Lalaji had been serious enough as he had been hit on the chest and he had long suffered from heart disease. Probably, in the case of a healthy youngman, the injury would not have been great, but Lalaji was neither young nor healthy. What effect this physical injury had on his death a few weeks later it is hardly possible to say definitely, thiough his doctors were of opinion that it hastened the end. But I think that there can be no doubt that the mental shock, which accompanied the physical injury had a tremendous effect on Lalaji. He felt angry and bitter, not so much at the personal humiliation, as at the national humiliation involved in the assault on him."

Meanwhile the sad news of Lajpat Rai's death gained currency like wild fire in the Indian press. In fact, he could not recover from the brutal and indiscriminate *lathi* blows of the police on him. *Hartal* was observed all over the Punjab and other towns of India as a mark of respect to the fearless soldier of freedom.[36] Prominent leaders expressed their sense of utter grief and sorrow at his untimely demise. Gandhi paid him glowing tributes. 'Lalaji's death had left a gap which it was difficult to be filled. His was a glorious death and he died a patriot. I do not believe that Lalaji is dead, but he lives.'[37] Motilal Nehru called him a 'prince among peace-makers.'[38] Jinnah stated, 'Lala Lajpat

Rai was undoubtedly a great figure in the political world of India and whether one could always see eye to eye with him or not, he was an earnest and sincere worker. His loss at this particular moment is a great misfortune to India.'[39] Besides other leaders like Madan Mohan Malaviya, C.P. Ramaswami Iyer, Tej Bahadur Sapru, C.Y. Chintamani, Raja Narendra Nath, Dr. Hari Singh Gour, Pheroze Sethna, Malik Feroze Khan Noon, Subhas Chandra Bose, Sankaran Nair, Abdul Qadir, M.C. Rajah and G.D. Birla sent there condolence messages. All praised Lalaji's courage, sacrifice, forbearance, nobility, heroism and patriotism.[40]

John Simon, when interviewed by the Associates Press, said, 'My colleagues and I greatly regret to learn of Lajpat Rai's death which means the removal of an ardent social worker as well as of a prominent political worker.'[41]

The sudden, unexpected and tragic death of Lala Lajpat Rai had greatly agitated the minds of the youths of the Punjab, who showed much respect and veneration for the great leader. The members of the Hindustan Socialist Republican Army at Lahore were particularly very sore over the maltreatment of reputed leader of Lalaji's stature by a British police official, J.A. Scott under whose order and supervision the police personnel had resorted to a severe *lathi* charge on a peaceful procession. The significant point at issue before the leadership of the H.S.R.A. was to wreak vengeance of his brutal action by directly hitting the Lahore police chief.

The task indeed was no easy. British imperialism in 1920s was in its hay days and it was not easy to touch a British official, particularly a police official and that too in the capital of the province, where he could have immense resources, departmentally or otherwise, to hit back with more force that might prove fatal and cause of serios destruction to the assailant. Such a kind of attempt had much involements of a risky venture, but it must be performed by one or two, devoted to the cause always preached and professed by Lala Lajpat Rai so long as he remained alive.

With the initiative of Sardar Bhagat Singh and his associates, Chandra Shekhar Azad and other senior members of the party were summoned at Lahore to execute this plan to a successful end. They ultimately decided to avenge the death of Lala Lajpat

Rai at the hands of the British police official. 'It was particularly the wish of every one present that the prophesy made by Lalaji at the Mori Gate meeting must come true and towards that end, the first step should be the liquidation of the offender who had insulted the whole nation by his wanton assault on Lalaji's person'.

It is indeed significant to know that the attitude and overall assessment of the progressive youths of the Punjab about Lala Lajpat Rai was not favourable in 1920s. It is also a fact that Lalaji was opposed by the members of the Naujawan Bharat Sabha during his election campaign in 1926. In fact, Sardar Bhagat Singh, Bhagwati Charan Vohra and their young associates criticised him on account of his deep linkage and association with Hindu Mahasabha which the revolutionaries openly labelled as a communal organisation. The revolutionaries, therefore, did not favour the idea that a leading and prominent national leader and above all, a nationalist of his stature should support any kind of communal organisation. They thought that 'we are all Indians and therefore, there was no scope for communal thinking.'

But at this point of time they thought it improper to rack up the past when the honour of the nation was involved. The best course they thought would be to get united for a concerted action to avenge Lala Lajpat Rai's death in the curcumstances which had directly hit the honour of the nation. This kind of action, taken against the British police official in the capital of the Punjab must establish the *bona fides* and identity of the young revolutionaries amongst the people of the country and must show how sincere, determined, dedicated and patriotic they were. Thus, the protest by the members of the Bharat Naujawan Sabha was louder and practical in every respect. A meeting of the Hindustan Socialist Republican Association was convened at once to chalk out the programme of executing such a responsible measure in a detailed manner. Any mistake or wrong planning could prove a sucidal measure for the youths participating in this kind of daring venture almost in the heart of the city. The task indeed was full of risks. For its successful execution, the venue of the meeting of the youths was the residence of Bhagwati Charan, and it was attended by Bhagat Singh, Chander Shekhar Azad, Sukhdev and other young revolutionary leaders. Each and every one present there expressed his emphatic criticism of the methods of British Raj and ultimately made a firm decision unanimously to wreak vengeance on J.A. Scott who was responsible for *lathi* charge on Lalaji and others.

Initially, Azad and Jai Gopal took the initiative in surveying the whole route of Scott—from his office to his residence and communicated each and every detail to his comrades. Proper places were alloted to every one of them. Bhagat Singh, Azad and Rajguru came fully armed riding on cycles which they left in the boarding house of the D.A.V. College. Bhagat Singh and Rajguru moved near the District Police Chief's office. Azad kept himself posted at the gate of the college and Jai Gopal stood at one end of the court road.

It was planned that Jai Gopal was to give a signal to Bhagat Singh and Rajguru as soon as Scott would come out of his office. The whole man well-discussed earlier, was to be executed meticulously by these four revolutionaries. The task was immense–a murder of police chief in broad-day light as well as the plan to escape–were to be completed without committing any kind of mistake by any one of them.

At the appointed time, a British official stepped out of his office and rode on a motor cycle. At once, the signal was given by Jai Gopal to Rajguru and Bhagat Singh who were anxiously waiting for the opportunity. At first, Raj Guru fired on the British official with a pistol shot which pierced through his neck and almost killed him. At this Bhagat Singh virtually pounced upon him and fired four or five shots with an automatic pistol. The British official died at the spot. He was not Scott but J.P. Saunders, the Assistant Superintendent of Police, a youngman of 21 and yet a probationer. It was a miscalculation on the part of Jai Gopal who failed to distinguish between Scott and Saunders. There may be much difference of ages and physical structures between the two officials. Thus, in a huff a wrong person was entrapped in the revolutionary snare. The mistake was detected soon after by the perpetrators of this murder, but it was considered as a great satisfaction to them with the feeling that a senior British police official had been done away with and it would be lesson-giving event to the British bureaucracy in India.

An Inspector of Police, Head Constable Chanan Singh and two constables were the eye-witnesses to this gruesome murder and all of them chased Bhagat Singh and Rajguru. But they escaped through the campus of the D.A.V. College where Azad was waiting for them. The hot pursuit by Chanan Singh cost him his life. He was shot dead by Azad.

With the murder of Saunders, Bhagat Singh and his associates gained nationwide fame and popularity. The people did not bother to call it an act of violence or terrorism, but, instead, it was rightly called the best method of vindication of the honour of Lala Lajpat Rai and through him of the nation.

The *Tribune* of 19 December, 1928 stated in its headlines thus: Assistant Police Superintendent Shot Dead. Constable who Gives Chase Also Meets With Same Fate: Police Surround D.A.V. College.[42]

The same day, the Additional District Magistrate went to the local D.A.V. College hostel and demanded the roll call of the boarders. The authorities arranged the roll call and it was followed by the search of the hostel which continued late at night. Besides, the adjoining hostels of the D.A.V. Middle School and the Aggarwal Ashram were searched. No clue however could be found out with these searches. Soon after the following persons were taken into custody. They were Dharamvir, Dhanwantri, H.R. Vohra, Kidar Nath Sehgal, Sant Ram, Abdul Majid, Mansur Ahmed, Virendra, Hari Ram Sethi, Ahmed Din, Satyavrat, Mohammad Afzal, Raj Kishore Singh and a few others.[43]

Next day a red poster was distributed all over Lahore. It explained thus:[44] 'It was indeed a great insult to the nation comprising of crores of people when an ordinary British police official murdered a most respected national leader, Lala Lajpat Rai. It was the foremost duty of each and every youth of India to perform this kind of sacred duty.

Today the whole world has seen how the people of India are fully conscious of their fundamental rights and how they are fully prepared to sacrifice anything in order to save the honour of their motherland ......we are sorry that we were compelled to take the life of an individual. But this official was a part and parcel of the bureaucracy which functioned in an inhuman and illegal way. We had to finish him once for all. By killing him we have put an end to a functionary of British bureaucracy. We are sorry to resort to this kind of killing, but it is very difficult to function for a revolution without any kind of bloodshed. Our aim is to work for such a revolution which would put any kind of cruelty to an end.

In 1947, J.A. Scott was D.I.G. of Police, Rawalpindi Division and he very much wished to come over to East Punjab after the partition of India. When he, along with a few other senior British police officials opted for East Punjab, his application was not accepted by the then Chief Minister of the newly-partitioned province on the plea that he had a highly questionable stigma with his name. Therefore, whereas other officials were permitted, he was not.

It was indeed a risky job to stay at Lahore even for a moment. The murder of Suanders had created panic and sensation in the capital of the Punjab. The police was alerted in every nook and corner not only in Lahore, but throughout north India. This kind of arrangement by the government was not unknown to Bhagat Singh who very cleverly and shrewdly changed his guise at the D.A.V. College; put on the dress of an Englishman and sought the help of Durga Bhabi who agreed to act as his wife during this daring political drama. He thus travelled by the Calcutta Mail along with Rajguru, Chandrashekhar Azad, Durga Bhabi and her infant son, Shachindra and not a single police man either at Lahore or during the long journey could detect his appearance. At Calcutta, he was welcomed by his comrades who had the information if his arrival there. This was indeed a daring escape from the scene of murder which had become a rendezvous of detectives who were commissioned by the government to arrest the culprits in the murder case.

On 17th December, 1928, the Secretary of State was seized of the critical situation which had developed in the Punjab with the murder of Saunders. He felt worried and much concern over the ghastly episode. In a telegram to the Viceroy, he enquired, 'Press here reports Saunders, I.P.S. Punjab and native clerk shot dead in Lahore. Please confirm or deny this report'.[45]

Besides, the Home Secretary, government of India enquired from the Punjab government on 19 December, 1928, 'Saunders murder. Please telegraph immediately action hitherto taken and keep government of India informmed regularly of developments of investigation'.[46]

In reply to this telegram, the Punjab government informed the Home Secretary on the same day.

'Jenkin, Superintendent of Police, Criminal Investigation Department, is in charge of investigation in Saunders's murder case, under direct supervision of D.I.G., C.I.D. Investigation is being pursued with greatest vigour and reasonable hope of success.'[47] A number of persons were arrested. They were Dhanwantri, Vir Indar, Hans Raj Vohra, Dharm Yash–members of the Lahore Students Union; Ahmad Din, Kedar Nath Sehgal, M.A. Majid, Mir Muhammad Afzal, Labhu Ram Partap, Sant Ram Pandha, Amolak Ram of Lahore, Hari Ram Sethi of Rawalpindi, Keshap Bandhu of Kashmir, Raj Kishore Singh of United Provinces.[48]

The Viceroy informed the Secretary of State on 20th December, 1928. 'Government of Punjab report that investigation into the murder of Saunders is being pursued with greatest vigour and reasonable hope of success. Sixteen persons most of whom are connected with Naujawan Bharat Sabha or with Lahore Students Union have been arrested on reasonable suspicion of murder, abetment of murder and or criminal conspiracy, and orders for arrest of three other have issued.'[49]

On the same day, the Home Secretary, government of India, showed much concern in his telegram to the Punjab government.[50] 'Increasingly inflammatory tone of speeches in Punjab particularly in connection with the death of Lala Lajpat Rai has recently been observed with some anxiety. If murder of Saunders can as they presume be attributed to these suggestive incitements to violence, they are of opinion that time has come to strike effective blow against those guilty of them. Please therefore report whether Punjab government contemplate launching prosecutions at once against all those who in last month or so have made speeches of this nature which afford strong grounds for prosecution and who are worth prosecuting. The men named below are among those whose speeches have been specially noticed by government of India, namely, Zafar Ali

Khan, Satyapal, Muhammad Alam, Abinash Chandar Bali and Gopi Chand. If prosecution of those who have really been inciting to violence follows murderous outrage promptly deterrent effect on such incitements for future should be considerable while, fact that outrage has occurred should help to secure heavy sentences. Of course, similar considerations apply to articles in newspaper.'

By 29th December, 1928, there was, in fact, no progress in locating the murderers of Saunders. 'I think we ought to inform the Secretary of State that the investigation in the Saunders' murder case is not making such progress. We might at the same time the opportunity of informing him of the policy of prosecuting seditious speakers.'[51]

When the Viceroy informed the Secratary of State on 29 December of the progress in the investigation of the murder of Saunders,[52] the latter felt disappointment over it '.........it is very disappointing to hear that progress of investigations is not so satisfactory. Punjab Government are I hope making every effort to bring matter to speedy and successful conclusion. . . . Please let me know if possibility been considered of proclaiming Naujawan Bharat Sabha an unlawful association if sufficient grounds for such action are provided by investigation.'[53]

On 10 January, 1929, the Viceroy informed the Secretary of State, 'Release on bail of all persons arrested has ended first phase of investigation. Accepted theory, which is probably correct, has been that murder was direct act of revenge for death of Lajpat Rai. There was secret information of complicity against some of those arrested, while ever since his death number of others have been indulging in inflammatory speeches. . . . There are several eye witnesses who profess ability to identify one or more of murderers. It is also reasonably certain that carefully chosen line of retreat throught D.A.V. College compound required intimate local knowledge on part of one or more of culprits who were probably seen by large number of students. It is also thought that fired cartridge cases bear sufficiently distinctive marks to lead to identification of firearms used if they are recovered. All these factors favour hope of ultimate success. Possibility of outside persons having been imported is being carefully examined, and every other likely line of enquiry is being followed up actively.'[54]

The Punjab government, was, however, not very serious take immediate action against Naujawan Bharat Sabha. It, therefore, informed the Home Secretary on 14 January, 1929,[55] Governor-in-Council doubtful whether any direct connection with Naujawan Bharat Sabha will be established by investigation of Saunders, murder, and until the result of prosecution of Sabha office-bearers are known and effect of consideration if obtained can be gauged, he would prefer to defer consideration of question of declaring Sabha unlawful association.

The Home Secretary, Punjab government, in a communication to the Home Secretary Government of India dated 14th January, 1929 admitted a few important facts about the murder of Saunders by Bhagat Singh and his associates.[56] Even prior to the murder episode, an atmosphere had been created favourable to commission of this kind of daring and fearless political outrage. Admittedly, Saunders was one of the police officials who helped to keep the crowd back from the barrier at the Lahore Railway Station on 30th October, when Lala Lajpat Rai was alleged to have been assaulted by the police, and the speeches made at the inflammatory meetings held in Lahore in connection with Lala Lajpat Rai's death tended directly to create and keep alive the impression that he and other police officials had caused Lajpat Rai's death and thus inculcate a spirit of revenge. These feelings tinged with violent sentiments were intensified on 16th December, 1928 when a meeting organised by the Naujawan Bharat Sabha and attended mainly by students was held in Lalore to celebrate the 'Kakori Day' and some particularly had speeches marked by incitements to violence and glorification of revolutionary assassins were made.[57]

The Home Secretary, Punjab government, admitted later on that some delay was caused by the police force to pursue the assassins of Saunders. At first the pistol reports did not alarm those in the police office as they were taken for motor cycle back fires when, however, the alarm was raised, a pursuit party was organised at once, but it was unable to come up with the assassins.[58]

On 19 April, 1929, the Viceroy informed the Secretary of State about some clear clues found out by the police soon after the Assembly Bomb episode in Delhi. 'Investigation of Assembly outrage, so far as it has proceeded, seem to have considerably improved prospects of a solution of the Saunders' murder..... The leaflets thrown down in Assembly by persons arrested were type on pink paper with printed heading which is identical in all respects with that used in threatening manuscript notices pasted up in Lahore after murder. Moreover for some time past suspicion has been hardening that Bhagat Singh, arrested in Assembly, was party to Saunders' murder and preliminary microscopic examination of automatic pistol found with his favours view that it was one of weapons used in actual shooting of Saunders. On this point proper scientific proof is being sought.'[59]

The following was the statement of Traffic Inspector of Police, W.J.G. Fearn.

'I was in the police office on the 17 December, 1928. I was with Mr. Saunders, Assistant Superintendent of Police, in his room from about 12-30 to 4 P.M. or a little later...... I had an appointment at about 4-30 p.m. in connection with an accident and so prepared to leave office. I was putting on my helmet and belt when I heard Mr. Saunders motor cycle start outside. I came out of my room and went straight to my motor cycle which was standing behind the gate pillar. As I got to my cycle Mr. Saunders was just cycling out of the gate. As Mr. Saunders got on to the road opposite an electric light standard, near the D.A.V. College, I saw two men step out from near the standard and fire at Mr. Saunders. Mr. Saunders was to move towards his right hand side of the road than the left hand side. Mr. Saunders fell forward on to his motor cycle. The cycle swerved to the left of the road and eventually fell over on to its left side. Mr. Saunders falling with his leg under the cycle. The two men who fired at Mr. Saunders crossed the road to where Mr. Saunders had fallen. One man stood in front of the cycle near the front wheel and the other man about half way down opposite the engine and both these men continued to fire at Mr. Saunders as he lay on the ground. Mr. Saunders was lying on the police office side of the road near a tree.

Mr. Saunders' Munshi Chanan Singh was standing talking to him when I came out to my motor cycle. I ran out to the gate in between the first and second firing followed by Chanan Singh. The two men who were firing at Mr. Saunders as he lay on ground ran off in the direction of court street. I ran after the man who had been standing in front of the motor-cycle. I ceased to observe the other man's movements. When we reached court street corner, I was overtaking this man. When we had gone up court street, a little distance, he turned and aimed at me. As he fired, I ducked, so he missed me. I continued running after him. My foot slipped in a small drain at the side of the road, and I came down very heavily. While I was on the ground, the man whom I was pursuing aimed at me again, but his shot misfired.

When I was getting up I saw Chanan Singh run past me going up court street towards the gate of the D.A.V. College. I did not see either of the assailants of Mr. Saunders going into the college gate. I did not see where they went. Chanan Singh went into the gate of principal's bungalow, and before he went in, I called out to him not to go inside (*andar na jao*). Very shortly afterwards there was a sound of another shot from inside the gate and the Chanan Singh came out a little later bleeding very badly from the right groin. Blood was flowing down from his right leg. He came up to me and said, '*sahib mar gaya*.' After saying this to me Chanan Singh collapsed.... I told sub-inspector Amar Singh who had arrived there to procure a gun. A gun was brought from the *kutchery* and taking the gun and some ammunition, I went into the D.A.V. College compound. I searched all the buildings behind the main block of the college and questioned some students who were sitting about the garden there, but could get no information about any persons having run through the compound.

The man standing in front of the wheels of Mr. Saunders' motor cycle looked like a student of about 5′-5″-6″ in height. He was slim built, wearing a Christy type of cap, a coat of dark cloth, white trousers and black Derby pattern shoes which I saw from close when I fell as this was the man who fired at me. The second man who was standing opposite the engine of Mr. Saunders' cycle was taller but dressed similarly. He was also slim built. To the best of my knowledge this man did not fire at me'.

Sohan Singh Josh reminisced thus in connection with his meeting with Bhagat Singh soon after the murder of Saunders.[60]

On December, 17 about afternoon, a police officer was killed by some revolutionaries while he was coming out of the police headquarters. In the evening rumours were afloat everywhere in Amritsar. Some said the murdered man was the SSP Scott, some said it was Saunders. On the same night (December 17) a little after 11 p.m. somebody knocked at my door in Bara Ghara, Islamabad. I was alone in the house, my family having gone to my village Chetanpura (Amritsar). I opened the door and to my utter surprise I found Bhagat Singh and Sukh Dev standing outside. I welcomed them but told them that it was rather risky to have come to my house because the police might raid it any time. But Bhagat Singh said: 'Don't worry, we have made all arrangements'. They came in and said: 'We are hungry, give us some thing to eat. I could offer only two *chapatis*, some vegetables and a glass of milk. I told them that we could cook fresh food. But they said, 'nothing doing, we shall talk and sleep'.

Bhagat Singh was wearing a flat hat and an English style suit. He was quite unrecognisable in those clothes. Sukh Dev was wearing an English hat and suit. Bhagat Singh took off his hat and placed it on a table nearby. He hung his pistol on a peg above the cot. Then after finishing the meagre meal, the first question he shot at me was, 'What is the reaction in general to Saunders' murder?' Now I came to know that it was Saunders who was murdered.

'The youth are happy,' I replied. 'But they would have been much happier if Scott had been killed.'

'We had gone there only for him (Scott), but the other devil came out,' he said. 'And we could not go back empty-handed after all the pains taken for the preparation. Any way: some beginning has been made'.

'There is another opinion also about this murder', I put in, 'that of Gandhi's followers.'

'We knew it beforehand,' he said. 'We discussed this before deciding upon this action.' Then he contemptuously added: 'Gandhi stabbed the nation in the back by withdrawing the non-cooperation movement (1920-22) after the *Chauri Chaura* incident. The people are still under the cloud of frustration and demoralisation which he brought to the country. But leave that aside. Do you know what has been the effect of Saunders' murder on the British rulers? There is a great panic among them. Some of them have already booked their wives' and children's passages for England. They are terribly frightened'.

'But this panic is temporary', I gave my opinion. 'It will wear off soon'.

'What do you think of this action?'

'My views you know. We have talked about this matter several times. Our Naujawan Bharat Sabha workers will be arrested. There will be greater repression and the movement will suffer, will be retarded.'

'I don't agree', he said, 'This action will rouse the masses and strengthen the movement.'

'During this whole talk, Sukh Dev did not say a word. He had met me for the first time.'

'Then Bhagat Singh asked me when I was going to Calcutta for the All-India Conference of the Peasants' and Workers' party, I replied, 'Tomorrow'.

'You go your way, we go ours.' "That ended our talk.'[61]

REFERENCES

1. *Halifax papers*. Secretary of State of Viceroy, September 23, 1926.
2. C.H. Setalvad, *Recollections and Reflections*, Bombay, 1946, p. 341.
3. *The Tribune*, 28 December, 1927.
4. Debates, House of Commons, 1927, Vol. 208, pp. 1974-75.
5. C.Y. Chintamani, *Indian Problems Since the Mutiny*, Allahabad, 1937, p. 171.
6. C.H. Setalvad, *Recollections and Reflections*, Bombay, 1946, p. 342.
7. C.Y. Chintamani, *op. cit.*, p. 171.
8. S.R. Bakshi, *Simon Commission and Indian Nationalism*, New Delhi, 1977, p. 25.
9. C.F. Andrews, *Indian and the Simon Report*, London, 1930, p. 32.
10. *Halifax Papers*. Secretary of State of Viceroy, May 5, June 9 and July 6, 1927.
11. The Earl of Halifax, *Fullness of Days*, London, 1957, p. 115.
12. The Earl of Birkenhead. *Frederick Edwin, Earl of Birkenhead: The First Phase and Last Phase*, London, 1933, pp. 251-52.
13. Debates, House of Commons, Vol. 210, 1927, p. 2219.
14. C.F. Andrews, *op. cit.* pp. 37-38.
15. A Liberal, *The Commission and After*, Bombay, 1928, pp. 27-28.
16. *Halifax* Papers. Secretary of State of the Viceroy, November 7, 1927.

17. Reforms Office, File 15-17 Misc. 1929.
18. For details see *Times of India*, 10 November, 1927.
19. See the resolution of the working committee of the Indian National Congress in *The Tribune*, 16 November, 1927.
20. *The Tribune*, 31 October, 1928.
21. Transcript of interview with Jai Dev Gupta, *op. cit*.
22. *The Tribune*, 29 October, 1928.
23. *Ibid.*
24. Transcript of interview with Durga Das Khanna, N.M.M.L.
25. *The Tribune*, 2 November, 1928.
26. *Ibid.*
27. *Ibid.*
28. *Ibid.*
29. See the complete statement of Gandhi in *Young India*, 8 November, 1928.
30. Quoted in Feroze Chand, *Lajpat Rai: Life and Work*, New Delhi, 1978, pp. 544-45.
31. *The Tribune*, 9 November, 1928.
32. *The Tribune*, 10 November, 1928.
33. *Ibid.*
34. Feroze Chand, *op. cit.*, pp. 540 ff.
35. Jawaharlal Nehru, *An Autobiography*, New Delhi, 1962, p. 174.
36. *The Tribune*, 19 November, 1928.
37. *Ibid*. Gandhi also stated that with Lalaji's death, a great planet has set in India's solar system.
38. *Ibid.*
39. *Ibid.*
40. *The Tribune*, 20 November, 1928.
41. *Ibid.*
42. *The Tribune*, 19 November, 1928.
43. *Ibid.*
44. Gopal Thakur, *Bhagat Singh: Vyaktitav aur Vichardhara*, New Delhi, 1980, p. 12.
45. Home Poll, File 4/7, 1930.

46. *Ibid.*
47. *Ibid.*
48. *Ibid.*
49. *Ibid.*
50. *Ibid.*
51. *Ibid.*
52. 'Progress of investigation into Saunders' murder does not appear to be coming up to expectations.... 'Home poll, File 4/7, 1930.
53. *Ibid.*
54. *Ibid.*
55. *Ibid.*
56. For details see this letter in Home Poll, File 4/7, 1930.
57. *Ibid.*
58. *Ibid.*
59. *Ibid.*
60. Proceedings of the Lahore Conspiracy Case, pp. 541 ff.
61. See 'My Meetings with Bhagat Singh' an article by Sohan Singh Josh in *Link*, 22 March 1981.

5 Bomb in the Assembly

THE WARNING

The daring escape from Lahore after the broad-day light murder of Saunders was swift and successful and soon Bhagat Singh felt slightly safe in the sense because he was out of the dangerous zone where the gruesome murder has taken place. He knew very well that his stay anywhere, in a big or small town, with a well-wisher or a party man, would be full of dangers which would land him into serious trouble. The police was after him and many of his comrades. To arrest them alive or to kill them in an encounter would have been considered an act of bravery by an Indian police man. But it was no easy job to accomplish such a hazardous, ticklish and risky task. the change of guise, wearing of various kinds of dresses, quick and speedy movement and changing of residential places at frequent intervals always put the police in an inexplicable suspense and doubt.

Bhagat Singh preferred to leave North India temporarily and made up his mind to shift at a place where his stay and work could be fruitful for the revolutionary movement. He also wished to have deep connection with his fellow-comrades in order to implement the vigorous anti-government programme of his party. It seems that after the murder of Saunders, he and his associates had the planning to execute a programme which could be more violent in action and effect. And for this kind of vigorous action, he shifted to Calcutta.[1] Soon he could contact J.N. Das and Phonindo Nath Ghosh and sought their advice and guidance for manufacturing bombs to be used by him and his associates in their anti-government activities at various places. Intially, such a work was taken up at the residence of Kanwal Nath Tewari in Calcutta. Bhagat Singh also learnt this art in a short time.

Meanwhile, Bhagat Singh kept on moving in the revolutionary circles in Bengal, U.P. and Delhi. A bomb factory was set up at Agra, the headquarters of the Hindustan Socialist Republican Army. Other bomb-manufacturing cells were organised at Lahore and Saharanpur by Sukhdev and Shiv Verma. Their effectiveness was duly tested out-of-the way places. This weapon greatly stengthened the hands of the revolutionaries who were yet to show their remarkable feat of bravery by throwing a bomb in the central hall of the Assembly.

In March 1929, the British government dealt a severe blow on the functioning of the trade union leaders in various provinces. Their movements were restricted by their arrests and convictions. As a result of this kind of repression, leaders like S.A. Danga, Muzaffar Ahmed, S.V. Ghate and 29 other labour leaders were arrested.[2]

The dire need for the performance of such a daring act was felt by Bhagat Singh and his associates at a time when the Central Assembly had taken up the Public Safety Bill and Trade Disputes Bill.

The young revolutionaries were of unanimous opinion that no Indian could expect fair justice under British imperialism. Their policy of suppression of the fundamental rights of Indians by one law or the other came in for severe criticism and condemnation. Under these cricumstances, these youths were not hopeful of any outcome that could emerge out of British administrative and judicial systems for the development of the country. Hence, their consensus was for sacrifice, indeed supreme sacrifice, of their lives in a way which should become a legend and a symbol for the whole nation.

A month prior to the finalisation of the act of throwing the bomb in the Central Assembly Hall, Sardar Bhagat Singh remained busy in revolutionary activities in the region between Delhi and Agra. During this period, as it is clear from the police reports, he happened to stay in Bazaar Sitaram, 15 Roshanara Mansion and at Banta Ashram in the Kucha Ghasi Ram–all places in Delhi.[3]

It is also evident that Bhagat Singh and B.K. Dutt got themselves photographed at Kashmere Gate, Delhi as these photos later on appeared in *The Pioneer, The Hindustan Times* and the *Bande Mataram*, Lahore. They managed their passes through an Indian member of the Assembly.

A daring decision to throw a bomb in the Assembly Hall was finally implemented in a detailed and meticulous way. The central idea of such an act was to express resentment for the bills being discussed by the Assembly and not to kill any member. Leaflets were to be thrown with the chanting of slogans like '*Inquilab Zindabad*' and the revolutionaries entrusted with this kind of daring mission were not to escape but to offer themselves to the police. The other idea was to the use the courts as the forums for the genuine expression of their revolutionary patriotic ideas before the people of India whose zeal and fervour for the freedom of the country could be rekindled in a better shape by this kind of voluntary gesture.

Personally Bhagat Singh never favoured the idea of escape after throwing the bomb in the Assembly. So with consensus, he and B.K. Dutt were chosen for this task. They made arrangements for the visitors' passes and two days prior to the occurrence they had the reconnaisance of the Assembly Hall and the kind of seating arrangement in it.

On 8 April, 1929, the Viceroy Lord Irwin was to deliver his speech in connection with those Bills. There was much rush both of visitors and press representatives. Bhagat Singh and B.K.Dutt dressed in *Khaki* shirts and *Khaki* shorts sat quietly in the visitors'gallery.

Just as the voting on the Trades Disputes Bill was over and the Bill had been declared carried by the President, and before the President started to give his ruling on Public Safety Bill, there was a hustle in visitors lobby and then a thundering noise, resulting in chaos and smoke.[4] A bomb or something like it fell, the atmosphere in the house became dark.There were shrieks in ladies, galleries, cries and noises below and before the people had got over first shock, there was a again second explosion. Another bomb fell. Thunder and smoke and shrieks, confusion and chaos all prevailed. Members were trying to rush out, visitors dashing for safety and women running for protection. And then two pistol shots were heard. The members and visitors all were terrified.

After sometime the smoke disappeared the members had all collected in the centre of House. Suddenly it was discovered that there was someone in Assembly visitors' gallery with bleeding hand. He offered himself for arrest to the police so did his companion. Immediately more members of the police force appeared on the scene and vacated to Assembly Chamber as well as the galleries. All doors of the Assembly were closed and no person including the members was allowed to leave the Chamber.[5]

A case was instituted under section 307 IPC for alleged attempt to commit murder. Bhagat Singh was sent to Central Police Station and B. K. Dutt to Raisina Police Station in lorries strongly guarded by police.

The Hindustan Times of Delhi reported thus

'Bombs and Pistols create chaos in Assembly: Two Bombs Explode: Pistol shots fired: Screaming Women from Ladies Gallery: Sir Fomanji Dalal Seriously Injured: Two Arrested: Sir George Schuster, Mr. S.C.Gupta and other officials received minor injuries.'[7]

Soon after this episode, a lightning raid was made by the police at Lahore in a house called Kashmir Building. Macleod Road and twenty-four bombs, some cartridges and some pistols were discovered.The Punjab Police arrested four youngmen: the building had been rented in the name of Bhagwati Charan in March last.[8]

On the other hand, the two young revolutionaries after the successful performance of their action were busy in rising their slogans like *'Inquilab Zindabad'* and Down with British Imperialism. They also threw the leaflets in the Central Hall of the Assembly in order to acquaint the members directly and the people of India Indirectly of their main aim object and mission. The contents of the leaf were as follows : 'It takes a loud voice to make the deaf hear. With these immortal words uttered on a similar occasion by Valliant a French anarchist martyr, do we strongly justify this action of ours'.

Without repeating the humiliating history of the past ten years of the working of the reforms (Montague-Chelmsford Reforms) and without mentioning the insults hurled at the Indian nation through this House–the so-called Indian Parliament— we want to point out that, while the people expecting some more crumbs of reforms from the Simon Commission, and are ever quarrelling over the distribution of the expected bones, the

Government is thrusting upon us new repressive measures like the Public Safety and the Trade Disputes Bill, while reserving the Press Sedition Bill for the next session. The indiscrminate arrests of labour leaders working in the open field clearly indicate whither the wind blows.

In these provocative circumstances the Hindustan Socialist Republican Association, in all seriousness, realising their full responsibility, had decided and ordered its army to do this particular action, so that a stop be put to this humiliating force and to let the alien bureaucratic exploiters do what they wish, but they must be made to come before the publics eye in their naked form.

Let the representatives of the people return to their constituencies and prepare the masses for the coming revolution, and let the Government know that while protesting against the Public Safety and Trade Disputes Bill and the callous murder of Lala Lajpat Rai, on behalf of the helpless Indian masses, we want to emphasize the lesson often repeated by history, that it is easy to kill individuals but you cannot kill the ideas. Great empires crumbled while the ideas survived. Bourbons and Czars fell.

We are sorry to admit that we who attach so great a sanctity to human life, we, who dream of a glorious future, when man will be enjoying perfect peace and full liberty have been forced to shed human blood. But the sacrifice of individuals at the alter of the "Great Revolution" that will bring freedom to all, rendering the exploitation of man by man impossible, is inevitable.

Long Live the Revolution

The wording and the ideas contained in this pamphlet were a serious challenge to existence and the functioning of the British Raj in India. The very fact that this kind of challenge emanated seriously from the dedicated youthful spirit of India, made the British bureaucracy from a District Collector to the Viceroy very cautious, watchful and alert in their functioning. They, in fact, had begun to realize that these revolutionary youths with fiery ideas, communistic ideology and last but not the least, with deadly weapons in their hands, would put a permanent blockage in the efficient and smooth functioning of the government. They therefore deviced stern means and used the official machinery to crush this kind of movement by arrests, convictions, deportations and hangings.

It was not a difficult task for Bhagat Singh and B.K. Dutt to dodge the usual vigil of the police after throwing the bombs in the central hall of the Assembly. A decision of this kind had already been made and at this point of time, it was no fun to change the earlier decision. Both the dauntless heroes stood like a rock at their places and they courted arrest with spontaneous smile and glee on their youthful faces.

It was not a part of their political decision to run. Instead of escaping from the scene, they stood like a rock, raised revolutionary slogans, threw leaflets in the central hall of the Assembly and willingly courted arrest when the police arrived there. By this kind of gesture which prove "suicidal" for them in the course of time, had a deep hidden meaning—a message for the nation and an expression of deep resentment and dissatisfaction against he existing laws of the Raj. This kind of model was patriotic, daring and sincere in its contents. It is true that thereafter Bhagat Singh was never let off and remained in the jail till 23 March, 1931 when he was hanged alongwith his two comrades, but the act was never forgotten and it made Bhagat Singh a symbol of the nation–a symbol to be honoured and respected and also to be emulated by the youths of India.

Soon after their arrests, the two revolutionaries were taken to the police *Kotwali* situated in Chandni Chowk. The assembly adjourned.

The accused admit throwing bombs in the Assembly Chamber they deny that either of them fired a pistol and deny that a pistol was seized from either of them. They alleged,[9] that a pistol was fired in the air by some other person whom they do not name.

They allege that the prosecution evidence regarding the seizure of the pistol is false and that some of the prosecution evidence regarding the throwing of bombs in also false.

'They affirm that they hold human life sacred and state that they dropped the bombs as a protest and as a warning. They had no grudge or malice against any one of the persons injured; they refer to the damage caused by the bombs which they characterise as slight and affirm that it was their intention that no serious damage would result.'[10]

The Judge stated in his judgement, 'I accept the direct and oral evidence produced before me as cogent proof that Bhagat

Singh and Datta each threw bombs into the Assembly Chamber, that Bhagat Singh fired a pistol and that Datta scattered leaflets in the Chamber. The facts which are essential to the charges are that each of the accused threw a bomb and I find it proved that each of them did it so.'[11]

The following was the historic and bold statement given by Sardar Bhagat Singh and B.K. Dutt in connection with the Assembly Bombs case on 6 June, 1929. It was made through an eminent advocate, Asaf Ali who pleaded this case in the court of the Sessions Judge, Delhi.

We stand charged with certain serious offences and at this stage it is but right that we must explain our conduct. In this connection the following questions arise:

1. Were the bombs thrown into Chamber, and, if so, why?
2. Is the charge, as framed by the Lower Court, correct or otherwise?

To the first half of first question our reply is in the affirmative, but since some of the so-called eye witnesses have perjured themselves and since we are not denying our liability to that extent let our statement about them be judged for what it is worth. By way of an illustration we may point out that the evidence of Sergeant Terry regarding the seizure of the pistol from one of us is a deliberate falsehood for neither of us had the pistol at the time we gave overselves up. Other witnesses, too, who have deposed to having seen bombs being thrown by us have not scrupled to tell lies. This fact had its own moral for those who aim at judicial purity and fairplay.

At the same time, we acknowledge the fairness of the Public Prosecuter and the Judicial attitude of the Court so far.

Viceroy's Views Endorsed

In our reply to the next half of the first question we are constrained to go into some detail to offer a full and frank explanation of our motive and the circumstances leading up to what has now become a historic event.

When we were told by some of the police officers, who visited us in jail that Lord Irwin in his address to the joint session of the two Houses described the event as an attack directed against no individual but against an institution itself, we readily recognised that the true significance of the incident had been correctly appreciated.

We are next to none in our love for humanity. Far from having any malice against any individual, we hold human life sacred beyond words.

We are neither perpetrators of dastardly outrages, and therefore, a disgrace to the country, as the pseudo-socialist Dewan Chaman Lall, is reported to have described us, nor are we 'Lunatics' as the *Tribune* of Lahore and some others would have it believed.

Practical Protest

We humbly claim to be no more than serious students of the history and conditions of our country and her aspirations. We despise hypocrisy. Our practical protest was against the institution, which since its birth, has eminently helped to display not only its worthlessness but its far-reaching power for mischief. The more we have pondered, the more deeply we have been convinced that it exists only to demonstrate to world India's humiliation and helplessness and it symbolises the overriding domination of an irresponsible and autocratic rule. Time and again the national demand has been pressed by the people's representatives only to find the waste paper basket as its final destination.

Attack on Institution

Solemn resolutions passed by the House have been contemptuously trampled under foot on the floor of the so-called Indian Parliament. Resolution regarding the repeal of the repressive and arbitrary measures have been treated with sublime contempt, and the government measures and proposals, rejected as unacceptable by the elected members of the legislatures, have been restored by a mere stroke of the pen. In short, we have utterly failed to find any justification for the existence of an institution which, despite all its pomp and splendour, organised with the hard-earned money of the sweating millions of India, is only a hollow show and a mischievous make-believe. Alike, have we failed to comprehend the mentality of the public leaders who help the Government to squander public time and money on such a manifestly stage-managed exhibition of India's helpless subjection.

No Hope for Labour

We have been ruminating upon all these matters, as also upon the wholesale arrests of the leaders of the labour movement. When the introduction of the Trade Disputes Bill brought us into the Assembly to watch its progress, the course of the debate only served to confirm our conviction that the labouring millions of India had nothing to expect from an institution that stood as a menacing monument to the strangling of the exploiters and the serfdom of the helpless labourers.

Finally, the insult of what we consider, inhuman and barbarous measure was hurled on the devoted heads of the representatives of the entire country, and the starving and struggling millions were deprived of their primary right and the sole means of improving their economic welfare. None who has felt like us for the dumb driven drudges of labourers could possibly witness this spectacle with equanimity. None whose heart bleeds for them, who have given their life-blood in silence to the building up of the economic structure could repress the cry which this ruthless blow had wrung out our hearts.

Bomb Needed

Consequently, bearing in mind the words of the late Mr. S.R. Das, once Law Member of the Governor-General's Executive Council, which appeared in the famous letter he had addressed to his son, to the effect that the 'Bomb was necessary to awaken Engalnd from her dreams', we dropped the bomb on the floor of the Assembly Chamber to register our protest on behalf of those who had no other means left to give expression to their heart-rending agony. Our sole purpose was to make the deaf hear and to give the headless a timely warning. Others have as keenly felt as we have done, and from under the seeming stillness of the sea of Indian humanity, a veritable storm is about to break out. We have only hoisted the 'danger-signal' to warn those who are speeding along without heading the grave dangers ahead. We have only marked the end of an era of Utopian non-violence, of whose futility the rising generation has been convinced beyond the shadow of doubt.

Ideal Explained

We have used the expression Utopian non-violence, in the foregoing paragraph which requires some explanation. Force when aggressively applied is 'violence' and is, therefore, morally unjustifiable, but when it is used in the furtherance of a legitimate cause, it has its moral justification. The elimination of force at all costs is Utopian, and the new movement which has arisen in country and of that dawn we have given a warning, is inspired by the ideals which guided Guru Gobind Singh and Shivaji, Kamal Pasha and Riza Khan, Washington and Garibaldi, Lafayette and Lenin.

As both the alien government and the Indian public leaders appeared to have shut their eyes to the existence of this movement, we felt it as our duty to sound a warning where it could not go unheard.

We have so far dealt with the motive behind the incident in question, and now, we must define the extent of our intention.

No Personal Grudge

We bore no personal grudge or malice against anyone of those who received slight injuries or against any other person in the Assembly. On contrary, we repeat that we hold human life sacred beyond words, and would sooner lay down our own lives in the service of humanity than injure any one else. Unlike mercenary soldiers of the imperialist armies who are disciplined to kill without compunction we respect and in so far as he lies in our power, we attempt to save human life, and still we admit having deliberately thrown the bombs into the Assembly Chamber. Facts, however, speak for themselves and our intention would be judged from the result of the action without bringing in Utopian hypothetical circumstances and presumptions.

No Miracle

Despite the evidence of the Government Expert, the bombs that were thrown in the Assembly Chamber resulted in slight abrasions to an empty bench and some slight damage to less than half a dozen cases while Government scientist and experts have ascribed this result to a miracle, we see nothing but a precisely a scientific process in all this incident. Firstly, the two bombs in exploded in vacant spaces with in the wooden barriers of the desks and benches. Secondly, even those who were within two feet of the explosion for instance, Mr. P. Rau Mr. Shanker Rao and Sir George Schuster were either not hurt or only slightly scratched. Bombs of the capacity deposed to by the Government

Expert [though his estimate, being imaginary is exaggerated] loaded with an effective charge of potassium chlorate and sesitive (explosive) picarate would have smashed the barriers and laid many low within some yards of the explosion.

Again, had they been loaded with some high explosive, with charge of this destructive pellets or darts, they would have sufficed to wipe out a majority of the members of the Legislative Assembly. Still again we could have flung them in to the official box, which was occupied by some notable persons. And finally we could have ambushed Sir John Simon whose luckless commission was loathed by all responsible people and who was sitting in the President's gallery at the time. All these things, however, were beyond our intention and bombs did no more than they were designed to do, and the miracle consisted in no more than the deliberate aim which landed them in safe places.

We then deliberately offered ourselves to bear the penalty for what we had done and to let the imperialist exploiters know that by crushing individuals, they cannot kill ideas. By crushing two insignificant units, a nation cannot be crushed. We wanted to emphasise the historical lesson that letters de cachets and Bastilles could not crush the revolutionary movement in France. Gallows and the Siberian mines could not extinguish the Russian Revolution. Bloody Sunday, and Black and Tans failed to strangle the movement of Irish freedom.

Can ordinances and Safety Bills snuff out the flames of freedom in India? Conspiracy cases, trumped up or discovered and the incarceration of all youngmen who cherish the vision of a great ideal cannot check the march of revolution. But a timely warning, if not unheeded, can help to prevent loss of life and general sufferings.

We took it upon ourselves to provide this warning and our duty is done.

Bhagat Singh was asked in the lower court what he meant by word "Revolution". In answer to that question, he said "Revolution" does not necessarily involve sanguinary strife nor is there any place in it for individual vendetta. It is not the cult of the bomb and the pistol. By "Revolution" we mean that the present order of things, which is based on manifest injustice, must change. Producers or labourers in spite of being the most necessary element of society are robbed by their exploiters of the fruits of their labour and deprived of their elementary rights. The peasant who grows corn for all, starves with his family, the weaver who supplies the world market with textile fabrics, has not enough to cover his own and his children's bodies; masons, smiths and carpenters who raise magnificent palaces, live like pariahs in the slums. The capitalist and exploiters, the parasites of society squander millions on their whims. These terrible inequalities and forced disparity of chances are bound to lead to chaos. This state of affairs cannot last long, and it is obvious, that the present order of society in merry-making is on the brink of a volcano.

The whole edifice of this civilisation, if not saved in time, shall crumble. A radical change therefore is necessary and it is the duty of those who realise it to reorganise society on the socialistic basis. Unless this thing is done and the exploitation of man by man and of nations by nations is brought to an end, sufferings and carnage with which humanity is threatened today cannot be prevented. All talk of ending war and ushering in an era of universal peace is undisguised hypocrisy.

By "Revolution", we mean the ultimate establishment of an order of society which may not be threatened by such breakdown, and in which the sovereignty of the proletariat should be recognised and a world federation should redeem humanity from the bondage of capitalism and misery of imperial wars.

This is our ideal, and with this ideology as our inspiration, we have given a fair and loud enough warning.

If, however, it goes unheeded and the present system of government continues to be an impediment in the way of the natural forces that are swelling up, a grim struggle will ensure involving the overthrow of all obstacles, and the establishment of the dictatorship of the proletariat to pave the way for the consummation of the ideal of revolution. Revolution is an inalienable right of mankind. Freedom is an imperishable birth right of all. Labour is the real sustainer of society. The sovereignty of the people is the ultimate destiny of the workers.

For these ideals, and for this faith, we shall welcome any suffering to which we may be condemned. At the altar of this revolution we have brought our youth as an incense, for no sacrifice is too great for so magnificent a cause. We are content, we await the advent of revolution. "Long Live Revolution".[12]

The judge remarked about the efficacy of the bomb used by Sardar Bhagat Singh and his associate. 'The force which is able to shattar wood of $1\frac{1}{2}$ inches thickness and to result in the embedding of fragments of metal in teak wood, I find to be sufficient to cause death if acting upon a vulnerable portion of a human body.'[13]

Very diverse opinions have been recorded by the assessors. One assessor considered that both the accused were guilty of an attempt to murder and that both were guilty under section 3 of the explosive substances act; he considered that all the persons injured were injured by the first bomb and not by the second. He, therefore, considered that Bhagat Singh caused hurt in an attempt to murder whilst Datta did not.[14]

Another assessor was of opinion that Bhagat Singh might have thrown both bombs and that possibly Datta did not throw either of them. He considered Bhagat Singh guilty of an attempt to murder in which he caused hurt, and also considered him to be guilty under section 3 of the explosive substances act. He was of opinion that Datta was not guilty of either of the offences with which he had been charged.[15]

A third assessor considered that both accused are guilty under section 3 of the explosives substances act, and that neither are guilty of an attempt to murder. His opinion was that there was no intention of causing death or other intention or knowledge necessary to the offence of attempted murder.[16]

The fourth assessor considered that the bombs were of such a nature that they could not cause death, and that neither of the accused had any intention beyond that of creating a panic. He considered that both committed very rash acts.[17]

Terry heard two pistol shots after the second explosion and saw several people pointing towards the public gallery to which he accordingly went.[18]

Terry, after hearing the shots, hurried to the public gallery, where he found two men standing shouting, he asserts that Bhagat Singh was gesticulating with a pistol in his hand, the witness arrested them and was then joined by Inspector

Johnson.... Terry handed him a pistol, and thereafter he searched the two men finding a loaded spare magazine on Bhagat Singh and some newspapers and too leaflets on Datta.[19]

All witnesses, who saw the arrest, agreed that the two accused offered no resistance.[20]

The two persons most seriously injured were Sir Bomanji Dalal and Sir George Schuster, neither of these has appeared as witness and there is no direct evidence as to which of the two explosions caused their injuries ...The evidence on the record leaves room for doubt as to whether Sir Bomanji Dalal's injuries were the result of the 1st or 2nd explosion. There can be no possibility of doubt that hurt was caused by both explosions.[21]

The Sessions Judge, Delhi stated,[22] 'I find it proved that Bhagat Singh threw the first bomb with the intention of causing death or with the intention of causing bodily injury which he knew to be likely to cause death. I find that by doing so he did cause hurt to Sir George Schuster, Mr. P.R. Rao and Mr. Shankar Rao. These facts constitute an offence punishable under section 307, IPC with transportation for life or with lesser punishment'.

'I find it proved that Datta threw the second bomb with similar intention and that by doing so he caused hurt to Mr. S.N. Roy and Rai Bahadur A.P. Dube....'

'I find both the accused guilty of both the offences with which they are charged and convict them accordingly.'

The acts of each accused constitute offences punishable under two different provisions of the law. One offence is included in the other. Under the provision of section 71 of the Indian Penal Code, the punishment which may be inflicted is not to be more severe than could be awarded for any one of such offences.[23]

Punishment can be regarded as retributive, preventive or deterrent. In these cases, both the accused appear to have been completely callous as to who might suffer, their acts might have resulted in the death of not only one but of several persons who had offered them no form of provocation and who were not even acquainted with their existence. The offence is a particularly heinous one and from the retributive point of view merits a severe punishment.

The accused have alleged that they hold human life sacred. Their allegation is negatived by their acts. Their attitude throughout has been that their acts are justifiable and justified. With such an attitude their acts are those of men who have not fallen in to crime on the spur of the moment, but by deliberate design. With such an attitude it is probable that what they have done once they may attempt to do again. From the preventive point of view their offences merit severe punishment.

The acts of the accused were acts which courted publicity. To a critical mind they might suggest imitation. From the deterrent point of view the offences demand severe punishment.

The accused are youngmen but their acts were deliberate and they had made preparation for those acts of a complicated nature. In these circumstances their youth must not be allowed to lead to the infliction of an inadequate punishment.

'I sentence Bhagat Singh and B.K. Datta to transportation for life.'[24]

About the Delhi Assembly Bomb Case, Durga Das Khanna reminisced thus, 'Finding me very inquisitive about it, Sukhdev did tell me why Bhagat Singh had been selected for Assembly action. I had actually remarked that we had sacrificed one of our best men in allowing Bhagat Singh to go and do that job, I remember telling him that they should have asked me to go instead. The life of Bhagat Singh was much more precious. But his reply was very straightforward. He felt that Bhagat Singh alone was suitable for the job. Nobody else, in his opinion was fit to handle it the way Bhagat Singh might. He wanted him to explain to the world why we felt compelled to resort to such an action and to enthuse the people in the cause of freedom. He said that he had discussed the whole issue threadbare with Bhagat Singh and persuaded him to undertake this assignment.'[25]

REFERENCES

1. Home Poll, File 192, 1929.
2. Gopal Thakur, *op. cit.*, p. 13.
3. Home Poll, File 192, 1929.
4. *The Hindustan Times,* 10 April, 1929.
5. *Ibid.*

6. *Ibid.*
7. *Ibid.*
8. *Ibid.*
9. See the Proceeding of Delhi Assembly Bomb Case, p. 28.
10. *Ibid.*
11. *Ibid.*, p. 36.
12. For More details see Delhi Assembly Bomb Case, National Archives of India, New Delhi.
13. *Ibid., pp.* 37-8.
14. *Ibid., pp.* 29-30.
15. *Ibid.*
16. *Ibid.*
17. *Ibid.*
18. *Ibid.*, pp. 9-12.
19. *Ibid.*
20. *Ibid.*
21. *Ibid.*, pp. 16-17.
22. *Ibid.*, pp. 39-40.
23. Copy of judgment of Messrs Bhagat Singh and B.K. Dutt, File 246.
24. Delivered by the Sessions Judge, Delhi on 12 June, 1929.
25. Transcript of the interview with Durga Das Khanna, *op. cit.*

6 The Lahore Conspiracy Case

On 11 July, 1929, the enquiry in the proceedings known as the Lahore Conspiracy Case commenced before a Magistrate and the accused in the case numbered 24 of whom five were absconding.[1] The offences alleged against the accused were both in their relation to the public security if 'unusually serious character'. They included the murder of Saunders, Assistant Superintendent of Police and Head Constable Chanan Singh in Lahore on 17 December, 1928; the establishment of bomb factories in Lahore and Saharanpur; the conspiracy leading to the throwing of two bombs in the Legislative Assembly in 8 April, 1929 and various other revolutionary activities. For the purpose of establishing these charges which were concerned with many different places and with events occurring over a considerable period of time, the prosecution considered that it would be necessary to produce about six hundred witnesses.[2]

Two of the accused had resorted to hunger-strike before the commencement of the enquiry. A number of others followed the same course shortly afterwards with the result that by 26 July, 1929, the case had to be adjourned owing to some of the accused being unfit to attend the Court. The case, therefore, had to be successively adjourned on the same ground until the 24 September. It was then resumed, but there were numerous interruptions by members of the public. On 4 February, 1930, most of the accused again went on hunger-strike and the case was on this account adjourned from the 8 February till the 8 March, 1930.

The enquiry thus had been in progress for about nine months, and during that time it had been possible to examine only 165 witnesses out of a probable total of 607. The spectacle of these proceedings, obstructed by unprecedented delays and repeatedly disturbed by disorderly conduct and revolutionary demonstrations, had tended to bring the administration of justice into contempt, and though the trial had lately been resumed, it was impossible to count upon obtaining a conclusion by the normal methods of procedure within any calculable period.[3]

The Viceroy stated, 'After anxious consideration I have come to the conclusion that neither the ends of justice not the interests of the accused are served by allowing these proceedings to drag out to a length, which cannot at present be foreseen. Public policy clearly demands that the grave charges against the accused should be thoroughly scrutinised and finally adjudicated upon with the least possible delay, by a tribunal of indubitable impartiality and authority, and the preliminary proceedings which have already extended over nine months and the end of which is not yet in sight should be terminated. It is also necessary to ensure that obstruction shall not further interrupt the course of justice. I have accordingly decided to avail myself of the authority conferred upon the Governor-General under section 72 of the Government of India Act and to issue an Ordinance which has the effect of entrusting the trial of this case to a tribunal to be constituted by the Chief Justice of the High Court and to invest this tribunal with powers to deal with wilful obstruction. By these means the accused will be assured of a trial before a court of the highest possible authority and it may be expected that a final and just decision will be reached with no unnecessary delay. I am convinced that the action which I have thought it right to take will best secure the achievement of the true ends of justice and re-establish respect for the administration of the Law.'[4]

In the Gazette of India Extraordinary dated Simla, May 1, 1930 was announced about the passage of the Ordinance No III of 1930.[5] The ordinance was called the Lahore Conspiracy Case and all cases pending in the court of Rai Sahib, Pandit Sri Kishan, First Class Magistrate Lahore against any or all the persons would be tried by the Tribunal to be constituted under section 4.[6] The Chief Justice of the High Court would constitute a Tribunal for the trial of the said cases consisting of three persons who at the time of such constitution were judges, additional judges or officiating judges of the High Court. The Chief Justice would appoint one of the members of the Tribunal to be president of the Tribunal. The Tribunal may pass upon any person convicted by it any sentence authorised by law for the punishment of the offence of which such person was convicted, and no order of confirmation would be necessary in respect of any sentence passed by it.[7]

The Tribunal shall have powers to take such measures as it may think necessary to secure the orderly conduct of the trial; and where any accused by his voluntary act has rendered himself incapable of appearing before the tribunal, or resists his production before it or behaves before it in a persistently disorderly manner, or in any way wilfully conducts himself to the serious prejudice of the trial, the Tribunal may at any stage of the trial, dispense with the attendance of such accused for such period as it may think fit and proceed with the trial in his absence.[8]

The judgment of the Tribunal would be final and conclusive and notwithstanding the provisions of the Code or of any other law for the time being in force, or of anything having the force of law by whatsoever authority made or done, there would be no appeal from any or sentence of the Court, and the High Court would not have authority to revise any such order of sentence or to transfer any case from the Tribunal, or to make any order under section 491 of the Code or have any jurisdiction of any kind in respect of any proceedings under this Ordinance.[9]

The Lahore Conspiracy Case held in the Poonch House at Lahore as the Special Tribunal started on 5 May, 1930 with Mr. Justice J. Coldstream as President and Mr. Justice Agha Haidar and Mr. Justice G.C. Hilton as its members. The Counsel of the Crown were C.H. Cardon Noad, Kalandar Ali Khan, Gopal and Bakshi Dinanath.[10] On the first day of the hearing of the case all the eighteen accused were present in person.[11]

The Tribunal took their seats at 10 a.m. and at two minutes past, the accused were brought.... They shouted revolutionary cries for a short time and then for a period of eight minutes altogether they chanted a revolutionary hymp.[12] One of the accused addressed the Tribunal stating that he wanted an adjournment for a fortnight in order to prepare and formulate arguments to the effect that the constitution of the Tribunal was *ultra vires*. He also stated that all the accused wanted time to file affidavits in connection with promulgation of the Ordinances. The Tribunal ordered that the proceeding could not be adjourned at present. The accused were not prepared to argue the matter forthwith.[13]

A petition was then handed in to the Tribunal by five of the accused asking for an adjournment for a fortnight to enable the petitioners to make necessary arrangements for their defence. This was rejected as premature.[14]

At 11-15 a.m. one of the accused, Shiv Ram alias Rajguru alias 'M' (no. 19) got up and began making a speech in some language unknown. It was explained later by another of the accused that the object of the speech of Rajguru was to ask for an interpreter as he did not understand the language of the court. At this, an interpreter was appointed.[15] Thereafter J.N. Sanyal read a speech on his behalf and on behalf of Mahabir Singh, B.K. Dutt, Dr. Gaya Prashad Nigam and Kundan Lal—all accused in the same case. This speech contained a violent political attack upon the British government. As the reading out of this speech in open court was highly improper being merely seditious propaganda and as what was being said was entirely irrelevant to the question of the guilt or innocence of the accused, the Tribunal stopped the reading. The paper was handed to the Tribunal and had been placed, drew the attention of the court to the final paragraph which ran as follows:

'For these reasons we decline to be a party to the farcical show and henceforth we shall not take any part in the proceedings of this case.'[16]

From the evidence of Wajid Ali Shah, Muhammad Ismail, Najaf Khan and Sayyad Asghar Ali, P. Ws., it was proved to the satisfaction of the Tribunal that Sat Guru Dyal, Bhagwati Charan, Chander Shekhar Azad, Kailash Pati alias Kali Charan and Yashpal were absconding and that there was no immediate prospect of arresting them. This finding was given under section 512 of the Criminal Procedure Code.[17]

The Tribunal asked each of the accused regarding his wishes in the matter of being represented by counsel at the expense of the government with the following result :

1.	Bhagat Singh	No
2.	Sukhdev	No
3.	Kishori Lal	Yes, but can name nobody, wants to consult Sardar Kishan Singh a member of the Defence Committee.
4.	Agya Ram	No
5.	Des Raj	Yes, cannot at present say whom he wants.
6.	Prem Dutt	Yes, cannot at present say whom he wants. Wants to consult Kishan Singh.
7.	Jai Dev	No
8.	Shiv Verma	No
9.	Gaya Parshad	States he will give no reply.
10.	B.K. Dutt	I refuse to answer any question by this court.
11.	Kanwal Nath Trivedi	No
12.	Ajoy Kumar Ghosh	Yes, cannot say whom until he sees the Defence Committee.
13.	Jatindar Nath Sanyal	States 'I give no reply'.
14.	Surinder Nath Pandey	No help from this court.
15.	Mahabir Singh	Says he will take no part in the proceeding.
16.	Shiv Ram alias Rajguru	No help.[18]

In the next hearing, all the accused except Sukhdev from the Borstal Institution, had not been produced in Court on 13 May, 1930, because they had refused to come unless brought by force. Each accused was asked individually to come to court, and he said:

'I will not come unless I am physically forced'. They gave as their reason the fact that they were mal-treated in the court and if the President of the Tribunal tendered an unqualified apology, they would attend the court.'[19]

In view of the disturbances that took place on 12 May, 1930, the President and members of the Tribunal decided that the proceedings of the Court must be conducted with judicial decorum and that no disorderly conduct was to be tolerated including singing and shouting while the Tribunal was sitting. 'While we are anxious that accused that the trial should be conducted with fairness and that the accused should have a reasonable opportunity to defend themselves, we consider that it is our duty to see that the proceedings are not obsructed and we want to make it absolutely clear to all the persons concerned that we will take such legal measures open to us, including the removal of the accused, as may be considered necessary for the proper conduct of the proceedings.'[20]

This kind of decision or court order clearly meant that it was going to take strong action against all the accused by removing them with force to the venue of the court with the help of the police.

So the next day, all the sixteen accused including Sukhdev refused to attend the court. Each said, 'I am not coming to court'. Sukhdev sent an application, which was written by Bhagat Singh and signed by Sukhdev.[21]

We, therefore, passed this order at 11-30 a.m. dispensing with the attendance of all the accused until 9 a.m. tomorrow and proceeding with the trial in their absence. This order is passed under section 9(i) of the Ordinance.

'With reference to the proceeding of yesterday and the above order we record that we are of opinion that each of the accused by refusing to attend court wilfully conducted himself to the serious prejudice of the trial within the meaning and intention of the section 9(i) of the Ordinance.'[22]

On 19 May, 1930, Major P.D. Chopra, Superintendent, Central Jail, Lahore stated before the Tribunal. 'Bhagat Singh and Dutt, the two accused in my charge, have not come to court today. They declined to come and offered resistance. I myself went to them. I asked them to come and they declined. We then brought them up to the main gate. Bhagat Singh came to the main gate without resistance, but B.K. Dutt had to be carried bodily there. At the main gate the police were asked to take charge of them for conveyance to court. They then both of them offered severe resistance.'[23]

It appears from the statement of the Superintendent, Central Jail how adamant Sardar Bhagat Singh and Dutt were in agreeing to attend the court. All kind of persuasion and force used by the government's official proved ineffective on them and, ultimately they were absent from the Court along with other revolutionaries who also acted in the same fashion.

Yesterday[24] Bhagat Singh, accused in this case was brought to the Borstal Institution and had a consultation with the other accused confined in that institution for three hours, in my presence (Bakshi Lal Chand, Assistant Jailor, Borstal Institution Lahore) but not in my hearing. Mr. Amolak Ram Kapur, advocate, Mr. Pran Nath, Pleader and Lala Feroze Chand, a member of the Defence Committee, were also present at the consultation.[25]

On 5 September, 1930, it was reported, "Bhagat Singh, accused refused to attend court today. He was brought to the main gate by me (The Assistant Jailor, Central Jail, Lahore) and when the police officer placing his hand on him and ordered him to attend court, he refused to do so and resisted his production. He ceased hunger striking yesterday and is quite fit to attend court."[26]

On 11 September, 1930, the court passed an order adjourning the case to the 8 October, 1930, and also dispensing with the attendance of the accused persons until that date. 'As we are now ready to announce today, we order that the accused persons should all be produced before us as soon as possible today in order that they may have an opportunity of being present when judgment is pronounced.'[27]

After the Assembly Bomb Case Judgment, Bhagat Singh was lodged in the Mianwali Jail, which was almost full of political prisoners convicted and undergoing the long imprisonments for their active participation in *Ghadr* movement Martial Law agitation and Babbar Akali Movement. This jail had become fairly notorious in its day-to-day dealing of the government officials with the life convicts. Even the simple demands of the political prisoners for their bare necessities were meted out with frown and mal-treatment. In spite of their protests and pleadings with the successive jail authorities, their pitiable lot was not improved. Nor could they hope for any kind of improvement in the near or distant future.

The arrival of Bhagat Singh changed the whole scene. He immediately took up the cause of the political prisoners for the grant of basic amenities to them. And before any kind of drastic step was taken in this regard, he apprised them of their fundamental rights and the hopelessness which they could only expect from the British Raj. He, therefore, gave them a novel idea of resorting on hunger—strike *en masse*. They all agreed to this kind of approach, which was to be practised by his associates as well who were lodged in the Lahore Jail.

Soon Bhagat Singh was in communication with the Inspector-General, Punjab Jails, Lahore. The letter given below was addresed by him on 17 June, 1929 from the Mianwali Jail through the Local Jail Superintendent.[28]

I have been sentenced to life imprisonment in connection with the Assembly Bomb Case, Delhi and I am obviously a political prisoner. We got special diet in Delhi Jail, but since my arrival here, I am being treated as an ordinary criminal. Therefore, I have gone on hunger strike since the morning of 15 June, 1929. My weight has decreased by lbs 6 than my weight at Delhi Jail in these two or three days.

I wish to bring to your kind attention that I must get special treatment as a political prisoner.

My demands being

1. Special diet (including milk and ghee, rice and curd etc.)
2. No forcible labour.
3. Toilet (soap, oil, shaving, etc.).
4. Literature of all kinds (History, Economics, Political Science, Science, Poetry, Drama or Fiction, Newspapers.)

I hope you will very kindly consider what I have said and decide favourably.[29]

Similarly, B.K. Dutt of the Assembly Bomb Case, communicated a letter to the Superintendent, Central Jail, Lahore. I want to let you know and the higher authorities that I demand the following things on the ground of being a 'Political Prisoner.'

After the Bomb incident in Assembly, Lord Irwin in his last speech said that, 'These bombs were not directed towards any individual but towards the *institution'*. Again, Mr. Midleton in his judgment mentioned that 'These persons. Dutta and Bhagat Singh) used to enter the court with the cries of 'Long live

Revolution'; Long Live Proletariat, etc. which shows clearly what sort of political ideas they cherish. In order to put a check in propagating these ideas I transport them for life.'

Again I must mention that when an European breaks an ordinary law in order to fulfil his selfish motive, he gets all kinds of privileges in the jail. He will get well-ventilated room with electric fittings, best food (such as milk, butter, toast, meat. etc.) and good clothing while we political are deprived of such things.

The comments of Lord Irwin and Mr. Midleton is sufficient to prove that we are politicals, and on this ground I demand that (Dutta and Bhagat Singh) should be treated as political. I must get better food as it is necessary to keep a man's health. At the same time, I must get all kind of literature and the newspaper in order to discuss the different politics. People call us rash, misguided and impatient youths. So we must be given a fair chance of studying the various books in order to see that whether we are really impatient, misguided youths or not, whether our life work is wrong or right.

My demands are as follows :

1. Better food, including loaf and milk in the morning, rice, dal and ghee, one vegetable and curd and sugar in the noon; and bread, meat and *chattni* at night.
2. No labour.
3. All kinds of literature and newspapers.
4. Toilet, including soap, oil and barber etc.
5. Better accommodation.
6. Civil dress.

I used to get all these things in Delhi Jail, before and after my conviction from the Jail expenses. But here I am deprived of all those things; that is why I have begun hunger-strike since 14 June, 1929. My comrade Bhagat Singh in Mianwali Jail is also on hunger-strike for these very reasons and I will not give up my hunger-strike till the government exceeds to our (I and Bhagat Singh) demands.

'Expect an early reply and will gladly discuss over this matter with any government officer whoever comes to me.'[30]

Soon after, Bhagat Singh was transferred to the Central Jail, Lahore and the idea of hunger-strike spread like wild fire in Borstal Jail where his other associates like Sukhdev, Jatinder Nath Das, Rajguru, Shiv Varma, Ajoy Ghosh, Gaya Prashad and B.K. Sinha were lodged. They also resorted to hunger-strike which attracted immense public support and sympathy through press and speeches by prominent leaders like Dr. Saifuddin Kitchlew, Dr. Gopi Chand Bhargava, Dr. Mohammad Alam and others.

Durga Das Khanna, who was a co-political prisoner with other revolutionaries, reminisced about the type of life in Lahore Jail. 'Jail is not the place where you are tortured. It is true that in the condemned cells you are not allowed to go out. You are handcuffed even when you are brought out in the enclosure attached to your cell. One bathed also with handcuffs on. There was no separate lavatory also. In a corner of the back wall was placed a pan. The inmate could pull it to ease himself. At the most, one may provide himself privacy by hanging one's blanket against the iron door of the cell.... Khan Sahib Akbar Khan, the Deputy Superintendent of Jail at that time, was a very nice man. He was the same man from whose custody Bhagat Singh had ultimately refused to be rescued, because he would not handcuff him while going out from the Central Jail to meet his co-accused in the Borstal Jail. He told me that he had deep respect for Bhagat Singh, Rajguru and Sukhdev who could be relied upon for anything and he always had faith in them. Therefore, he allowed us to move about and meet one another whenever it was time to do so. There was no restriction imposed on us within the condemned cells' enclosure on such occasions. We were, later on allowed to keep our safety razors with us and shave daily, if we so liked. These are things, which ordinarily are not allowed within a condemned cell lest one commits suicide and cheats society or law of its retributive action.'[31]

The public demand to redress the grievances of the youthful revolutionaries had no much effect on British bureaucracy and instead it resorted to forcible feeding of the hunger-strikers.

On the issue of hunger-strike by the revolutionaries, Jawaharlal Nehru expressed his concern thus[32] on 5 July, 1929. 'I have learnt with deep grief of the hunger strike of Bhagat Singh and Dutt. For 20 days or more they have refrained from all food and I am told that forcible feeding is being resorted to. The two youngmen may have done wrong, but no Indian can refrain from admiring their great courage and our hearts must go out them now in their great and voluntary suffering. They are fasting not for any selfish ends but to improve the lot of all political prisoners. As days go by, we shall watch with deep anxiety this hard trial and shall earnestly hope that the two gallant brothers of ours may triumph in the ordeal.'

In fact, Jawaharlal Nehru paid a visit to the Central Jail and the Borstal Jail, Lahore and saw Sardar Bhagat Singh, Batukeshwar Dutt, Jatindar Nath Das and all the other accused in the Lahore Conspiracy Case, who were on hunger-strike.[33] Attempts had been made for many days past to feed them forcibly, and in the case of some of them, the result of this kind of forcible method were so injurious that, all forcible feeding had to be given up in the face of a greater danger. And some of the revolutionaries were just maintaining measure of strength on account of forcible feeding which was given twice a day. Nehru stated, ' It was very painful for me to meet these extraordinarily brave youngmen and to see their manifest suffering. I gathered from them that they would adhere to their resolve, whatever the consequences to their individual selves might be. Indeed, they did not care very much for their own selves. They could not undergo such tremendous suffering for a little personal comfort in future. They feel strongly, however, that the lot of political prisoners in India is bad and must be improved'.

The position, as explained to me by Sardar Bhagat Singh, was that all political prisoners, with one exception if necessary should be given special treatment. This exception was the case of an actual perpetrator of murder.

'I can only hope that the great sacrifice which these youngmen are making will bear fruit.'[34]

The A.I.C.C. expressed its serious concern about the hunger-strike and the general plight of the young revolutionaries in various jails. In a letter to Damodar Swarup Seth[35] who was one of the accused in the Banaras and Kakori Conspiracy Cases, Jawaharlal Nehru expressed his opinion thus.[36] ...The resolution of the A.I.C.C. you refer to was passed at the express desire of many persons intimately concerned. I do not think that under the circumstances the A.I.C.C. could have done otherwise... It may even be better to die rather than submit to continuous suffering and degradation. But the weapon can be misused or overused and then it results in additional suffering only and sometimes in humiliation and demoralisation. There can be no doubt that Jatin Dass death and the hunger-strike of Bhagat Singh and Dutt and others created profound sensation in the country and at the same time forced the issue on the public mind. Undoubtedly the government's hands were also forced to a large extent and many privileges have been given to political prisoners which they never had before. A continuation however of these methods by many others had a great measure of danger in it from many points of view.... I am very sorry indeed that the Kakori prisoners had not benefited at all by the recent agitation. If you will kindly send me the facts we shall try to give publicity to them as much as possible...[37]

In a letter to R. Brigdeman on 23 July, 1929, Jawaharlal Nehru has opened his mind about the Lahore Conspiracy Case ...In the Lahore Conspiracy Case the accused are kept even in court handcuffed with a policeman on either side and policemen have actually thrashed them in court while the magistrate is trying to look the other way. When an application was made for a transfer of the case from this magistrate's court it was thrown out as being frivolous. It was ordered however that handcuffs need not be kept on inside the court room.... Meanwhile, the hunger-strike of Bhagat Singh and Dutt is in its sixth week.[38]

To Mahatma Gandhi, Nehru explained: '.... In Delhi I had stated that we could not help sympathising with Bhagat Singh and Dutt during their long fast. As a matter of fact I am not in favour of hunger-strikes. I told this to many youngmen who came to see me on this subject but I did not think it worthwhile to condemn the fast publicly.[39]

The successful hunger–strike by Bhagat Singh, J.N. Das and their associates was indeed an enigmatic problem which proved a nightmare for the British bureaucracy in the Punjab. It was left with no alternative except to yield to the basic demands or the hunger-strikers and therefore, it appointed the Punjab Jails Inquiry Committee on 2 September, 1929.

On 6 September, 1930, the Lahore Conspiracy Case hunger strikers sent a comprehensive note to the Chairman, Punjab Jail

Enquiry Committee and Members of the Hunger strike Sub-committee, Simla and brought the following points to their notice.[40]

They made it clear to the committee that they did not abandon the hunger-strike, but merely suspended it pending the decision of the government. 'We are surprised to note that this point has not been even mentioned in the press statement given by the members of the hunger-strike sub-committee as published in civil and Military Gazette dated the 4 September, 1929. However, we hope you will do so at the earliest opportunity.' They further clarified the point that they suspended the hunger-strike not only on the assurance that they and the remaining members of the Enquiry Committee would make unanimous recommendations practically meeting all their demands to their satisfaction.[41]

Besides, you gave us further assurance that in compliance with our strong desire Comrade Jatindra Nath Das would be released immediately and unconditionally, in view of his critical state of health. Secondly, that our demands as under-trials, the most important of which was to keep all of us together (including Comrades Bhagat Singh and Dutt) in a general association barrack would be accepted by the Government within a day or two.

But our fears came true when, despite the strong and unanimous recommendations of all the members of the sub-committee, the government did neither agree to release Comrade Das nor to keep Comrades Bhagat Singh and Dutt with us.

Thus, we have been furnished with immediate proofs of the fact that the Government does not care for your recommendations, and we hope you will excuse us when we say that we believe that all the government wanted was to exploit your individual positions as public men in getting our hunger-strike broken. We may further mention that before we suspended our hunger-strike we carefully considered how far we could rely on the promise of the Enquiry Committee. On that, Comrades Bhagat Singh and Dutt suggested that the present occasion would serve as a test case. Now that we find that the Government has not paid any heed to even two most ordinary recommendations of yours; we have been forced to resume hunger-strike immediately.

The condition of Comrade Das is now absolutely hopeless, and if the Government thinks that after his death, we will shirk our duty, it is a fatal mistake. Let us all state that we are all prepared to share his fate.

For the sake of convenience, however, and keeping the idea of continued fight in view, we are dividing ourselves in two groups, the first of which is resuming hunger-strike at once.

It is resolved that, as soon as a member of the first group meets his death, one member from the second group will come forward to fill the gap.

We have arrived at this decision in full realisation of its gravity. There is no other proper and honourable course left to us now but to follow in the footsteps of our Comrade Das.

We regard our cause as just and honourable, which any fair Government would have conceded without forcing the necessity of such a serious step. We repeat that we are going into this fight with a firm conviction that nothing can be more glorious and honourable than to fight till death for a just and noble cause.

In conclusion, we feel that we fail in our duty if we do not express our heartfelt thanks for the sincere interest and great trouble that you have taken to uphold our cause before the Government.[42]

When a copy of this letter reached Duni Chand, Advocate and a member of the Jail Enquiry Committee, he advised the under trial prisoners in Borstal Jail thus[43]. It is quite true that you had from your point of view merely suspended the hunger-strike, but in my opinion there is hardly any difference between the suspension and the abandonment of hunger-strike as you can resume hunger-strike at any time if you so wished or willed....It is quite true that it was after full discussion with you as to the concessions that the Government was prepared to grant and even after disclosing to you precisely what the Jail Enquiry Committee had secured for you tentatively that you had agreed to give up hunger-strike. It was at the end of our deliberations with you that you had brought in the question of the release of Mr. Jatinder Nath Das. So far as the concessions other than those of the release of Mr. Das and the association of Messrs Bhagat Singh and Dutt with other under trial prisoners of Lahore Conspiracy Case are concerned, you do not say that they have been withheld or even whittled down. So far as the unconditional release of Mr. Das and the association of Messrs Bhagat Singh and Dutt with others are concerned, we had not arrived at any understanding with the government before we left Simla though we knew the mind of the government as to all other concessions.

You had decided to go through agony of a long drawn out hunger-strike according to you not for your sake but for the sake of political prisoners, all over India and forced the issue upon the Government. If that was the object as I also believe you had succeeded well. According to the communique issued by the Government a more or less uniform policy as to the better treatment of political prisoners throughout India had been decided upon and it was in pursuance of this policy that the Punjab Jail Enquiry Committee had been appointed. If the concessions with regard to food, books, magazines, newspapers, furniture, clothes, etc. had been granted to your satisfaction, in my opinion there was no justification for you to resume hunger-strike on the ground that Mr. Das had not been released. The Government had taken a tremendous responsibility in keeping him in jail while he was lying there almost in a dying condition. With all the sincerity of purpose and with all the carestness that I can command I beseech you not to sacrifice your valuable lives through hunger-strike. You will be perfectly justified to resume hunger-strike if the Government withholds or even minimises the concessions that have been promised to you. As to your allegation of the Government wanting to exploit our individual position as publicmen, I must repudiate the implication. I have shown in the past and shall show it in future that I am incapable of being exploited either by the Government or by any other person however great.

'As to the condition of Mr. Das being absolutely hopeless I pray you to save him if you can and wish the Government not to make a fetish of false prestige as nothing enhances the genuine prestige as the respect for public opinion. As to your determination to kill yourself one by one through hunger-strike, the very idea of it is most shuddering to my mind. I presume you all to innocent unless the contrary is proved against you. I shall not forget the pathetic scene of a number of youngmen I suppose varying between 18 and 25 being placed in the position in which I found you. It may be that all or many of you may be spared to serve the country which you have so much and again most solemnly ask you to desist from the resolve of sacrifice yourself.'[44]

On 18 September 1929, the Governor of Punjab telegraphically informed the Home Secretary, Government of India, about the hunger-strikers at Lahore.[45] 'Please convey following to Emerson. If Bhagat Singh and Dutt give up hunger-strike it would be feasible to give them *qua* under trials same special treatment as Punjab Jail Committee have recommended for under trials in conspiracy case except as regards prison dress and few details of discipline applicable to convicts. It would be made clear that this treatment would be given only while they are under trials in conspiracy case and pending conclusion on general recommendation of Jail Enquiry Committee. Bhagat Singh and Dutt will remain in Central Jail where they are now confined but will be permitted to freely associate with each other. Under-trials confined in Borstal Jail will be permitted to see them reasonably frequently on the understanding that *bona fide* object of interview is to discuss and concert line of defence in conspiracy case. Punjab Government are taking steps of convey these conclusions to Bhagat Singh, Dutt and to the members of Provincial Jail Committee who have made recommendations on the subject. Our justification of this exceptional treatment is desire that they *qua* under trials should be enabled adequately to arrange for their defence in unusual lengthy trial on serious charge. Please be careful to avoid flowery admission that *qua* convicts Bhaghat Singh and Dutt can be given special treatment in view of nature of crime, which they already been convicted.'[46]

The Viceroy informed the Secretary of State on 13 September, 1929 of Jatindra Nath Das's death. 'Jatindra Das, hunger-triker in the Lahore conspiracy case, died this afternoon at 1 p.m. Last night five of the hunger-strikers gave up their hunger-strike, so there are now only Bhagat Singh and Dutt who are on strike....'[47]

In another telegram, after a few days, the Viceroy informed the Secretary of State of the unprecedented reception, the dead body of Jatindra Nath Das received in Calcutta.... 'The procession in Calcutta is stated to have been of record size and to have consisted or five lakh of people.... the crowd was undoubtedly enormous.... Meetings of sympathy with Das and of condemnation of Government have been held in many places, but no report has yet been received of any clash with the authorities.'[48]

The Deputy Commissioner of Lahore, F. H. Puckle, reported on Jatindra Nath Das's death on September 1929.[49]

'J.N. Das died yesterday...at about 1.10 p.m. his brother K.C. Das had received Rs.600 from Subhas Bose from Calcutta to pay for the carriage of the body by car to Sardul Singh Kaveeshar's residence in Nishat Road and from there to take out a procession. Eventually, however, the procession started from the Borstal Jail at about 4 O'clock. It consisted of Dr. Gopi Chand Bhargava and other prominent Congressmen and Congress volunteers—about eighty all told. In the city numerous shops on the way were closed. Outside the Delhi Gate, a huge meeting presided over by Dr. Muhammad Alam was arranged. He and Dr. Bhargava declared their resignations from the membership of the Legislative Council.'[50]

After the meeting concluded, the assembly broke up and the body was taken by a few persons to Shahid Ganj near Naulakha Police Station, where it was placed in a coffin and afterwards taken to the Railway Station. The coffin was accompanied by six attendants upto Calcutta.[51]

The trial court, its venue and proceeding had become a very romantic phenomenon in Lahore. As the main gate of the court faced towards the road, most of the students of schools and colleges assembled thereafter being free from their institutions. So there was always a huge crowd of the youths and they were often heard singing:

Kabhi who din bhi ayega
Ke jab azad hum honge
Yeh apni hi zamin hogi
Yeh apna asman hoga
Shahidon ki chitaon par
Lagenge har baras mele
Watan par marne walon ka
Yehi baki nishan hoga[52]

Their other common patriotic song was as follows :

Sarfarosi ki tamanna ab hamare dil mein hai
Dekhna hai zor kitna bazuai katil mein hai
Waqt ane de bata deinge tujhe e asman
Hum abhi se kya batain, kya humare dil mein hai

Following are the important points in judgment of Lahore Conspiracy Case :

1. Bhagat Singh, Rajguru and Sukhdev proved conclusively to have taken prominent part in various projects of the Hindustan Socialists Republican Army since its inception in September 1928.
2. That sentence on Bhagat Singh, Rajguru due to part played in the murder of Saunders and Chanan Singh.

Tribunal found that Rajguru was the expert marksman specially brought to Lahore for this murder. Rajguru fired first shot which brought down Saunders under his motorcycle and whilst in this helpless position Bhagat Singh fired several shots at him from his automatic pistol at close range.

Sukhdev proved to have been the brain of conspiracy with Bhagat Singh, its right arm. He was proved responsible for recruiting new members of party, proved privy to plot ending in murder of Saunders and privy to plot for bombing Assembly Delhi. He organised bomb-making at Agra and later at Lahore. Tribunal found that most important fact against him was connection with Lahore factory. When this was raided by police, Sukhdev who attempted to use his revolver, was arrested inside. From the factory were recovered live bomb, 8 bombshells, store of chemicals and apparatus and notebooks containing bomb-making formulae.

By the middle of September 1930, when it became evident that death sentence would be awarded to Bhagat Singh, Sardar Kishan Singh made an attempt to save his son from the gallows by writing petitions to the Tribunal trying the case and the Viceroy. He, in fact, wanted to seek permission to prove that Bhagat Singh was not in Lahore on the day Saunders was murdered.

Sardar Kishan Singh stated, In this case, the accused persons wanted to produce defence evidence after the perusal of the prosecution evidence. They wanted time to find out the material from the prosecution evidence because they could not produce the defence evidence without fully knowing what they had to meet. The time asked for was about a week, but the Hon'ble Members of the Tribunal for the reasons best known to them refused to allow time. I, therefore, beg to submit the following points for the consideration of the Hon'ble Judges.

1. No reliance should be placed on the evidence of the allieged eye-witnesses, for when Bhagat Singh was brought from Delhi to Lahore during the course of the investigation of this murder case of Mr. Saunders, he was not taken to the Central Jail or the Borstal Institution where the prosecution witnesses could have no opportunity to see him before the formal identification parade held by the Magistrate at the Lahore Cantonment Police Station. The distance between the Lahore Cantonment Police Station and the Central Jail is only two miles. Bhagat Singh could very easily have been brought to the Central jail, and the identification parade could have been held there. At the Cantonment Police Station, the witnesses were procured by the investigating staff, and the magistrate, who had to hold the identification parade was also sent by the investigating staff. There could be no other object of the police to go out of the way, and to arrange the identification parade at the Cantonment Police Station than give an opportunity to the witnesses to see Bhagat Singh before the force of an identification parade. I at once made an application to the District Magistrate, Lahore that the identification parade was of no value and referred 21 P.W.R. 19, 1917 (Cr. Ruling) in that application drawing the attention of the learned District Magistrate to this abnormal conduct of the investigating officer. It has been clearly laid down by the Punjab High Court that the evidence of identification is considerably declared, if the witnesses get an opportunity to see the accused person before holding the identification parade. That application of mine was published in the local newspapers *Milap* and very probably in *The Tribune*. No weight, therefore, should be attached to the evidence of those witnesses, who identified Bhagat Singh at the identification parade. You, yourselves, are great judges and presumably read the newspapers. Photos of Bhagat Singh were published in almost all the newspapers of india after the "Assembly Bomb Case" and the witnesses should be presumed to have seen these photographs

of Bhagat Singh before the present identification parade took place.

2. There is no manner of doubt that Mr. Fearn, European gentleman and Traffic Inspector of Police who had plenty of opportunity to see the real criminals could not identify the culprits. This man being a Traffic Inspector had developed his sense of identifying the natives by virtue of his procession and calling in life. He could not pick out Bhagat Singh, but it is curious that Ganda Singh, Head Constable, and a Naib Court Police Constable and other witnesses who were accidentally present on the spot, could spot Bhagat Singh. It means that accused was shown to those witnesses before the identification parade.

3. No reliance be placed on the evidence of the approvers in this case, because the provisions of Sec. 167 Clause (iii) of the Cr. Procedure Code have been abused by the Magistrate in remanding the accused persons to police custody. Bhagat Singh and other persons, who have been admitted or likely to the Lahore Fort and other different police lock-ups for about 3 months continuously. They were not shown the air of the world. Magistrates extraordinarily went over to the lock-ups and remanded the accused persons for fortnights. Instead of being the governors of the police, they were at the beck and call of the police. The object of taking remands in this extraordinary way was that the public might not come to know that grievances the accused persons who were confined in the strange lock-ups, made before the Magistrate at the time of the remands. Presumably, the police did not want any legal practitioner to contend before the Magistrate at the time of the remands that there are no sufficient reasons for further remanding the accused persons to police custody. The accused persons had no opportunity to know the reasons for which the British subjects were being detained by the police. In 90 days, any amount of evidence can be prepared; the accused confined can be made to talk by the notorious method of the police well-known to courts. In Z.C.W.N. page 457, the Hon'ble Judges of the Calcutta High Court have held that the evidence of the accused person, who has confessed and has been admitted or is likely to the admitted as approver, and who has been detained in the police custody up to the time of the trial, is open to the greatest suspicion that the police have arranged his statements so as to fit with any evidence that they may have obtained elsewhere.

4. About a hundred persons, including the Superintendent of Police, Deputy Superintendent of Police and Inspectors were on the investigating staff in this case. They were the officers of the C.I.D. and the local Police Board vying with one another to contribute some material evidence in this case. It is for the protection of the accused persons and to prevent the fabrication of false evidence in this case that Sec. 167, Cr.P.C. and other similar sections were enacted. In 90 days, even stones can be pulverised into smooth powder. In this case, the accused persons were boys of easy living habits and delicate nature. They could be very easily rehearsed and drilled for a theatrical representation. The C.I.D. keeps record of suspicious persons and their activities, they are in possession of the seditious literature, and have got inter-provincial communications in the country. They could very easily get the seditious literature and the prescriptions (formulae) for bomb-making and fit them in the statements of the approvers purchasing their immunity at the sacrifice of the lives of others. And the fiction appears to be more real than the truth. The officers investigating the case, like the experienced craftsmen and engineers, have built up a structure by the violation of the remand law. I, therefore, pray that the orders of the remands may kindly be pursued at the time of weighing the evidence of the approvers. These persons were certainly kept and detained by the police without any sufficient reasons against the Punjab Chief Court Ruling No. 24 of 1902 Cr. No person can be detained in police custody without the commencement of the trial for more than 15 days. The law protects the accused persons.

5. The witnesses for the prosecution appeared at a very late stage of the investigation and in this country witnesses can be procured and they come forward to give evidence in order to achieve their own private ends, and the police officer investigating big cases did get witnesses from their friends and hungers on to corroberate the approvers. Sec. 179 Cr. Procedure Code has been made to take the assistance of the Police diaries to find out the dates on which their statements were recorded by the police. It is also essential for the prosecution to reveal before the Tribunal, how all the witnesses were traced out. I, therefore, pray to the court to see whether it had been done or not.

6. It is, therefore, in this case that the accused persons have not cross-examined the prosecution witnesses, but the Bench is

composed of judges of experience. They themselves should apply the tests for testing the varacity of the witnesses. Bhagat Singh was in Calcutta on the day of the occurrence and he actually wrote and despatched a letter to one, Ram Lal, Manager of the *Khaddar Bhandar*, Pari Mahal, Lahore, which was duly received by him. There are respectable gentlemen to swear that Bhagat Singh was in Calcutta on the day of the occurrence. I can produce them if I am given an opportunity, according to justice or they may be called as Court witnesses in the interest of justice, equity and good conscience. The question in this case is of life and death. The right of defence is to be jealously preserved for the accused. If an opportunity of defence would have been given, I would have exposed, according to the Evidence Act Sec. 155, who the witnesses for the prosecution are, and what is their position in life, and what are their objects in giving the evidence, when and how they were made witnesses. I still humbly pray that Bhagat Singh may be given an opportunity to produce his defence.

As a matter of principle and the strict follower of an ideology which basically differed with that of his father, Bhagat Singh was the last man to offer any kind of defence in his case. He, therefore, did not approve of the efforts his father was putting into permit his son to have his defence in the case[53]. He stated, I was astounded to learn that you had submitted a petition to the members of the Special Tribunal in connection with my defence. This intelligence proved to be too severe a blow to be borne with equanimity. It has upset the whole equilibrium of my mind. I have not been able to understand how you could think it proper to submit such a petition at this stage and in these circumstances. In spite of all the sentiments and feelings of a father, I don't think you were at all entitled to make such a move on my behalf without even consulting me. You know that in the political field, my views have always differed with those of yours. I have always been acting independently, without having cared for your approval or disapproval.

I hope you can recall to youself that since the very beginning you have been trying to convince me to fight my case very seriously and to defend myself properly. But you also know that I was always opposed to it. I never had any desire to defend myself, and never did I seriously think about it, whether it was a mere vague ideology or that I had certain arguments to justify my position, is a different question and that cannot be discussed here.

You know that we have been pursuing a definite police in this trial. Every action of mine ought to have been consistent with that policy, my principles and the programme. At present, the circumstances were altogether different, but had the situation been otherwise, even then I would have been the last man to offer defence. I had only one idea before me throughout the trial i.e. to show complete indifference towards the trial in spite of the serious nature of the charges against us. I have always been of opinion that all the political workers should be indifferent and should never bother about the legal fight in the law courts and should boldly bear the heaviest possible sentences inflicted upon them. They may defend themselves but always from purely political consideration and never from a personal point of view. Our policy in this trial has always been consistent with this principle. Whether we were successful in that or not is not for me to judge. We have always been doing our duty quite disinterestedly.

In the statement accompanying the text of the Lahore Conspiracy Case Ordinance, the Viceroy had stated that the accused in this case were trying to bring both law and justice into contempt. The situation afforded us an opportunity to show to the police whether we were trying to bring law into contempt or whether others were doing so. People might disagree with us on this point. You might be one of them. But that never meant that such moves should be made on my behalf without my consent or even without my knowledge. My life is not so precious—at least to me—as you may probably think it to be. It is not at all worth buying at the cost of my principles. There are other comrades of mine whose case is as serious as mine. We had adopted a common policy and have so far stood shoulder to shoulder, so shall we stand to the last no matter how dearly we have to pay individually for it.

Father, I am quite perplexed. I fear I might overlook the ordinary principles of etiquette, and my language may become a little bit harsh while criticising or rather censuring this move on your part. Let me be candid. I feel as though I have been stabbed in the back. Had any other person done it, I would have considered it to be nothing short of treachery. But, in your case, let me say that it has been a weakness—a weakness of the worst type.

This was the time when everybody's mettle was being tested. Let me say, father, you have failed. I know you are as sincere a patriot as one can be. I know you have devoted your life to the cause of Indian Independence, but why at this moment have you displayed such a weakness? I cannot understand.

In the end, I would like to inform you and my other friends and all the people interested in my case, that I have not approved of your move. I am still not at all in favour of offering my defence. Even if the Court had accepted that petition submitted by some of my co-accused regarding defence etc., I would have not defended myself. My application submitted to the Tribunal regarding my interview during the hunger-strike were misinterpreted and it was published in the press that I was going to offer defence, though in reality I was never willing to offer any defence. I still hold the same opinion as before. My friends in the Borstal Jail will be taking it as a treachery and betrayal on my part. I shall not even get an opportunity to clear my position before them.

'I want that the public should know all the details about this application and, therefore I request you to publish this letter.'[54]

The judgment was delivered on 7 October, 1930. Bhagat Singh, Sukhdev and Rajguru were sentenced to death, Kamal Nath Tiwari, Bejoy Kumar Sinha, Jaidev Kapur, Shiv Verma, Gaya Prasad, Kishori Lal and Mahabir Singh were sentenced to transportation—for life. Kundan Lal was given seven years R.I. and Prem Dutt three years R.I. Therest were released. The news of the judgment[55] spread like wild fire. The sympathy for these youths was spontaneous and a wave of indignance gripped the whole country, *Hartals* were observed in numerous towns and meetings of students and prominent political bodies were addressed by the leaders who severely criticised the action of the British Government. A legal battle to save these youths was yet to follow.

The youths were not happy to see their leader like Bhagat Singh to be in the Jail for a long time and thus become a victim of British law which indeed was very strict in its operation against the revolutionary activities of the members of the HSRA. The youths outside had therefore, expressed sentiments of their keenness and a strong desire to get Bhagat Singh and his associates free from this kind of bondage, which had greatly affected the party. A scheme was finally devised to make use of a strong tactics of throwing a bomb near the main gate of the Lahore Central Jail on the police party at a time when Bhagat Singh was to be brought to the court for evidence in the Lahore Conspiracy Case.[56]

This kind of function was entrusted to Bhagwati Charan who readily agreed to do it. He stated exphatically, '*Mein koi tarak nahin karna chahta, Lekin chahta hun ke is ghatna mein bagh lun.*'[57] Before the final act was to be performed, it was suggested to test the efficacy of the bomb so that it should prove effective. So Bhagwati Charan, Sukhdev Raj and Bachhan (Vishwanath)—all the three picked up their cycles and went towards the banks of river Ravi. They took a boat, went across the river and entered a thick forest. Bhagawati Charan tested the bomb but as its trigger was loose, it burst in his hands. The result was fatal for Bhagwati Charan whose hands were cut off, sustained serious injuries on stomach and face, which were bleeding profusely. All efforts to save his life proved ineffective and this brave and dauntless worker of the HSRA breathed his last in the forest where he was secretly cremated. His sudden death was indeed an irreparable loss to the HSRA. The kind of work he was to undertake to save the life of Bhagat Singh could not be executed by anyone.[58]

In a speech at Allahabad on 12 October, 1930, Nehru made a bold statement in which he greatly praised the courage and bravery of Bhagat Singh. '.... whether I agree with him or not my heart is full of admiration for the courage and self-sacrifice of a man like Bhagat Singh. Courage of the Bhagat Singh type is exceedingly rare. If the Viceroy expects us to refrain from admiring this wonderful courage and the high purpose behind it, he is mistaken. Let him ask his own heart what he would have felt if Bhagat Singh had been an Englishman and acted for England.'[59]

The Home Secretary, Government of India, informed all the local Governments on 4 November, 1930.[60] The present position in regard to the Lahore Conspiracy Case is that an application has been made on behalf of most of the persons convicted, for leave to appeal to the Privy Council. There will, therefore, be delay of some weeks in the further proceedings. The Government of India have arranged with the Punjab Government to be informed in due course of the date of the execution of the sentences if the proceeding before the Privy Council are unfavourable to the accused, and in view of the probability of popular demonstrations being held, they will communicate the date to other Local Governments.

The Punjab Government was reluctant to prohibit meetings since the prohibition would be difficult to enforce without a series of clashes with the police. It, however, proposed to prosecute 'without delay' persons who were to make actionable speeches at such meetings.

On this issue H.W. Emerson, Secretary to the Government of India opined on 13 December, 1930, 'Since it appears that a uniform policy should be pursued, Government of India suggest for the consideration of local Governments and Administrations that similar arrangements be made elsewhere, subject to such variations as may be desirable having regard to local conditions and practice e.g. the Government of India do not desire to suggest that meetings in sympathy with the convicts should be allowed it is the present policy to forbid political meetings.

Local Governments will doubtlessly appreciate the desirability of keeping the arrangements secret and of avoiding prohibitory orders on the part of District Magistrates unless there is definite information of an intended procession. In particular it is very desirable that prohibitory orders should not be issued in connection with the application pending before the Privy Council until the result of the application is known since these might be interpreted as prejudging the decision.'[61]

The Secretary of State in a telegram to the Viceroy on 12 February, 1931 communicated thus : 'Privy Council appeal Bhagat Singh and others versus the King emperor application for leave to appeal in above-mentioned case heard by Judicial Committee Privy Council. Their Lordship decided to recommend to His Majesty that it should be dismissed. Departing from the usual practice in these cases their considered reasons at a later date. It is not possible to say at present when these will be published.'[62]

Pandit Madan Mohan Malaviya sent the following telegram to the Viceroy on 14 February, 1931.[63] May I appeal to Your

Excellency to exercise your prerogative of mercy in cases of Bhagat Singh, Rajguru and Sukhdev to commute sentences of death passed upon them into those of transportation for life. I do so only because I am opposed on grounds of humanity to infliction of death sentences upon a fellow man but also because the execution of these youngmen whose action was prompted not by any personal or selfish consideration but by a patriotic impulse, however, misguided will give a great shock to public feeling in the country. While the purpose of Law and State will be fully met by a sentence of transportation for life, such an act of mercy on Your Excellency's part will, at this juncture, produce a very beneficial effect on Indian public opinion'.

A public memorial sent to the Viceroy stated: May it please Your Excellency, we the undersigned request that the death sentences passed by the Tribunal at Lahore on Messrs Bhagat Singh, Sukhdev and Rajguru be commuted on the following, among other grounds.'[64]

That the trial was held according to the ordinary form of law before an ordinary Court of Law.

That the trial was conducted ex-parte in the absence of the accused by an extraordinary Court of Law.

That the accused were not permitted to appeal to the High Court.

'That when Sardar Kishan Singh, father of S. Bhagat Singh requested to be permitted to produce documentary and oral evidence to disprove the prosecution story regarding the murder of Mr. Saunders, the request was not granted...'

A telegram followed by a petition was sent to the Government of India by Vidyavati, mother of Sardar Bhagat Singh, on 17 and 19 February, 1931 respectively and prayed for the stay of execution of death sentence passed on her son. Pray stay execution death sentence passed on my son Bhagat Singh by Special Tribunal appointed under Ordinance Third of 1930. I petition for mercy on grounds of youth of Bhagat Singh and special circumstances of the case. Detailed petition being submitted through post. Bhagat Singh lodged Central Jail, Lahore.[65]

The petition dated 19 February, 1931 was as follows. 'Humble petition of Vidyavati, mother of Bhagat Singh condemned prisoner in the Lahore Conspiracy Case, now confined in the Central Jail, Lahore, most respectfully showeth.

1. That the aforesaid Bhagat Singh was, along with other prisoners put on his trial before the Special Tribunal at Lahore which was appointed under the Ordinance passed by Your Excellency the charge against him being under Sections 302, 102-B and 131 of the Indian Penal Code and Sections 34 and 5 of Explosive Substance Act.
2. That the sentence passed on him is one of death and his appeal to Privy Council has been dismissed.
3. That your petitioner is his mother and naturally is anxious to save his life. She does not propose to raise any legal or political arguments, but she would respectfully urge that the conviction is based on evidence led by the prosecution which was never tested by cross-examination, and though the Tribunal might have felt itself justified in basing the conviction on much untested evidence, yet the petitioner feels that if it had been subjected to proper to cross-examination, his innocence would have been established and the Tribunal, in any case, would have been able to appraise that evidence properly.
4. That the petitioner would further urge that under the form of trial prescribed by the Ordinance he was deprived of the right of appeal to the High Court which he would have had under the code of criminal procedure but for the special procedure laid down by the Ordinance.[66]
5. That the petitioner therefore prays that your lordship may be graciously pleased to exercise your prerogative of mercy by commuting the sentence of death passed on my son and by substituting the sentence of imprisonment'.

The Home Department, Government of India informed the Punjab Government on 17 March, 1931, 'your telegram of the 16. Governor-General-in-Council has declined to interfere on behalf of the persons under sentence of death in Lahore Conspiracy Case. Namely, Bhagat Singh, Shiv Ram Rajguru and Sukh Dev. The Government of India accept the view of Local Government that advantages lies in not waiting until after

Karachi Congress, but they consider execution should be carried out not later than Monday 23rd and earlier if practicable. We are giving preliminary warning to Local Governments. Kindly communicate actual date by cypher wire.'[67]

The same day the information was given to other Local Governments, 'Please refer to Emersons demi-official of 28 February, regarding Lahore Conspiracy convicts. Petitions of mercy have been rejected. It is probable that execution will take place than 23rd but further information as stated in the demi-official letter will be given in due course. Meanwhile, this information should be treated as very secret.'[68]

Next day, the Home Secretary, Punjab Government infromed Home Secretary, Government of India, "Your telegram of the 17 instant No. 797-S. Bhagat Singh, Rajguru and Sukhdev will be executed at 7 on the evening of March 23. The news will be made known in Lahore on early morning of March 24".[69]

The Viceroy informed the Secretary of State on 23 March 1931.[70] Petitions of mercy of Bhagat Singh and two other condemned have been rejected and execution has been fixed for this evening. In meantime their friends have filed last minute applications in High Court at Lahore. We understand they will be heard today. If they are rejected existing arrangement will be carried out. If High Court reserves judgment, it will be necessary to postpone execution.

There has been considerable agitation by Youth Associations and extreme left of Congress and there is undoubtedly strong feeling in these quarters. So far there have been no clashes between police and sympathisers and excitement has not been so high or extensive as we apprehended. Days immediately following execution are, however, more likely to see trouble.

Earlier the Punjab Government delivered a telegram to the Home Secretary, Government of India, on 27 November, 1929 informing him of the intensity in the activities of revolutionaries at Lahore.[71]

Kali Pado Bhattacharya and Pulin Behary Roy, both from Howrah, were arrested in a kitchen in a stunned condition as a result of an explosion of bombs in Ramgali. The police found photographs of Bhagat Singh and B.K. Dutt and a formidable dagger from them and also another bomb was recovered from the kitchen. On investigation, the accused stated that two revolvers and their baggage were stolen from them near Amritsar while they were travelling in a train. According to their own statement accused had been four days in Lahore seeking an opportunity to murder Bengali approver in the Conspiracy Case. Prosecution sanctioned under Expolosive Substances Act and accused remanded for investigation. Original suspicion is confirmed that was confederate.[72]

The Additional District Magistrate, Lahore convicted both of these revolutionaries to seven years rigorous imprisonment. In its judgment, in court as reported in the press, found them guilty of having in their possession dangerous bombs and considered that they would, had the accidental explosion not taken place, in all probability have bombed either the court of the Special Magistrate trying the Lahore Conspiracy Case or one or more officials.[73]

On 23 December, 1930, on the occasion of the convocation of the Punjab University at Lahore, six shots were fired at the Governor, Sir Geoffrey De Montmorency who received two minor wounds, one at his back above left hip and another on his left arm. Besides, two police officers were also hurt as also one lady doctor. Two students were arrested in this regard by the police one of whom alleged to have been seen actually firing shots.[74]

No bullet appears to have penetrated body. Governor was taken to hospital where his wounds were dressed and he walked out of hospital to his car smoking a cigarette and proceeded to Government House.... Assailant was arrested in possession of a revolver.[75] The Home Secretary, Government of India in a telegram to the Governor of Punjab on the same day stated, "Government of India are very shocked to hear of dastardly attempt on your life, but greatly relieved to hear your providential escape. They hope you will make rapid recovery from injuries".[76]

Sardar Makhan Singh, the Proprietor, The Naresh, Lahore criticised this kind of violent cult and in a caption 'what is our Duty', he stated, '....in my opinion this attempt is not only an attempt on the life of His Excellency, but on all the peace loving population of Punjab. It is, therefore, the duty of every Punjabi to condemn the cowardly attack in the strongest possible language and thank God who saved His Excellency's life. It is my proposal that everywhere in the Punjab arrangements should be made to convene public meetings wherein resolutions of condemnation of the attack and congratulations to His Excellency should be passed and prayers should be made for His Excellency's speedy recovery. I myself convened such a meeting in my own village on 27 December, 1930.

I invite all responsible public men to cooperate with the Government to find out the nature of this conspiracy which led to this attack. It is my firm conviction that this attack is an outcome of a branch of anarchism, which should be discouraged and resented by all Indians.

At the end I request all those who happen to go through this circular to contribute their share of opinions on this attack so that in the next issue of the *Naresh* I may be able to widely circulate them for creating a healthy atmosphere for the future.

At the end I earnestly pray for His Excellency's long life and ever increasing prosperity.[77]

On 3 March, 1930, the Superintendent of Police, Jalandhar,[78] informed the Inspector-General of Police, Punjab[79] of a serious conspiracy of the revolutionaries to bomb the British officials at Jalandhar. But the conspiracy, before it could mature, was unearthed with the connivance of an approver who leaked out all kinds of details to the district police chief.[80]

On 3 March, Newman received reliable information from one of the men in touch with the conspirators that they had decided to bomb the Deputy Commissioner or him or both that night. He atonce consulted the Commissioner who agreed with him that action should be taken as soon as possible.[81]

The informer told us that the party would meet at 6 p.m. at a certain house in the city of which we already knew the whereabouts and then the men selected to do the bombing would be provided with the necessary bombs.... As they had spies posted on the Lines and City I had to send into Cantonment for the raiding party and the police headed by Fazal Imam. The District Inspectors made the raid on the meeting place and a couple of the dwelling houses of the revolutionaries. The metting house turned out to be a regular bomb factory. We found two readymade bombs, one of them of the coconut type. There was prepared material for filling another bomb, a quantity of bomb material and seditious, literature, also a daggar. A couple of stones for lithographing purposes and some filled in enrolment forms signed in blood. Incriminating staff and chemicals, bullets, etc. was also found at the other places. Muni Raj Dhanda and six of his companions were arrested on the spot red handed.... I have some 24 more arrests pending, these include about a dozen students of the local D.A.V. College. Amongst the pending arrests is that of Ujjagar Singh who has been giving us so much trouble lately.[82]

REFERENCES

1. Home Poll, File 172/30, 1930.
2. *Ibid.*
3. *Ibid.*
4. *Ibid.*
5. *Ibid.*
6. *Ibid.*
7. *Ibid.*
8. *Ibid.*
9. *Ibid.*
10. Proceedings of the Lahore Conspiracy Case, 1930. Part I Crown vs. Bhagat Singh and others, p. 1.
11. *Ibid.*
12. *Ibid.*
13. *Ibid.*
14. *Ibid.*
15. *Ibid.*, pp. 1-2.
16. *Ibid.*
17. *Ibid.*, p. 4.
18. *Ibid.*, pp. 13-14. Bhagat Singh put in an application stating that he wanted a legal adviser to watch the proceedings of the tribunal and give him advice on lines of cross-examination. The Tribunal sanctioned the arrangement proposed.
19. *Ibid.*, p. 44.
20. This statement was duly signed by the President and the members of the Tribunal on 13 May, 1930.
21. *Ibid.*, p. 46.

22. *Ibid.*, p. 47.
23. *Ibid..* p. 81.
24. On 31 August, 1930.
25. *Ibid.*, Part II, p. 653.
26. *Ibid.*, part II, 672
27. *Ibid.*, p, 691.
28. Home Poll, File 244 and K.W. 1930.
29. *Ibid.*
30. *Ibid.*
31. Transcript of the interview with Durga Das Khanna, *op.cit.*
32. Quoted in *The Tribune*, 7 July, 1929.
33. *The Tribune*, 10 August, 1929.
34. *Ibid.*
35. He was released on medical grounds and joined Congress in U.P.
36. A.I.C.C. Papers, File C-40 (ii) (Pt. III). 1929. This letter was written on 7th October, 1929.
37. *Ibid.*
38. A.I.C.C. Papers, File F.D. 23/1929-30.
39. Quoted in S. Gopal (ed.), *Selected Works of Jawaharlal Nehru*, Vol. IV, New Delhi, 1973, p. 157.
40. Home Poll, File 244 and K.W. 1930.
41. *Ibid.*
42. *Ibid.*
43. *Ibid.*
44. *Ibid.*
45. *Ibid.*
46. *Ibid.*
47. Home Poll, File 21/63, 1929.
48. *Ibid.*
49. *Ibid.*
50. *Ibid.*
51. *Ibid.*
52. Virendra Sandhu, *Amar Shaid Bhagat Singh*, Delhi, 1974, p. 46.

53. See *The Tribune*, 4 October, 1930.
54. *Ibid.*
55. See the judgment in proceedings of the Lahore Conspiracy Case.
56. Rajendra Kasvan, *Karantikari Bhagwati Bhai*, Delhi, 1975, pp. 100ff
57. *Ibid.*
58. *Ibid.*
59. S. Gopal, *op. cit.*, pp. 394-95.
60. Home Poll, File 4/21, 1931.
61. *Ibid.*
62. Home Department, Judicial, File, 152/1, 1931.
63. Home Poll, File 4/20, 1931.
64. See *The Hindustan Times*, 18 February, 1931.
65. Home Department, Judicial, File, 152/1, 1931.
66. *Ibid.*
67. Telegram from Home Department, Government of India, to the Punjab Government, 17 March, 1931 in Home Poll, File 4/21, 1931.
68. See Home Poll, File 4/31, 1931.
69. *Ibid.*
70. *Ibid.*
71. Home Poll, File 4/5, 1930.
72. *Ibid.*
73. *Ibid.*
74. *The Hindustan Times*, 25 December, 1930.
75. Home Poll, File 4/10, 1930.
76. *Ibid.*
77. *Ibid.*
78. He was F.L. Newman.
79. He was C. Stead.
80. Home Poll, File 4/14, 1930.
81. *Ibid.*
82. *Ibid.*

7 Hunger-strike in Jail

Although conceivable, people awaited wondering the fate of the revolutionaries, Bhagat Singh and others. In the year 1929, 7 May, started the hearing of the case of Central Assembly bomb dropping in the court of Mr. Pool, inside Delhi prison. Afterward this case, as we are already aware of, was transferred to the court of Mr. Middleton, special magistrate. The Indian press and the world press gave importance o this case as a *cause celebre*. In the past Khudiram (hanged on 11 August, 1908) and Kanhailal (hanged on 20 November, 1908) and been given great importance. Mandanlal Dhingra's hanging in England on 16 August, 1909, was naturally international news. Poets, most of them unknown, sang songs on them.

But Bhagat Singh transcended them all, because of one great factor—the statement which they issued on the 6 June 1929 in which the party's commitment to socialism was explained. In that statement they discussed the fact of the case first :

We stand charged with serious offences and at this stage we venture to explain our conduct.

The following questions arise—

(1) Were bombs thrown into the chamber, if so, why?

(2) Is the charge as framed by the lower court correct or otherwise?

To the first half of the first question our reply is in the affirmative, but some of the so-called eye-witnesses have committed perjury. By way of illustration we may point out that the evidence of Sergeant Terry regarding the seizure of pistol from one of us is a deliberate falsehood for neither of us had a pistol at the time we gave ourselves up.

In our reply to the next half of the first question, we are constrained to go into some detail to offer full and frank explanations of our motive and the circumstances leading to what has now become a historical event. When we were told by some of the police officers, who visited us in the jail that Lord Irwin in his address to the joint session of the two houses after the event in question, described it as an attack directed against not individual, but against the constitution itself, we readily recognised that the true significance of the incident had been correctly appreciated.

We are next to none in our love for humanity and so, far from having malice against any individual, and holding human life sacred beyond words, we are neither perpetrators of dastardly outrages and therefore a disgrace to our country as the pseudo-socialist Diwan Chamanlal is reported to have described us, nor are we lunatics as *The Tribune* of Lahore and some others would have the people believe.

We claim to be no more than serious students of history and the conditions of our country and human aspirations, and we despise hypocrisy.

Our practical protest was against the institution, which since its birth has eminently displayed not only its worthlessness, but also its far-reaching power for mischief. The more we have pondered, the more deeply we have become convinced that it only exists to demonstrate to the world India's humiliation and helplessness, and it symbolises the overriding domination of an irresponsible and autocratic rule.

Time and again the national demand has been pressed by the representatives of the people, only to find the wastepaper basket as its final destination. Solemn resolutions passed by the House has been contemptuously trampled underfoot on the floor of the so-called Indian Parliament Resolutions regarding the repeal of repressive and arbitrary measures have been treated with sublime contempt and Government measures and proposals, rejected as unacceptable to the elected members have been restored by just a stroke of the Viceregal pen.

In brief, in spite of earnest endeavour we have utterly failed to find any justification for the existence of an institution, which despite all pomp and splendour organised with the hard earned money of sweating millions of India, is only a hollow show and a mischievous make-believe.

In the same manner we failed to comprehend the mentality of public leaders, who help to squander public time and money on so manifestly a stage managed exhibition of India's helpless subjection. We have been ruminating upon all this, as also on the wholesale arrests of the leaders of labour movement. The introduction of the Trade Dispute Bill brought us into the Assembly to watch its progress. The course of the debate only served to confirm our conviction that the toiling millions of India had nothing to expect from an institution that stood as a menacing monument to the strangling of the exploited and the serfdom of the helpless labourers.

Finally an insult, which we considered inhuman and barbarous, was hurled on the devoted heads of the representatives of the entire country and the starving and struggling millions were deprived of their primary rights and the sole means of their economic welfare.

None who has felt like us for the dumb driven labourers could possibly witness this spectacle with equanimity, none whose heart bleeds for those, who have given their lifeblood in silence to the building up of the economic structure of the exploiters, of whom the Government happen to be the biggest in the country, could repress the soul-agonising anguish, which is so ruthlessly wrung out of our hearts. Consequently, bearing in mind the words of the late Mr. S.R. Das, once the law member of the Viceroy's council executive, which appeared in the famous letter he addressed to his son, to the effect that the bomb was necessary to awaken England from her dreams, we dropped the bombs on the floor of the Assembly Chamber to register our protest on behalf of those, who had no other means left to give expression to their heartrending agony. Our sole purpose was to make the deaf hear and to give the needed timely warning.

Others have as keenly left as we have done and from under the sea of the Indian humanity a veritable storm is about to break out. We have hoisted a danger signal to warn those who are speeding along without heeding grave danger ahead. We have only marked the end of an era of utopian non-violence of whose futility the rising generation is convinced beyond a shadow of doubt. Out of sincere goodwill and love for humanity we have adopted this methods of warning to prevent untold suffering, which we like millions of others clearly foresee.

Utopian Non-violence

We have used the expressions utopian non-violence in the foregoing para, which requires more explanation. Force when aggressively applied is 'violence' and is therefore unjustifiable. But when it is used in the furtherance of a legitimate cause, it has its own moral justification. Elimination of force at all costs is utopian and the new movement which has arisen in the country and of which we have given a warning is inspired by the ideals which guided Guru Gobind Sigh, Shivaji, Kamal Pasha, Reza Khan, Washington, Garibaldi, Lafayette and Lenin. As both the Indian government and the Indian public leaders appeared to have shut their eyes and closed their ears against the existence and voice of this motive, we have felt it our duty to sound the warning, where it could not go unheard.

Our Intentions

So far we have dealt with the motive behind the incident in question and now we must define the intention. It cannot be said that we have no personal grudge or motive against anyone of those, who received slight injuries or against any other person in the Assembly. On the contrary we hold human life sacred beyond words and would sooner lay down our own lives in the service of humanity than injure any one else. Unlike mercenary soldiers of imperialist armies, who are inclined to kill without compassion, we respect and in so far as it lies in our power, we attempt to save human life. And still we admit to have deliberately thrown bombs into the Assembly Chamber. Facts, however speak for themselves and intention should be judged from the result of action without drawing upon hypothetical circumstances and presumptions. Despite the evidence of government experts, the bombs thrown in the Assembly Chamber resulted in slight damage to an empty bench and slight abraisons in less than half a dozen cases. While the government scientist ascribed this to a miracle, we see nothing but a precise scientific process. The two bombs exploded in vacant spaces within the wooden barriers of desks and benches. Secondly even those who were within two feet of the explosion, for instance Mr. Rau, Mr. Sanker Rao and

George Schuster were either not hurt or received slight scratches. Loaded with an effective charge of Potassium Chlorate and sensitive, Picrate, the bombs would have smashed the barriers and land may low within some yards of the explosion. Again had they been loaded with some other high explosive with a charge of destructive pellets or darts, they would have sufficed to wipe out a majority of the members of the Assembly. Still again we could have flung them on the official benches chockful with people of note. And finally we could have ambushed Sir John Simon, whose luckless commission was hated by all reasonable people and who was at that time sitting in the presidential gallery. All this was however beyond our intention and the bombs did not do more than what they were designed to do and the miracle consisted of no more than a deliberate aim which landed them in safe places.

We then deliberately offered ourselves to bear the penalty for what we had done and to let the imperialist exploiters know that they can crush individuals but, they cannot kill ideas. By crushing the insignificant units the nation cannot be crushed. We wanted to emphasise the historical lesson that *lettres de cachet* and Bastilles could not crush the revolutionary movement in France. Gallows and the Siberian mines could not crush the Russian revolution. Can ordinances and safety bills snuff out the flames of freedom in India? Conspiracy of youngmen who cherish the vision of the greater ideal could not check the march of revolution. But timely warning, if not unheeded, can help to prevent loss of life and general suffering.

What is Revolution?

Bhagat Singh was asked in the lower court as to what he meant by revolution. In answer to that question, we would say that revolution does not necessarily mean sanguinary strikes, nor is there any place in it for individual vendetta. It is not the cult of the bomb or the pistol. By 'Revolution' we mean that the present order of things, which is based on manifest injustice must change. Producers or labourers in spite of being the most necessary elements of society, are robed by their exploiters of the fruits of their labour and are deprived of their elementary rights. On the one hand, the peasants who grow corn for all, starve with their families. The weaver who supplies the world markets with textile fabrics cannot find enough to cover his own and his children's bodies. Masons, smiths and carpenters, who build magnificent palaces live and perish in slums. On the other hand, capitalists, exploiters, parasites of society squander millions on mere whims. These terrible inequalities and forced disparity of chances are heading towards chaos. This state of affairs, cannot last and it is obvious that the present order of society is merrymaking on the brink of a volcano and the innocent children of exploiters, no less than millions of the exploited, are walking on the edge of a dangerous precipice. The whole edifice of this civilisation, if not saved in time, shall crumble. Radical change is therefore necessary, and it is the duty of those who realise this to reorganise society on a socialist basis. Unless this is done, and the exploitation of man by man and nation by nation, which goes masquerading as a civilising force, but in reality is imperialism, is brought to an end, the suffering and carnage with which humanity is threatened today cannot be prevented and all talk of ending wars and ushering in an era of universal peace, is undisguised hypocrisy. But revolution we mean the ultimate establishment of an order of society, which the sovereignty of the proletariat should be recognised and as a result of which the world federation should redeem humanity from the bondage of capitalism and the misery and the peril of wars.

Fair and loud enough warning. This is our ideal. With this ideology for our inspiration we have given a fair and loud enough warning. If, however, it goes unheeded and the present system of government continues to be an impediment in the way of the national forces that are swelling up, a grim struggle must ensure involving the overthrow of all obstacles and the establishment of the dictatorship of the proletariat to pave the way for the consumination of the ideal of revolution. Revolution is the inalienable right of all men. Freedom is the imprescriptible birthright of all. The toiler is the real sustainer of society. The sovereignty of the people is the ultimate destiny of the workers. For these ideals and for this faith we shall welcome any suffering to which we may be condemned. To the altar of this revolution we have brought our youth as incense, for no sacrifice is too great for so magnificent a cause. We are content to await the advent of the revolution.

Long Live Revolution!

Bhagat Singh and Dutt from the very first day of their trial used the courtroom as a launching pad for their ideological missiles. They utilised every small occasion to issue a statement. After some time they angled their attack on a different plane. They were being treated as ordinary criminals. During British rule the European or pseudo-European criminals were, as a rule, treated better than Indian criminals. This was totally a racist policy. The Kakori prisoners had fought against it and had won a limited, and as it proved later on, a temporary victory some 3 years ago. They were extended European treatment on medical grounds, but as soon as they were convicted and their bargaining power was diminished, they were deprived of this privilege. To protest against this they went on hunger strike, which they broke at the insistence of Ganesh Shanker Vidyarthi who had been duly assured by the Government that special treatment would be offered to them. But the Government did not stand on this promise. Thus, the position in Indian jails had gone back to square one as in 1925

Bhagat Singh and Dutt picked up the fight from where it had been left by their predecessors, specially the Kakori prisoners, who at least, had secured a temporary victory. As has been repeated time and again the revolutionaries did not think like Gandhi that an imprisoned freedom fighter should give up all fight. Revolutionaries believed that prison only changes the *modus operandi* of the struggle. Therefore they smuggled out articles, even whole books from jail and they made the best use of the courts.

On the 12 June, Bhagat Singh and Dutt were sentenced to transportation for life. Immediately Bhagat Singh was transferred to Lahore jail and Dutt was sent to the jail at Mianwali.

They were separated, but Bhagat Singh impressed the English sergeant so greatly that he allowed him to meet Dutt during the journey to their respective jails. Bhagat Singh knew what was going to happen. He knew that he had only a few days to live and he decided to make the best use of those days. He instructed Dutt to go on hunger-strike as soon as he reached Mianwali jail. Accordingly, they both went on hunger-strike from the 14 June, 1929 in their respective jails.

In the meantime, the police had decided to reopen the Lahore conspiracy case. Though some arrests had been made, they were still in the process of nabbing other. From Delhi jail, Bhagat Singh and Dutt had been sent to stand their trial in this case. Later on, the Government decided to exclude Dutt in this trial, in his case transportation for life was supposed to be enough because there was not evidence to implicate him in the Saunders murders case, so there was not much chance to hang him.

The hunger-strike started by Bhagat Singh and B.K. Dutt developed into an all-India affair. 30 June was celebrated throughout India as Bhagat Singh Day. But the Government did not give in. On the 10 July, the revolutionaries arrested to try in this case alone, were brought together in jail for the first time. All the comrades were excited and wanted to jump into the fray. But Jatin Das of Calcutta opposed this emotional approach and advised caution. He said, 'It is a long struggle different from and more difficult than gunfights.' He further said, 'Inching to death in a hunger-strike is far more difficult than death in a gunfight or on the gallows. It would be against revolutionary traditions to withdraw from the strike without attaining the objective. It is better not join the strike than to suffer a premature withdrawal.'

Before we proceed to describe the full story of this epic hunger-strike let us recall the story of the martyrdom of Bhagavaticharan as described by Vishwanath Baishampayan.

Thus, Jatin Das advanced towards, meeting his end. The whole country was woked up. Subhas Bose despairing of compromise, sent Rs. 600 for his body to be sent to Calcutta. Bombay and the Punjab come forward to bear the expenses. The whole of India prepared for his glorious martyrdom. The Government immemely tense that his body might be taken out in a procession. A discordant note was aired by certain sticklers for non-violence that Das was not a believer in violence, that is why he was dying so gloriously. Indeed it was Gandhi, who said this after his death, trying thus to glorify non-voilence. Anyway, Jatin Das died at 1-5 p.m. on the 13 of September. The doctors for some reason could not force-feed him even for a day. This was an achievement in fasting. Terence Macswiney, the Irish mayor of Cork, lasted 74 days and our Jatin died on the 63 day.

His body was escorted by train from Lahore to Calcutta. Large crowds turned out to pay tribute at all stations. When it reached Calcutta, a procession of 6 lakh mourners accompanied the body to the cremation ground. Only Tagore at a later date was given such a homage. Gandhi kept mum over the whole affair, and when he did speak after a few days, he most inadvertently spoke of violence and non violence. He prophesed that Jatin Das did not belong to the 'School of Violence.' The revolutionaries had a good laugh at Gandhi, because they knew that Jatin was an ardent revolutionary.

The Plot at Lahore

The explosion on the 23 of October, during the *Dashera*, holidays, in 1928, elucidated certain fact that created the suspicion that Bhagat Singh was connected with some grave conspiracy. But as yet the police were just in the dark. On the 15 April, 1928 the police raided a house and arrested Sukhdev, Jaigopal and Kishorilal. Jaigopal opened up within 8 days of his arrest, though in Bhagat Singh's estimation, he was a jewel. On 27 May a house was searched in Saharanpur resulting in the arrest of Shiv Verma and Jaydev. Hansraj Vohra became a witness.

On the 7 of June a dacoity was reported from a village named Maulania in Bihar. Regarding this Phanindranath Ghosh was arrested and though he belonged to the old guard, deposed as king's witness. Thus, the case started with 16 accused –(1) Sukhdev, (2) Kishorilal, (3) Shiv Verma, (4) Gayaprasad, (5) Jatin Das, (6) Jaidev Kapur, (7) Bhagat Singh, (8) B.K. Dutt, (9) Kamal Nath Tiwari, (10) Jitendra Nath Sanyal, (11) Asharam, (12) Deshraj, (13) Premdutt, (14) Mahabir Singh, (15)Surendra, (16) Ajoy Ghosh. The absconders—Bejoykumar Sinha, Rajguru and Kundanlal were arrested in Bareilly, Pune and UP respectively. B.K. Dutt, in the end excluded in the conspiracy.

When the trial started, the revolutionaries involved were crystal clear in their views as to how to make the best use of the courtroom. Bhagat Singh constituted a 3-member committee for this purpose, which comprised of himself, Bejoykumar Sinha and Sukhdev. Thus, Bhagat Singh and his colleagues proved to be unbearable annoyance to the judges and police officers threating them at every step, with the prisoners always managing to publicise revolutionary propaganda in court. In prison, visitors were discouraged and correspondents were harassed. Bhagat Singh was against all this. This trial began with slogans of *Long Live Revolution, Down with Imperialism and Workers of the*

World Unite and the singing of *Vande Mataram*. During these performances the judge and the officials looked like guilty and helpless by-standers. But the court had to do something to demonstrate its authority, so it ordered all the accused to be handcuffed. More slogans. When an approver made some stray remarks, the accused shouted 'Shame', but the youngest of them Premdutt, disgruntled with this hurled his slippers at him. The proceedings were stopped and it was ordered that henceforth the accused must remain handcuffed in court. Bhagat Singh's immediate reaction was –"Under these circumstances we won't attend the court."

Despite all efforts the accused could not be forced to attend court. Only five accused were somehow commuted to the gate of the jail, where the court was sitting, in a vehicle, but they could not be made to get down from it. So the court had to compromise. It was agreed that the accused would be handcuffed before reaching the court, but once inside the courtroom, their handcuffs would be taken off. The accused kept to their part of the agreement. They came to court in handcuffs. But the proceedings started without taking off their handcuffs. The accused kept quiet at this breach of trust. At noon their handcuffs were taken off to enable them to take lunch. After lunch they started handcuffing them again, but they refused. This gave way in a scuffle and the Pathan police was called to deal with them, tilting the struggle a communal. These simple Pathans of the frontier viewed they were dealing with dangerous criminals. They swooped down on the prisoners, specially on Bhagat Singh, on whom 8 Pathans fell and began to beat him with sticks and shoes. All this happened in broad daylight in the presence of visitors and correspondents. The judge just sat still, looking on. While this continued for some time, the visitors and correspondents were asked to quit. The government hoodlums got tired, but the accused did not surrender. Ultimately the police authorities disposed the court that the accused would rather be killed, but could not be 'disciplined.' The story of this gruesome assault was printed in the papers with big captions and was condemned by everybody. Gandhi kept mum again, although what the accused were going through was nothing but non-violent passive resistance. The government realised that it could not overpower. The judge had to cut his own words and annul his orders. Jitendra Sanyal, one of the accused, has written that the news of this judicial vandalism reached the world press and a Polish lady sent some money. Also money poured in from Japan, Canada and far away South America. The whole country in protest celebrated Bhagat Singh day. Top leaders came to see the accused—Subhas Chandra Bose, Jawaharlal Nehru, Baba Gurdit Singh, Nariman, the Raja of Kalakankar (a patron of litterateurs and patriots), Rafi Ahmed Kidwai, Mohanlal Saksena (a lawyer for the Kakori prisoners and later member of Nehru's cabinet), Ganesh Shanker Vidyarthi, the idealist editor of Hindi *Pratap*, and the dean of Congress leaders Motilal Nehru.

Although Gandhi ostentaciously talked of non-voilence all time, many of his archbishops admired the revolutionaries. Motilal Nehru saw Chandrashekhar Azad many times and encouraged him to keep up. In reality, the Nehru family was close to the revolutionaries. Jawaharlal Nehru writes about an interview with Azad in his Autobiography, in which he unfortunately says, "This of them, it seem to me have definitely the Fascist mentality." This was a complete mis-statement, because he knew that they were not at all Fascists, on the other hand, they were poineers of the socialist ideology.

A few names in this socialist heritage were Madame Cama (who attended the International Socialist Congress at Stuttgart in 1907), M.N. Roy, Birendra Chattopadhyay and, of course, Bhagat Singh. It seems that Bhagat Singh went to the Nehrus for some money after the Saunders murder, but came back empty handed, because they did not know him. Later on, when they got to know him, he was helped. No detail of this incident is available.

The publicity gained by the Lahore case prisoners caused unrest in the dovecote of British bureaucracy. A solution was suggested that the presence of under trials in the court should be dispensed with by an ordinance, and that the presence of their lawyers should be deemed sufficient. Finally, the Government passed the decision and in violation of all legal norms the necessary ordinance was made public. The accused attended court, but they insisted on singing the National Anthem before the proceedings started. The court now asked the police and jail authorities to control this, it was reiterated by them that they could kill the accused, but could not stop their singing. Ultimately the accused decided not to attend court.

Sardar Kishan Singh was deadsure that Bhagat Singh would certainly be sentenced to death. Somebody, convinced him that he should forward a petition to the Government that on the fateful day, Bhagat Singh was far away from the place of occurrence. Even a letter beating a postal stamp was produced to substantiate this alibi. Sardar Kishan Singh writes in detail and argues the cause of his son being not guilty.

This was published in all the papers. In view of the statements of the approvers this plea appeared ridiculous and childish. Bhagat Singh was very much embarrassed as he thought that some people might get the notion that all this was being done with his consent. He wrote a strongly worded letter to his father in which he said :

"I was very much surprised to note that you have written a petition to the special tribunal in my defence. This distressed me very much and cannot take it lying down. As a son I have the greatest respect for your paternal sentiments, at the same time I think you had no business to send such a petition without my consent. From the very beginning you have tried to impress upon me that I should give the highest priority to my legal defence, I have always thought that political workers should ignore the court and should accept and bear the heaviest punishment with a smile on their faces.

I assure you that my life is not as precious as you think. As least I do not hold life so important as to imperial the priceless ideals to save it. Had somebody else done what you have done. I would have straightaway branded him a traitor, but your case is different. I must however accuse you of a low type of sloppy sentiment. This is an occasion when you, I, everybody is on trial. I must say that you have in this trial. I know that you have been a tried battle-scarred patriot. I fail to understand why you could not rise to the occasion in the case."

Under Bhagat Singh's instructions this letter to his father was printed in all the papers, as the mischief wrought by Sardar Kishan Singh's 'petition' could only be negated by this method.

When attending court, Bhagat Singh made good use of the occasions. Everyday he gave some message to the youths. Lenin day, Kakori day and other revolutionary days were celebrated after informing the court. His object was to inspire the youths to read the works of Lenin was not an arm-chair politician. Bhagat Singh maintained that clarity of thinking should not be kept apart from struggle. Thus, Bhagat Singh, within the course of a few months, emerged as the greatest factor contributing to the understanding and study of Marxism-Leninism. I have already shown that Madame Cama lit the flame of socialism in 1907, M.N. Roy, Birendranath Chattopadhyay and others made the word meaningful to some intellectuals, but Bhagat Singh burst like a bomb to make its fame encircle, enrich and fill every aspect of the freedom struggle and even Jawahar Lal Nehru was forced to declare himself a socialist and a republican in the Lahore Congress. This aspect has not been conceded in importance it deserves.

When approver Phanindra Ghosh came to depose in court that he had learnt how to make explosives, Shiv Verma, at the urge of Bhagat Singh subjected him to a rigorous and detailed cross-examination. This object aimed at teaching youngmen how to make explosives, because detailed report of the court proceedings reached the press. During the hunger-strike, Bhagat Singh had sent telegrams to jails where political prisoners had gone on hunger-strike sympathizing with the Lahore prisoners. These telegrams were sent through the court. He asked his father to send similar telegrams too. When he learnt on the 5 April, 1930 about the passing away of the veteran revolutionary Shyamji Krishna Verma in Europe, he sent a telegram C/o Hindustan Association of Europe, Berlin, which read—

"We condole the death of Shyamji, pioneer and veteran freedom fighter. His life-long struggle for independence is a national heritage that will inspire generation of freedom fighters."

In the same manner Bhagat Singh mourned some Hungarian freedom fighters who had passed away in jail. These telegrams were sent on behalf of the Lahore prisoners.

His lawyers put their foot down against celebrations of Lenin day, Kakori day, May day and other such days, because in their legalist eyes this constituted an indirect corroboration of the charges levelled against them, but the revolutionaries ignored such warnings.

As time passed Bhagat Singh began to realise about the fact that the hunger-strike in which Jatin Das conceded his life had not as yet yielded any results although a jail commission had been set up. There was no doubt that the Government was using the jail commission only to hoodwink the Lahore prisoners and the masses. Bhagat Singh foresaw that it was his duty to make sure that the supreme sacrifice of Jatin Das be made meaningful before he himself was hanged. The Government was waiting for the case to finish and Bhagat Singh etc. to be hanged. Then the Jail commision could escape by producing a futile report full of banalities signifying nothing.

Bhagat Singh and his youngmen saw through the making and retook to the hunger-strike with the same old demands. Public leaders had promised them that they would fight, declaring that it was now their fight. But they had failed to show results. Bhagat Singh was certain that even if only a single Lahore prisoner were sentenced to death, it would be he, so the fight for special treatment for freedom fighters Rardly personally concerned him. It was a fight, which concerned the future of all except the condemned prisoners.

His attitude towards life and death was like a born fighter. He didn't mind hanging, but not like a fatalist. And, in the meantime, he wished to use every minute of his life for the fight, which was the salt of his life. After being sentenced to death, he wrote to B.K. Dutt from the condemned cell :

"I am sentenced to death and you are sentenced to transportation for life. You shall live and show to the world that revolutionaries can die as well as live for their ideals in the face of heavy odds. It would be wrong to welcome death as a means of escaping from worldly pinpricks. Revolutionaries, who are spared hanging by chance, should demonstrate to the world that they defy the life of torture in dark cells."

What Bhagat Singh said was in line with ideas of revolutionaries. In the same manner Rajendranath Lahari (hanged on 17 December, 1927) had told of me on the day he was sentenced to death, 'I don't care. In my case the agony would be over within a few days, but you have to trudge for years and years'.

The hunger-strike started on the 4 February, 1930. The Lahore Congress had been convened in the meantime and

Jawaharlal Nehru created quite a stir by declaring 'I am a socialist and a republican'. This was, in fact, a success for Bhagat Singh, Chandrashekhar Azad and his youths that after Bhagat Singh had named his party a socialist republican party, Jawaharlal endorsed his words inside he Congress. No Doubt it was clever on the part of Nehru. Very few can recapitulate what Nehru actually said in the Congress. He said :

"I must frankly confess that I am a socialist and a republican and am no believer in kings and princes or in the order which produces the modern kings of industry, who have greater power over the lives and fortunes of men than even the kings of old, and whose methods are as predatory as those of the feudal aristocracy. I recognise, however, that it may not be possible for a body constituted as is the national congress and in the present situation of the country to adopt a full socialistic programme. But we must realise that the philosophy of socialism has gradually permeated the entire structure of society the world over and almost the only points in dispute are the pace and the methods of advance to its full realisation. India will have to go that way, if she may evolve her own methods and may adopt the ideal to the genius of her race."

After nearly 50 years of its existence, the Congress had, finally declared complete independence as its objective and was poised for a Gandhian type of fight. It was against this background that Bhagat Singh and his brave colleagues engaged on hunger-strike. This electrified the atmosphere and freedom fighters, lingering in jails all over India, took part the strike. Kakori prisoners—Rajkumar Sinha, S.N. Bakshi, Mukundilal and Manmathnath Gupta—who and already spent more than four years in jail, joined the strike on the 7 February, 1930, i.e., 4 days after the Lahore comrades. Other prisoners also jumped in. The Government had before hand knowledge of this hunger-strike and the blueprint of an 'Operation Hunger-strike,' technically perfect, was all set to tackle with the strike. It was found out that although Bhagat Singh, Dutt and other had been on hunger-strike for a longer period than Jatin Das, they did not die because they were force-fed everyday. Jatin Das could not be force-fed, although a few attempts were made to do so. The Government deduced that force-feeding hunger-strikers gave them more days for propaganda and thus psychologically helped them. It was therefore decided to lessen force-feeding to the minimum, to be taken up only when the prisoners were about to pass away and to be abandoned as soon as they revived a little. This new policy was meant to keep the growing pangs of hunger always alive and thus increase chances of surrender. Medical science and psychology were requisitioned to derail the freedom fighters.

But this new policy did not bear any fruit. Political leaders, editors and philanthropists visited the Lahore and the Kakori prisoners. Bhagat Singh and other told their interviewers that their object was to ascertain that the supreme sacrifice of Jatin Das was not meaningless. Thus, a movement was created through the length and breadth of the country. This movement naturally helped to increase the strength of the bigger movement that was being launched by the Congress. The new policy of force-feeding only to keep the lamp of life burning called for a quick solution, because the Government had realised that one Jatin Das was enough, they coud not afford to let another freedom fighter starve to death at this very crucial moment. Quick consultations were held and on the 19 February, 1930 the Government came out with a communique, creating A, B and C classes of prisoners. This classification saw the end to the racist discrimination prevalent in Indian jails till now. European convicts were now rechristened B class prisoners and Indians with higher standard of living, with higher cultural and educational backgrounds were now entitled to this class. Class A was reserved for people of status convicted in crimes not involving 'moral turpitude'.

Thus, the demands for which Jatin Das had given his life were not fully attained, but it had at least removed racial discrimination. It was no doubt a victory, but at the same time it was not a gull victory. Bhagat Singh and his colleagues thought that they should consider this enough for the time being, and called off the hunger-strike. But Kakori prisoners at Bareilly jail, refused to call it off, as they had been cheated once. Mukandilal, however, broke the strike. The remaining trio continued. Granted that now there existed a B class, they argued, what was the guarantee that they would be kept in this class? In spite of telegrams from Bhagat Singh, Sardar Kishan Singh and other public leaders they did not give in. The new policy of force-feeding reduced them very soon to skeletons, each striker having lost much weight. Many leaders came to see them, but they remained dogged. To make the story shorter on the 53rd day of their hunger-strike when they were assured, that on breaking the strike, they would be given B class, they called off the strike. By this time each of them had lost 50 to 60 Ibs of weight. Thus, they became the first three to benefit from this new classification. There is a sequel to this story showing how the bureaucracy took its revenge. Bhagat Singh, Rajguru, Sukhdev were of course hanged, but others of the Lahore case were not given B class.

In parenthesis, we must note one thing that is very important. Although in 1921, 1930 and 1942 large numbers of Congress prisoners, were put in jail, it was the revolutionaries who fought for and created this classification, which is still prevalent in Indian prisons. In the 1930 and the 1942 movements, hundreds of Congress prisoners enjoyed the awards of this classification. But neither Gandhi nor any Congress leader ever gave any credit for this to Jatin Das or Bhagat Singh because this naturally would open the uncomfortable question—'Who won independece for India?' The battle begun by Ramrakha in the Andaman jail (although fought on a lower key) was thus brought to a meaningful end by Bhagat Singh. The supreme sacrifice of Jatin now yielded some tangible result.

8 M.A. Jinnah's Statement in Legislative Assembly

"Sir one is placed somewhat in a difficult position when one has got to deal with a speaker like the last one. It was his maiden speech, and it is the tradition of this house, that when a Member makes his maiden speech, he is in a privileged position and is not to be attacked. Whatever reasons or grounds, therefore, he may have given me for criticising him, I will not wish to depart from that tradition which, I think, ought to be maintained in the House. But I would say this, that in his concluding portion he remarked that the Hon'ble Members may have admiration and sympathy for the accused in the Lahore case. I think I am speaking on behalf of a very large body of people when I say that, if there is sympathy and admiration for the accused, it is only to this extent, that they are the victim of the system of government. It is not that we approve or applaud their action if they are guilty, which still remains to be proved. If they are guilty of the offences of which they are charged, then I am sure it is not that we admire them or approve of their action, but on the contrary, I am sure a large body of thinking people fell that these youngmen, whatever be the provocations, are misguided in resorting to actions for which they now stand charged.

Now, Sir, the Hon'ble Home Member asked the House that we must approach this question without prejudice, and impartially. Sir, I am sure the Hon'ble Home Member himself tried his best to follow the same principle, but has he been able to apply the same principle when he brings this before the House? Do the facts justify that? The last speaker, whom I am not going to attack, almost gave away the case in his concluding remarks when he said that the only way to break the hunger-strike is to pass this Bill.

Well, I am not concerned at present so much with the account that was given by the Hon'ble Member with regard to the treatment in jails of various classes of prisoners, but one thing is clear, and it is this. From the statement that was issued by Bhagat Singh and Dutt, what is an admitted fact now, even from the speech of the Hon'ble Member who spoke last, is that they were not given the treatment—not on racial grounds—but according to the standard and the scale which is laid down for Europeans in the matter of diet and bare necessities of life. It is not a mere question that they want to be treated as Europeans. As a matter of fact, according to the admission and the definition given by the Hon'ble Member who spoke last on behalf of the Treasury Benches, so far as I know, Bhagat Singh and Dutt wear topees, and their figures appeared in shorts. Therefore, they ought to have been treated as Europeans. The Hon'ble Member in reply to a question said that whether the man is a European or an Indian—and he accepted the definition of my honourable friend Mr. Neogy—if one wears a topee, then one is a European for the purpose of jail rules. Then why should you not treat Bhagat Singh and Dutt, who wear topees and European clothes, as such for the purpose of treatment in jails? Why do not the Punjab Government given them the treatment that they are entitled to, at once, and be done with? They wear topees and they are entitled to that treatment.

What do they say in their statement which was read out? This is what they say :

"We, Bhagat Singh and Dutt, were sentenced to life transportation in the Assembly bomb case, Delhi, on 19 May, 1929. As long as we were under trial prisoners in Delhi jail we were accorded very good treatment and we were given good diet. But since our transfer from the Delhi Jail to Mianwali Jail and Lahore Central Jail,—

Which is represented by the Hon'ble member, who spoke last—the Punjab seems to be a Terrible place . . .

Mian Muhammad Shah Nawaz (West Central Punjab) : Don't go there.

M.A. Jinnah: I won't. To continue what they say :

"We are being treated as ordinary criminals".

So, in Delhi they received very good treatment and in the Punjab they are treated as ordinary criminals. Surely, Sir if the government of the Punjab was not wanting in statesmanship, if the Government of the Punjab had any brains, they would have found a solution to this question very easily and long ago. But, Sir, it is a question—the more I examine it and the more I analyse it, I find—it is a question of declaration of war. As far as the Punjab Government are concerned, the Government do not merely wish to bring these men to trial and get them convicted by a judicial tribunal, but Government go to war against these men. They seem to me in this form of mind : "We will pursue every possible course, every possible method, but we will see that you are sent either to the gallows or transported for life, and in the meantime we will not treat you as decent men."

Sir, the whole spirit behind this is that and nothing else. I do not for a moment wish to say that the Government are not bound—in fact, it is their bounded duty—to prosecute those people that commit offences. I do not wish to say that the Government should not do every thing in their power to see that their convictions are secured. But may I ask, with whom are you at war? What are the resources of these few youngmen who, according to you, have committed certain offences? You want to prosecute them, and after due trial, you want to secure their convictions. But before they are convicted, surely this is not a matter on which there should be this struggle, that you should not at once yield to their demands for bare necessities of life. After all, so far as the Lahore case prisoners are concerned, surely they are political prisoners and undertrial. You ask me, what is a political prisioner? It is very difficult to define a political prisoner. It is very difficult to lay down any particular definition. But if you use your common sense, if you use your intelligence, surely you can come to the conclusion with regard to the particular case and say, here are these men who are political prisoners, and we do not wish to give them proper treatment. We want to give them treatment as undertrial prisoners. If you had said that, the question would have been solved long ago. Do you wish to prosecute them or persecute them?

Sir, I do not wish to base my opposition to this Bill on this issue of bad treatment, because this is only one aspect of the issue, or rather one aspect of the Bill before us. This Bill has got to be looked at, as far as I can see, from three point of view. The first, form the point of view of criminal jurisprudence; second, political point of view or the policy of the Bill; and third, treatment to the accused when they are undertrial. I think it will be admitted, I think even the Hon'ble Home Member conceded, that by the Bill which he has brought before the House, he is introducing a principle in the criminal jurisprudence, of a very unprecedented character. I do not think, Sir, there is any system of jurisprudence in any civilised country where you will find such a principle in existence as is involved in this Bill. Some of the Hon'ble Members who are not lawyers might not have appreciated fully the implications of this Bill. This Bill not only dispenses with the presence of the accused at the trial, but I will give you a picture as to what will happen under this Bill. Under this Bill the Government will apply to the Magistrate before whom the inquiry is going on and say: "Here is a law which we have secured from the Legislature. Now the accused have voluntarily made themselves incapable of attending the Courts and, therefore, you have to dispense with their presence". The inquiry will then proceed *ex parte* before the Magistrate. Evidence will be led, oral and documentary, which will go without being tested by cross-examination. The documentary evidence will go without being even seen by the accused, against whom it is produced, and how will you identify the accused in their absence? Then we know, and particularly those who are lawyers would know, that when the Magistrate has concluded the recording of the evidence for the prosecution, under Section 209 of the Criminal Procedure Code, he must ask the accused whether he has any explanation to offer with regard to the evidence which is recorded by him against the accused. It is after that statement is made that the Magistrate has got the power either to commit or discharge the accused. That statement of the accused under Section 209 is absolutely obligatory. It is not the choice of the Magistrate. The Privy Council has laid down that an omission in that regard would vitiate the whole trial. Under this Bill the accused will not be there to give any explanation to the Magistrate with regard to the evidence that has been already recorded *ex parte*.

Then, Sir, we come to important Sections. Under Section 287 that statement again will have to be made before the Sessions

Court. There also, the accused will not be present. The evidence before the Sessions Court will be recorded *ex parte* and if it is a jury, the jury will be asked to return their verdict. If it is a case of assessors, they will be asked to express their opinion, and the Judge will pass his judgment or sentence, as the case may be. I ask the Hon'ble Home Member, and I ask the Hon'ble Law Member of the Government of India whether that will be a trial or a farce?

Sir Brojendra Mitter (Law Member) : Not a farce. The accused can always go before the Court if she chooses to.

Gaya Prasad Singh : But what about the evidence that has already been recorded in his absence?

M.A. Jinnah : I am very glad that the Hon'ble Law Member has given me a reply. Then you want by this Bill really to break the hunger-strikers. You want this House to given you a Statute laying down a principle generally in the criminal jurisprudence for this particular case, so that you may use it for breaking the hunger-strike in the Lahore case. Remember, you have no other case that you can cite. One swallow does not make a summer. It is the Lahore case. Well, you know perfectly well that these men are determined to die. It is not a joke. I ask the Hon'ble Law Member to realise that it is not everybody who can go on starving himself to death. Try if for a little while and you will see. Sir, have you heard anywhere in the world except the American case, which may honourable friend Mr. Jamnadas Mehta pointed out, of an accused person going on hunger-strike? The man who goes on hunger-strike has a soul. He is moved by the soul and he believes in the justice of his cause; he is not an ordinary criminal who is guilty of cold-blooded, sordid, wicked crime.

Mind you, Sir, I do not approve of the action of Bhagat Singh, and I say this on the floor of this House. I regret that, rightly or wrongly, youth today in India is stirred up, and you cannot, when you have three hundred and odd millions of people, you cannot prevent such crimes being committed, however much you may deplore them and however much you may say that they are misguided. It is the system, this damnable system of Government, which is resented by the people. You may be a cold-blooded logician : I am a patient cool-headed man and can calmly go on making speeches here, persuading and influencing the Treasury

Bench. But, remember, there are thousands of young men outside. This is not the only country where these actions are resorted to. It has happened in other countries, not youths, but greybearded men have committed serious offences, moved by patriotic impulses. What happened to Mr. Congrave, the Prime Minister of Ireland? He was under sentence of death a fortnight before he got an invitation from His Majesty's Government to go and settle terms? Was he a youth? Was he a youngman? What about Collings? So what is the good of your putting forward this argument? You have got a situation which you have got to meet, not by introducing and enacting measures which go to the root of the fundamental principles of criminal jurisprudence, and lightly, saying, "Oh! But it is common sense!" Law is common sense : it is not common sense of one individual.

Mr. President : I hope the Hon'ble Member is not inconvenienced when I ask him to resume his speech at the next meeting.

Pandit Madan Mohan Malaviya : Sir, cannot we go on for another 15 minutes?

Mr. President : What is the idea of going on for another 15 minutes? I can understand the House asking me to sit till 6 o'clock, but there is no idea in sitting for another 15 minutes only.

The House was then adjourned. Mr. Jinnah concluded his speech at the next sitting, after the adjournment motion had been admitted for discussion.

"Sir, when the House last adjourned I was dealing with this Bill from the point of view of criminal jurisprudence—and I brought to the notice of the House what would be the position if this Bill was passed, so far as the trial and proceedings of this particular case, or any other case under it, were concerned. It is quite clear, as I said, that the trial will be a travesty of justice. Let us consider the point further. The trial would proceed in the absence of the accused. I ask the Home Member, is there a Judge or jury who would feel that they were administering law or justice in that case? The moment this Bill is passed, the prosecution can go before the Court and say: "Here is a voluntary act of the accused person; he has or they have incapacitated himself or themselves, and we ask you now to proceed *ex parte*". Remember,

Sir, that in a particular case that procedure may be adopted from the very start. Even the plea of the accused may not be recorded, guilty or not guilty. Then the Judge will be asked to proceed to empanel a jury and the jury will be empanelled : You will have a Judge on the Bench and the jury by his side. What will they do? They hear the *ex parte* evidence, oral and documentary. I ask the Home Member, I ask this House, what would you consider of that Judge, what would you think of that Judge or jury, sitting there solemnly, seriously, proceeding with a charge of murder, going through this farce as His Majesty's Court—what conclusion do you think any jury can come to under those circumstance? That prisoner stands already condemned. What is the good of this farce? I say that no Judge who has got an iota of a judicial mind or a sense of justice can ever be a party to trial of that character and pass sentence of death without a shudder and a pang of conscience. This is the farce which you propose to enact under this procedure ! I say this, that if ever there was a conscientious Judge and he was strong enough, if he had a judicial mind, and if he had any independence, let me tell you, that, in spite of this provision of yours, he would say, "True, the law has to be administered; I am obliged to make the order that the trial shall proceed *ex parte*; but I realise and I feel that it will be a travesty of justice and I cannot be a party to it; and I shall, therefore, adjourn this case until further orders". Have you considered that? I suppose you have not. It seems to me, Sir, that the great and fundamental doctrine of British jurisprudence, which is incorporated and codified in the Penal Code and the Criminal Procedure Code, I have very wisely not made such an absurd provision in the criminal law of this country and I am not satisfied that there is a lacuna in our system of criminal law.

The Home Member said that it is a well-known doctrine and a fundamental doctrine of criminal jurisprudence that the man is taken to be innocent until he is proved to be guilty. May I remind him of another doctrine which goes to the very root of the criminal jurisprudence, or for the matter of that of even civil law, that no man is to be condemned until he is given a hearing? Sir, I think there cannot be the slightest doubt that we are now engaged in considering a cardinal principle, a principle of very vital and paramount character, to be introduced into the criminal jurisprudence of this country. It must be admitted that this is a most revolutionary, unheard of, unprecedented change that is proposed in our criminal jurisprudence. I know the Home Member will tell me, "Yes, the doctrine is that no man shall be condemned unless he is heard and until he is given a hearing; but here it is the voluntary act of the accused, and if he chooses not to go there and insist upon his being heard, it is his fault." Sir, this is not a new question; it has been considered in England and there is a long history about it and behind it and you will find that in old days there was the strictest formality observed as to the recording of the plea of the prisoner. And if the prisoner was mute of malice, that is to say, if he refused deliberately to open his mouth when he was arraigned in a Court of law and when the question was put to him as to whether he pleaded guilty or not—he had to make his plea, and there are cases where he refused to speak, and the old law was—even England has advanced—in that case he was condemned and executed or must be committed to imprisonment...

E.L. Price (Bombay : European): Torture.

M.A. Jinnah : I am glad that you are up to date. I know that. I am only dealing with this one point, that he used to be executed or committed to prison. Further, when it was thought that it was rather a serious thing that, because a man was mute of malice, he should be condemned to death or imprisonment—then comes the point of my learned friend over there, who I understand is a member of the Bar—that they resorted to torture. Torture for what? That he should make his plea, not that an *ex parte* trial should proceed. That is what you want to do here by this Bill, that *ex parte* trial should proceed. The old law was then altered, because the result of the torture was that some of them died and the form of torture was the most cruel form of torture, and I will read to you a passage from the Stephen's History of Criminal Law:

> *If he was accused of felony, he was condemned, after much exhortation to the peine forte et dure, that is to be stretched, naked on his back, and to have iron laid upon him as much as he could bear and more', and so to continue, fed upon bad bread and stagnant water on alternate days, till he either pleaded or died.*

But they did not proceed *ex parte*. Then the old form of trial was trial by ordeal. That was done away with because the plea that a prisoner had to put forward was in a particular form. When he was asked he had to say that he wanted to be tried "By God and by my country". That was the trial by ordeal. That was done away with and in 1827 by a Statute it was enacted that in such cases a plea of not guilty should be entered. Now, Sir, before that Statute was passed there is one case which I will bring to the notice of this House and which will illustrate how much importance was attached to the form and the procedure even in olden days. Of course, my honourable friend Sir Darcy Lindsay will say that matters of this kind can be decided by the common sense of a single individual such as himself. Sir, I must remind him—for he is a man of place, and especially when we get old we love peace, and common sense is sometimes regulated by that state of mind— I will remind him, and I think the House will agree with me, that law is nothing but the essence of common sense, that law is the concentrated essence of experience, of knowledge, of practice, of centuries and generations, and even Sir James Stephen will point out to you that, when these rules, when these forms have been laid down as the essence of common sense and experience of generations, they are not lightly to be departed from.

What do we find in this House now? Have we not got forms and are we not slavishly following them? Some of them would appear to the strangers in the gallery or any outsider to be most absurd and against common sense, at first sight. If any one passes across between you and the speaker he will be guilty of a gross breach of the forms of this House and you would call him to order at once. Why is that ? Without meaning? Without reason? Without experience? What common sense is there? Why should the man not pass across? It is, therefore, no use treating these matters lightly and saying that we have got to decide everything by the common sense of an individual. The instance that I was going to refer to is this. In one case :

> Mr. Pike produces some evidence to show that in the early part of Edward I's reign, people who refused to put themselves on their trial were executed...

Better, people who refuse to put themselves to trial, execute them, rather than go through the force of an *ex parte* trial; much better.

> "...but this practice was opposed to the statute which provided that notorious felons' and which openly be of evil name and will not put themselves in inquests of felonies that men shall charge them with before the justices at the King's suit, shall have strong and hard imprisonment, as they which refuse to stand to the common law of the land."

Then he cites a case which I think will interest the House. He says this :

> 'But this is not to be understood of such prisoners as be taken of light suspicion.' According to Barrington this meant that the prisoner who refused to plead was to be starved till he died, but not tortured—(so they improved later on)—and he quotes in proof of it a pardon granted in the reign of Edward III to a woman who *pro eo quod se tenuit mutam* was put in *areta prisona* and there lived without eating or drinking for forty days, which was regarded as a miracle."

Well, Sir, I know that here is a passage which is likely to be quoted in this House in Stephen's *Digest of Criminal Procedure*. It is a curious thing that the Government of India, who have hardly given this House even seven days' notice and call upon this House to endorse a vital, cardinal principle of a novel or unheard of character, do not possess in their library even an edition of the Law of Criminal Procedure by Stephen of a later date then 1883. And they seriously ask this House, "The Government case is that they find that a deadlock is created. The law is paralysed, and in fact, even the government of India might tumble down altogether, and we, therefore, call upon the Legislature to come to our rescue—we admit it is unprecedented, we admit it is unheard of, we admit it is unknown to any system of jurisprudence: but you as a responsible body—would you not endorse this Bill straightaway within these few days' notice?" You do not possess in your library an edition of a textbook which is the standard book except of the year 1883! And it is a tall order to ask the House to pass the Bill now and here. I will read the passage how, which is likely to be quoted, and I want the House not to be misled by it. But before I do so, I will request the Law Member, to consider what I am going to submit. That is a branch of the law which comes under the category of contempt of Court, and we know that the King's Bench in England and Superior Courts in India, who have inherited the jurisdiction under the Charter, have got unfettered power to deal with cases of contempt. That is the one branch of the law which is neither codified nor restricted by any law. It is entirely left to the Supreme Court or the High Courts in India to deal with cases of contempt as they think proper. That is a branch which comes under that doctrine of law of contempt of Court and even there, while the Courts have asserted that they have the power to refuse to hear the party who is guilty of contempt of court, the footnote says that it has never been done in a criminal case. I will read to you what it says:

> "The Prisoner has a right to be present at the trial so long as he conducts himself properly, but the Court may, in its discretion, permit his absence in cases of misdemeanour, and may proceed with the trial in his absence in cases in which he has pleaded to an indictment or information in the High Court (Queen's Bench Division)."
>
> "If a prisoner so misconducts himself as to make it impossible to try him with decency, the Court, it seems, may order him to be removed and proceed in him absence."
>
> The footnote says this:
>
> "I have never known or heard of this being done, but Lord Cranworth (then Rolfe, B.) threatened to have Rush removed from Court, at his trial for murder at Norwhich in 1849, if he persisted in a singularly indecent and outrageous course of cross-examination. I have heard from eye-witness an account of a trial before Shee, J. (then acting as Commissioner) at Dorchester, where the prisoner (a convict at Portland, tried for the murder of a warden) behaved with such desperate violence that it was necessary to fasten him down with chains and straps. He was not, however, removed from the Court, and it is obvious that in capital cases, or indeed in any trial involving severe punishment, almost any measures, short of removing the prisoner, should be resorted to."

The raison d'etre of this principle is very different and requires no more words to understand it. Now, Sir, I shall not weary the House with any further legal quotations. I am driven to think the object of Government in bringing in this Bill is political, but if their real object is to supply a lacuna, not for the purpose of this particular case, but in the general interest of the country and the administration of justice, if that is their object, let them remove this case from their mind, for Heaven's sake. Come to us dispassionately and without prejudice. Let them tell us that they find a lacuna, and that it is necessary to make some provision. If that is their object, then their honest and straightforward course is to come before the House and place all the facts before us. Now, I do not admit for a moment that there is a lacuna, and I do not admit that such a principle should be introduced in the criminal jurisprudence of our country, especially and admittedly when it does not exist anywhere else I am prepared to assume that you honestly and sincerely believe that it is necessary, in the interest of the people and the administration of justice, that some such measure of the kind should be introduced. Then your honest course is to go slowly. Pause and consider. Let those outside this House who ware competent to speak, express their opinion. What are you going to lose? What is the harm that will be done? Remove from your mind this Lahore conspiracy case. But if you say that this course will cause you inconvenience and that you want this instrument now and at once, then I say that I am not satisfied with your plea and I can't support it, nor am I satisfied with the version that you have placed before the House about your difficulties. I am not going to give you this power standing on the floor of this House, today, now and here.

Sir, can you imagine a more horrible form of torture than hunger-strike? If rightly or wrongly, these men are inflicting this punishment upon themselves and thereby you are inconvenienced, is that any reason why you should ask us to abandon one of the cardinal principles of criminal jurisprudence? If these youngmen pursue this course, and I am sorry to hear that one of them has died, what will happen? Is this a matter which can continue indefinitely? Certainly not. As I say, I am not satisfied with the version that you have placed before this House. I understand that some of the prisoners are not on strike. If you are solicitous and anxious that their trial should proceed and should not be delayed, then split up the trial. Proceed against them and bring home the guilt to them if you can. I am told that it means expense. I am told that 400 witnesses are going to be produced and 200 more may be added. Now, I appeal to the common sense of the House and not only of Sir Darcy Lindsay. Can you imagine that 600 witnesses are necessary to prove the case against each one of the accused? And Sir, I ask, is it not an amazing fact that, in order to prove this case, 600 persons should have been cited as witnesses? Well, Sir, it may seem a joke and it may seem that I am making fun of the statement made to this effect, but the first impression that one gets is that, when a case cannot be proved without the testimony of 600 witnesses, that case is a very bad case. Therefore, I say that it is open to Government to split up the case. You think of expense? But are we here to abandon this cardinal principle because it is going to cost some money to Government? Is that the reason? Is that a plea which can be accepted by any responsible Legislature?

Well, Sir, I was told that some of them go on a hunger-strike for a short time and then they get better for a little while and again they start, and so it goes on. Sir, I cannot understand the anxiety of the Government to proceed with this trial when these men are inflicting the greatest possible punishment upon themselves by prolonged fasting? Is it your fault? Does it mean that you are not treating them properly and, therefore you are compelling them to resort to these extreme methods? Well, then I appeal to you with all the emphasis I can command, do not be vindictive. Show that you are fair, generous, that you are willing to treat these men decently. At any rate, before they are released or sentenced, give them proper treatment. What treatment do they want? What is it that bothers them? Do they want spring mattresses? Do they want dressing tables? Do they want a set of toilet requisites? No, Sir, they ask for nothing but bare necessities and a little better treatment. I ask you in all decency, why cannot you concede this small thing? Well, Sir, if this Bill is passed, perhaps I might ask the Hon'ble Member when he goes to Court how would he base his application? Will he base his application on the point that the period of a hunger-strike which has already taken place for a short period is not to be counted? Or is it to be counted? Supposing I tried to put myself in the position of a Judge when the application is made that the presence of the accused in this case should be dispensed with, because by their own voluntary act they have rendered themselves incapable. Now, from what period shall I take the disability? From the period after this Statute is passed? Shall I disregard the disability which has already taken place before the passing of the Act? Supposing something else happens to these men on hunger-strike and they do not get well for two or three months. Will the trial not be delayed? Do you think you can avoid considerable delay even if the Bill is passed? Further, can you give a guarantee that all the prisoners will be well enough in the course of these two or three months from now to stand their trial. Even if they abandon hunger-strike? When you say that this Bill will not have retrospective effect, how is it going to work? Then will you give them notice that in view of the fact that this measure is passed, if you do not cease your hunger-strike from today and if you are not better within two or three months, as you ought to be, then we shall apply to the Court that your presence will be dispensed with and we shall proceed *ex parte*? Does it not come to this, that you want to carry this Bill, you want to have this Bill placed on the Statue-book, and then you want to given notice to the prisoners that, unless they cease their hunger-strike within a certain period, you are going to proceed *ex parte*? Under that threat you think these prisoners will cease their hunger-strike? Can you give the House that assurance, and if they do not cease their hunger-strike, what will you do? You will proceed *ex parte*? Just imagine the absurdity of the whole position.

Sir, now I have finished from the point of view of the jurisprudence. I do not wish to go into details so far as their treatment is concerned. I have, in the course of my speech, already indicated their grievances and how they can be met. But there is a political aspect of this bill and the policy underlying this measure. I think the Hon'ble the Home Member must admit that this is not a measure which is only brought here for the purpose of putting the law in order. Sir, it reminds me of a story, an old persian story. A man got stomachache because he had eaten some very rotten bread. So he went to the doctor and told him that he had stomachache. The doctor said, yes, and he promptly started treating his eyes. Then he said, "What have my eyes got to do with my complaint?" Then the doctor said, "Well, if you had eyes, you would never have got stomachache because you would not have eaten rotten bread". Similarly I would say to the Hon'ble the Home Member, "Have you got eyes? Well, if you had, you would never gave go, this stomachache". Now, will you open your eyes? Will you have a little more imagination? Have you got any statesmanship left? Have you got any political wisdom? This is not the way you are going to solve the root cause of the trouble. You may temporarily, provisionally, get over this particular trial. But now let us see what is the real cause of the trouble.

I ask this House to consider this. Is there today in any part of the globe a civilised government that is engaged, day in and day out, week in and week out month in and month out, in prosecuting their people? You have read the daily papers for the last six, eight months. You will find prosecutions in Bengal, prosecutions in Madras, prosecutions in the Punjab, prosecutions all over the country. In fact, I am afraid you will soon have to open a new department and to have an additional Member to manage these prosecutions if you go on at this rate and in this way. Do you think that any man wants to go to jail? Is it an easy thing? Do you think any man wants to exceed the bounds of law for the purpose of making a speech which your law characterises as a seditious speech, knowing full well the consequences, that he may have to go to jail for six months or a year? Do you think that this springs out of a mee joke or fun or amusement. Do you not realise yourself, if you open your eyes, that there is resentment, universal resentment, against your policy, against your programme?

Then, Sir, what has happened so far as this House in concerned? What have you done since 1924 with regard to the protests that we have made session after session? Have you accepted the proposal or suggestion of any reasonable section of this House? I do not wish to go into the details, Sir, but what has been the attitude of the Government towards this House and the country outside over the constitutional reforms since 1924, leave alone the past prior history? The reply is: "We have appointed the Simon Commission and we must await its Report." Well, the Simon Commission was not accepted by this House— out that does not matter. What is the answer in regard to the Indianisation of the Army? You appointed a Committee to go into that very important question : I attach more importance to it than to any other question. What have you done with the unanimous Report of the Skeen Committee which was endorsed by this House, without a division, the responsible House as you call it today and to which you appeal today in the name of "responsibility"? This House endorsed that Report without a division. What have you done with it? The attitude of Government has been an amazing one. The Army Secretary stood there on the floor of this House last session and said : "We cannot get even 20 suitable candidates". Sir, the apparent untruth of the statement is enough to condemn the Government. You cannot get 20 youngmen out of 300 odd millions of people, who are suitable candidates for the King's Commission?

Then, there are many other matters. What has been your attitude always? Don't you think that, instead of trying to proceed with an iron hand and pursuing a policy of repression against your own subjects, it would be better it you realised the root causes of the resentment and of the struggle that the people are carrying on? Don't you think that it is high time that you made your position more clear? I understand that there is something in the atmosphere—I hope it is true—that some satisfactory announcement is going to be made in Parliament very soon, when it meets next, which I trust will satisfy this House and the people. Do you want to prepare an atmosphere for it, or you do not? Do you want reconciliation betwen the Government and the people or you do not? Don't you think that these difficulties and troubles of yours are of a temporary character? They are an obstruction in the trial of this particular case which can be managed by other methods, but that is a very small matter when you compare it with the bigger issues which are awaiting the decision of the Government, this House and the country.

Sir, the Hon'ble Member asked, what are the Government to do? I think I understood the Hon'ble Member aright when he said that the Government have no other course. What are the Government to do? They are, therefore, compelled to bring this Bill. Now, let me tell you that your course is to open your eyes, have more imagination, do not be guilty of bankruptcy of statesmanship, do not merely sit there as if the wheels of the Secretariat must not be clogged at any cost, but try and understand the root cause and deal with the situation as politicians, as statesmen and not as bureaucrats, who can see no other way but to come forward before this House and ask for more statutory powers the moment any difficulty arises. You have got several courses open to you. The first and the foremost course open to you is this. Give these men decent treatment, and I think you will get over your difficulty. At least I hope so. If you do not, you will, at any rate, be exonerated in the eyes of the public and at the Bar of public opinion. Behave as a humane and decent Government, and that is enough for you. I am not going to urge upon the Government to withdraw prosecution cases against men if they have evidence enough to bring home to them their guilt. So try that better treatment first. Secondly, if you do not succeed, split up the trials. Try those with whose trial you can proceed, and leave the rest. After you have made it clear to them that you stand for a decent treatment being given to them and they still wish to torture themselves and follow that course, then you cannot help it; and I venture to say that it will not last very long or indefinitely. And the last words I wish to address the Government are, try and concentrate your mind on the root cause and the more you concentrate on the root cause the less difficulties and inconveniences there will be for you to face, and thank Heaven that the money of the taxpayer will not be wasted in prosecuting men, nay citizens, who are fighting and struggling for the freedom of their country."

Legislative Assembly Debates, Vol. IV, Part I, pp. 752-55 and 757-65.

9 Arguments of Government Advocate

The full text of Government Advocte Carden Noad's opening speech.

"There are 32 persons involved in the case of whom 7 are approvers, 9 are absconding and are still at large and 16 are place on their trial present in Court. They will be tried under the ordinary criminal law of the land for offences alleged to have been committed by them while evidence will be recorded under Section 512 of the Criminal Procedure Code against the absconding accused.

I desire to emphasise the fact that this is an ordinary trial under ordinary law (though of singular importance) and that these individuals alone are upon their trial. No political action or system is in any way involved. No social, religious or educational body or institution is or can be affected by the outcome of this prosecution except so far as it is in their interest of all citizens of a civilised community that offences against the law of the land shall, if proved according to law, be suitably punished.

I wish also to say on behalf of myself and my colleagues, Khan Sahib Kalandar Ali Khan and Mr. Gopal Lal, that we shall do our best to assist the Special Magistrate in giving the accused fair, patient and impartial enquiry and I confidently ask for the cooperation of the learned counsel appearance on behalf of the defence in attaining this object. It may not be out of place at this stage to recall the occurrence of the murder of Mr. Saunders, ASP and Chanan Singh, Head Constable. Two unarmed men were shot down in broad daylight in the streets of Lahore on the 17 December, 1928 and the police were unable at that time to apprehend the culprits. Coupled with universal condemnation of this dastardly murder severe criticism was levelled against the police in Council and in the newspapers because of the delay which took place in the detection of the culprits. The Special CID with K.B. Abdul Aziz and his staff all working under the direct instructions and orders of Mr. Stead, Inspector General of Police, have now discovered the facts and are prepared to prove that these murders were committed in pursuance of a widespread conspiracy as a part of a series of criminal acts and designs of the most serious nature. I am confident that every member of the public will now be interested in seeing that justice is done. I may not be misunderstood. We desire the Court as well as the public to hold the scales evenly between the case of the Crown and the case of the accused now before the Court.

Constitution of Revolutionary Party

I should like to give a short summary of the various intentions, designs and acts which form part of the subject-matter of the case to be placed before the Court.

The accused above-mentioned were members of a revolutionary party which became active throughout Northern India. At a meeting held at Delhi in August 1928, a Central Committee was constituted representing different provinces. In that meeting the following plans and resolutions were adopted and passed.

1. Phonindra Nath, approver was elected officer-in-charge of Bihar and Orissa. Sukhdev and Bhagat Singh accused were to be in charge of the Punjab. Shiv Varma, Bijoy Kumar Sinha and Chandrashekhar Azad, the last two are absconding, were to be in charge of the United Provinces. Kundan Lal alias Partap absconding was elected for Rajputana and the Central Office. Chandrashekhar Azad was also to be in charge of the Military Department.

2. It was decided that officers in charge should be held responsible for any work or action to be accomplished in the Province under their orders and that if any outside assistance were required in any provincial action the case should be submitted to the Central Committee which would issue final orders.

3. That all matters relating to finance, income and expenditure were to be dealt with by the central body.
4. That all arms and munitions should be placed with the central body to be issued for use by member of any province wherever and whenever required.

Aims and Objects

The main aims and objects of this revolutionary party as will be proved by the evidence of witnesses and of documents were as follows :

1. To establish a Republican Government by means of an organisation known as the Hindustan Republican Association and Indian Republican Army. For this purpose the policy of non-violence was to be discarded and armed forces organised with a view to overthrow the present Government and to overawe all officials and persons interested in the Administration.
2. To establish a reign of terror by the murder of officials who took a prominent part in such cases as the Kakori Conspiracy Case and other persons who were for various reasons obnoxious to the conspiracy. By such murders it was hoped to obtain the approval and financial support of persons in foreign countries interested in the propagation of revolution in India and such murders were definitely advocated as a means for obtaining funds abroad.
3. To organise the escape of convicts undergoing sentences in the jails for complicity in the Kakori conspiracy and similar cases.
4. To raise funds by every possible means by voluntary subscription, by dacoity or by contributions from abroad. Money thus collected was to be utilised for purchasing arms, manufacturing bombs and helping the members in spreading their republican propaganda and obtaining recruits throughout India.
5. The seduction of educated youths with a view to enlist them in the India Republican Army.

Fictitious Names

Evidence will be led to show that in prosecution of the objects of the conspiracy secret meetings were held by the members at different places for the constitution of Committees and for the arrangement of various crimes. The accused were moving about from place to place and from province to province under fictitious names some of which were as follows :

Sukhdev	Dayal, Swami Villager
Kishori Lal Rattan	Dev Dutt, Mast Ram Shastri
Agya Ram	Masterji
Prem Dutt	Master, Amrit Lal
Surindra Nath Pandey	Stone
Jai Dev	Harish Chandar
Shiv Varma	Parbhat, Har Narain, Ram Narain
Gaya Prashad	Dr. B.S. Nigam, Ram Lal, Ram Nath, Desh Bhagat
Mahabir Singh	Partap
Bhagat Singh	Ranjit
Batukeshwar Dutt	Battu Mohan
Ajoy Kumar Ghosh	Negro-General
Shachindra Nath Sanyal	Sachin Sanyal
Absconders	
Chandrashekher Azad	Panditji
Bijoy Kumar Sinha	Bachu
Kailash Patti	Kali Charan
Raghunath	'M', Ram Guru
Bhagwat Charan	B.C. Vohra
Kundan Lal	Partap, No. 1 of Benares
Kailash	Gunthala of Jansi
Approvers	
Jai Gopal	Harbans Lal, Gopal, Krishen Chand
Hansraj Vohra	Tarlok Chand
Phonindra Nath Ghosh	Dada
Brahm Dutt	Manmohan
Manmohan Bannerji	Manohar Bannerji

Over Acts

The overt acts committed in furtherance of the conspiracy included the following :

1. *Saunders and Channan Singh Murder*. The Committee of the revolutionary party deputed Jai Gopal, approver, Bhagat Singh, Chandrashekhar Azad, and Raghu Nath, the last two are still absconding, with arms to murder Mr. Scott. The said party of four culprits used to frequent the neighbourhood of the police office with a view to watch Mr. Scott's movements and to know the locality better. It so happened that Mr. Scott did not attend the office for a few days before the occurrence while Mr. Saunders attended the office daily. On 17 December, 1928, when Mr. Saunders came out of the office and was about to get on his motorcycle he was shot by the culprits in mistake for Mr. Scott. Hearing the report of the shots, Channan Singh, Head Constable, rushed towards the spot, ran and followed the accused when he too was fired at Mr. Saunders died instantaneously and Channan Singh died shortly after. The culprits after shooting these men ran always.

2. *Assembly Bomb Outrage*. With a view to create terrorism Bhagat Singh and Batukeshwar Dutt were deputed to throw bombs in the Assembly Chamber, Delhi. Consequently, these two accused threw bombs and fired shots in the Assembly Chamber on 8 April, 1929 causing severe injuries to Sir Bomanji Dalal and others. Both the culprits were arrested at the spot and placed on trial with the result that both of them were sentenced to transportation for life.

3. *Dacoity at Punjab National Bank, Lahore*. When the course of activities in Lahore was a house in Mozang, a meeting was held at which several of the accused were present. One of the members, namely, Panditji proposed a raid on the Punjab National bank in order to secure funds. The members who formed a party for this raid were fully equipped with arms and specific duties were assigned to each of them. Bhagat Singh and Partap had to bring a taxi there in order to take away the body. Consequently all the member detailed for the dacoity arrived on the appointed day, i.e., 4 December, 1928 at the premises of the Punjab National Bank and waited for the arrival of Bhagat Singh and Partap. At about 4 p.m. only Partap turned up in a tonga and informed the conspirators that a taxi could not be obtained. The project was then for the time being dropped.

4. *Dacoity at Maulina in Bihar and Orissa*. In order to raise funds the members of the revolutionary party resolved to commit

dacoity at Maulina. With the object in view a dacoity was conducted on 7 June, 1928 in the house of a rich man named Dank Mahton Koori, a Hindu gentleman. The owner of the house was shot and died later on and a quantity of jewellery was taken by the culprits.

5. *Attack on Mr. Bannerji, DSP, CID of UP.* Mr. Bannerji was an officer in the CID of UP who took a leading part in connection with the Kakori Conspiracy Case. The revolutionary party decided to do away with him and for this purpose two of them, namely, Mani Bannerji and Tarak Nath, were deputed. Mani Bannerji happened to Meet Mr. Bannerji, DSP in Benares on 13 January, 1928 who shot at him with a revolver. Mr. Bannerji got injuries but luckily survived them. Mani Bannerji was arrested, tried and convicted.

6. *An Embezzlement of Rs. 3,199.* Kailash Patti alias Kali Charan, an absconder, who was an employee in the Post Office, Burhal Ganj, District Gorakhpur, was one of the members of this revolutionary party. He embezzled Rs. 3,199 from that post office on 26 June, 1928 to be utilised by the party in furtherance of their common object.

7. *Manufacture of Bombs.* The revolutionary party learned how to manufacture bombs and during the course of their activities they were manufacturing bombs for the purpose of using them when occasion arose. Members of the conspiracy manufactured bombs at Lahore, Sharanpur, Calcutta and Agra. The factories at Lahore and Saharanpur have since been captured. On search, bombs, revolvers, ammunitions, implements for manufacturing bombs, books on bomb making and various prescribed literature were found. The Saharanpur and Agra cases have also been transferred to this province by order of the Government of India as they form an integral portion of the conspiracy under trail.

Crimes not Carried Out

Certain crimes were discussed and planned by the conspirators but for various reasons not carried out. Among them were the following:

1. Proposal to blow up the train carrying the members of the Simon Commission by means of dynamite. For want of funds this plan could not be carried out.

2. Proposal to make arrangements for the escape of Jogesh Chandra Chatterji, a convict in connection with the Kakori Conspiracy, and Sachin Sanyal, another convict. These also could not be carried out for want of funds and also because the convicts were well guarded. The conspirators were apparently not prepared to face the personal risk involved.

Having briefly discussed the activities of the accused the next point I will deal with is how the case has been discovered.

How the Police Got Information

On the occasion of Dussehra festival in 1928 a bomb was thrown on a crowd near the Roshanai Gate in Lahore which resulted in numerous deaths and severe injuries. As a similar outrage on the occasion of the Dussehra festival in 1926 had taken place and the case had remained untraced, the Punjab Government deputed Khan Bahadur Abdul Aziz, Superintendent of Police, Montgomery to investigate this outrage. During the course of investigation of these bomb outrages, it transpired that two ex-students of the Oriental College had been frequenting the Boarding House situated on the 2nd floor of Roshanai Gate, the place where the latter bomb explosion had taken place. Enquiries further showed that these two persons belonged to the Revolutionary Party.

As a result of a statement made by one of them, the police for the first time came to know that Bhagat Singh accused was one of the murders of Mr. Saunders and that Bhagwati Charan an absconder, a member of Naujawan Bharat Sabha, was his Chief Lieutenant in the Punjab. Bhagat Singh accused could not be found in spite of the fact that strenuous efforts for his arrests were made in the Punjab, UP and Bengal. He suddenly appeared in the Assembly as one of the perpetrators of the Assembly Bomb outrage.

Lahore Bomb Factory

Shortly before these certain persons had engaged some iron moulders of Lahore to make certain oblong implements which on enquiry they stated were intended to be parts of a gas machine. The curiosity of a local workman was aroused and he happened to mention these facts to a constable of his acquaintance. The information was passed onto the police who instructed their informant to watch the individuals who had given the orders and to follow them to their house. Sukhdev accused happening to pass by was duty followed to No. 69, Kashmir Buildings and this house was pointed to the police. The enquiry showed that the tenant of the premises was Bhagwati Charan who has been named as the Chief Lieutenant of Bhagat Singh and of the conspiracy in the Punjab. The house appeared to be locked and empty and a strict watch was kept to ascertain when it was visited. In the meantime, information from Delhi showed that the bomb thrown in the Assembly corresponded closely with the description of the alleged oblong gas machine parts. The careful watch kept on the house eventually resulted in information which led to a raid on 15 April, 1929. Sukhdev, Jai Gopal and Kishori Lal, accused were captured in the house. From the facts disclosed by these accused, the whole history of the revolutionary organisation came to light. The lengthy statement of Sukhdev cannot be referred to by me in this statement except so far as it led to discoveries which render it admissible under the Evidence Act. But it is sufficient to say that from the moment when these accused were capture, information in the possession of the police led them steadily and by regular steps to the unravelling of the whole conspiracy and to the detailed knowledge of its activities which will be placed before the Court in evidence in this case.

The Charges

The charges against the accused will include murder, abetment of murder and conspiracy to murder, conspiracy to revolution and other offences against the State and also offences under the Explosive Substance Act. With regard to offences against the State a complaint has been that in accordance with the requirements of law by the Senior Superintendent of Police, Lahore. The facts which I have very briefly mentioned will be fully proved by the evidence which will be laid before the Court."

—*The Tribune*, July 11, 1929, pp. 4 and 13

10 The Verdict

Views of Jury

Finally arrived the day of judgement, judgement that was already anticipated. The Lahore prisoners had their last supper. In many respects, it showed semblance to the last lunch of the Kakori prisoners on their judgement day (6 April, 1927), but was different as some jail officials also joined it. According to the revolutionary traditions everybody was in his Sunday best. They knew what the morning was to bring for them. The accused did not attend court in its final stages. But the trial had continued.

The judgement was pronounced by an emissary of the tribunal. The government was aware of the fact that judgement would be followed by a tremendous demonstration which would shake the whole nation. It appears that the day of the judgement was not disclosed and not even to the accused. That is why the last supper was held 2 or 3 days earlier.

The judgement was delivered on the 7 October, 1930, and Bhagat Singh, Rajguru and Sukhdev were sentenced to death. Bijoykumar Sinha, Kamalnath Tiwari, Jaidev Kapur, Shiv Varma, Gaya Prasad, Kishorilal and Mahabir Singh were sentenced to transportation for life. Kundanlal was given 7 years R.I., Premdutt 3 years R.I. The rest were freed.

The judgement could not be kept under cover and people came to know of it immediately. It was a fifty page document. Wherever the news reached, it resulted in a spontaneous hartal and a wave of anger and disobedience gripped the country. On the 8 October not only Lahore, but all cities in northern India witnessed strikes. Some institutions closed automatically, other were forced to close. Naturally Lahore was the most agitated. Many students and seventeen women were arrested. A crowd that had gathered round the Government College was attacked. The sky blazed with the cry of "Bhagat Singh, Rajguru, Sukhdev Zindabad." The police entered D.A.V. College and beat up 80 students and one professor practically to death. The Government was ready with its oppressive bulldozers.

The *Naujawan Bharat Sabha* convened a meeting of students and youth at Bradlaugh hall, once the centre of activities of Bhagat Singh and Bhagwaticharan. In this meeting, the revolutionary leaders were eulogised and very exting speeches were made. On the field outside Mori Gate, 12 thousand men collected in a meeting presided over by the veteran freedom fighter Parvati Devi.

Eminent personalities like Jinnah took upon themselves to deliver the message to the British Raj by way of presenting the case of Bhagat Singh and others. He amply supported the unhappiness of the youth with the suppression by British. A legal battle was begun to save the heroes. An appeal was made in the Privy Council. The public agitation gathered momentum every day. Many people were arrested, others were lathicharged. People were aware that the appeal to the Privy Council was an exercise in futility, in spite of this it was made, to allow time for the public agitation to consolidate.

Seen from a purely legal point of view, so the legal pundits said, the appeals had a number of good points and any just appellate court could crush the judgement to shreds because the case had been conducted without the participation of the accused.

Bhagat Singh, Rajguru and Sukhdev were now lying in condemned cells. Now that the courtroom was no longer available to propagate the revolutionary propaganda,they sent an appeal to the Privy Council, to highlight the high-handedness of the tribunal and trumpet the fact that the revolutionary party in India stood for socialism. The agitation to get Bhagat Singh released very soon, got on its feet. Had Gandhi wanted to, he could have utilised it to give fire to the movement that was in the offing. But he did not do this, as it would have meant boosting up revolutionaries.

Basically Gandhi stayed away from all this, because he was mortally afraid of revolution. All the time, he brandished the big stick of revolution, but in the pit of his stomach he always wanted a compromise, because he was aware of the shortcoming of this weapon–*Satyagraha*. Bhagat Singh's thoughts on the subject were recorded in a letter, which though written on this time could only be published on 2 February, 1931, in the *Punjab Kesari*. The letter addressed to his comrades said —

The Punjab Kesari

"Dear friends,

Our fight for freedom is passing through a critical period. After a year of hard struggle the Round Table Conference has pinpointed on certain positive reforms and the Congress leaders have been asked to assist in shaping them. Under the circumstances, the leaders of the congress seem to be heading towards switching off the movement. It does not matter much to us, if they stop the movement or continue it. Their present agitation can only end in a compromise, just now or after some time.

In reality, compromise is not as detestable as people make out, on the contrary judicious compromises are sometimes necessary to advance the struggle. A nation struggling against a despotic system meets with initial defeat, but in its long struggle it becomes stronger and stronger through reforms acquired and through compromises. Thus gradually, it becomes so powerful that its final assault breaks the backbone of the system. Even at the final stage a compromise may give it a breathing space. This is illustrated in the Russian struggle against the Tsar.

In 1905 waves of revolution started in Russia. The revolutionary leaders were very hopeful. Lenin returned from abroad and took the reins in his own hands. People slew a handful of capitalists and burnt a few houses, the revolution however did not come off. But the Government was forced to concede some reforms and the 'duma' was established. At that time Lenin said that the 'duma' should be accepted. But in 1906 he started opposing it. Again he said in 1907 that one should go in the 'duma', although the powers of the 'duma' had been curtailed in the meantime. He wanted to convert the 'duma' into a platform for his agitation.

In the same manner when the question of peace arose after 1917, everybody, except Lenin was against the compromise. But Lenin said 'Peace at all cost. Peace even if we have to cede some districts to the German militarists'. When some Bolshevik leaders opposed this, he said, "At present the Bolshevik Government is weak, just now our first duty is to consolidate our government."

What I want to impress upon you is that compromise is a weapon that has to be used during a political struggle to give respite to a tired nation for some time, so that it can pick up the thread of struggle with renewed vigour at a later date. But during all these compromises we should not lose sight of the ideal, which should remain as a target before our eyes all the time. We should be very clear and determined about the goal of our struggle. If you are fighting for 16 annas and you get only one anna, pocket that one anna and continue the fight for the rest. What I despise about the Indian 'moderates' is that, they lack a goal. They agitate to get one anna with the result that they get nothing.

The Congress aim is to liberate the country, but after liberation it does not seek to liberate the *mazdurs* and *kisans* from the clutches of the capitalists and the landlords. The liberation struggle is manned by middle class people, naturally its goal is very limited. The Congress wants to pressurise Great Britain through the capitalists and shopkeepers and thus secure certain rights, but this would not set the teeming millions, the *mazdurs* and *kisans*, free. The real fight for freedom can only be fought by mobilising the *mazdurs*, *kisans* and the common people. Along with liberation from the foreign yoke, they have to get rid of capitalists and landlords.

I maintain that the Congress does not stand for total revolution. They want to pressurise and secure certain rights. They want to secure certain privileges for the burgeoisie, that is why I think that the Congress agitation can only end in the smoke of some kind of compromise or failure.

Under the circumstances the youths should remember that bad times are ahead. They should fight against frustration and confusion of ideas. Having experienced two agitations sponsered by Mahatma Gandhi, it has become necessary to formulate precise aims and programme. Having said this let me spell out what I want. *Long live Revolution* has become your battle cry. But it is very sacred and we should use it with good care. I take it that you stand by the slogan you raise. During the Assembly Bomb Case I thus defined Revolution —'By revolution I mean that the present set up and system must be uprooted. For this purpose we have to grab the state machine, which is now in the hands of the capitalists. For the good of the common people and for giving a practical shape to our ideals, we must wrest the state machine according the principles of Marx. This is the object of our fight. Keeping in view this objective, we must educate the masses.'

What should be the yardstick for measuring and evaluating the reforms for those who are engaged in the fight for revolution. All reforms must stand these three tests--

1. To what extent the administration is passed on to Indians.
2. What is the character of the government that is called upon to take over and to what extent the people are called upon to participate in it.
3. What are the future prospects and to what degree its progress in blocked.

Universal suffrage must be advocated.

The type of provincial autonomy proposed by the Round Table Conference, is, according to my opinion, not provincial autonomy, but provincial *Zulam* (tyranny) because of the class on which it confers power. Having considered all this, I have come to the conclusion that we must have a clear-cut picture before us. Compromise may not mean always a surrender, it may add up to only one step forward, and then there may be a pause. At the same time we must all the time be very clear that this is not our ultimate destination and not a point for final pause.

I would like to say something on the object and the means of our party. It is named 'socialist republican', its object is to establish a socialist society. The difference between the Congress and our party is that the Congress after the power has passed from the hands of the British to the hands of Indians, will rest on its oars, but our object is to bring power to one and all, who are committed to socialism. For this the toiling masses have to be mobilised., because for them it won't matter much if Lord Reading is replaced by Sir Tejbahadur Sapru or Purushottamdas Thakurdas.

Our party means all this by complete independence. Even during the Lahore Congress (where the Congress ceremonially passed the resolution of complete independence) the Mahatma said, 'We have not banged and bolted the door to compromise it is still open'. This means that he was aware of the fact that his type of struggle could only end in some sort of compromise. His aim was a half-hearted advocacy of complete independence. It is this half-heartedness that we abhor.

To youths I say, they should enlist as workers in this cause, as for leaders we have them galore. Our party does not need leaders. If you are a worldly man, a family man, don't come to us. However, if you are sympathetic to our cause, help us in other ways. Only strictly disciplined people can take a movement forward. It is not necessary for the party to worked in secret for these objectives. We may propagate our ideas everywhere through leaflets, pamphlets, booklets, small libraries, lectures, private conversations.

Our party should have a military wing. Let me make myself clear. It is said that I am a terrorist, but in reality, I have been all along a revolutionary with definite ideals and ideology. I may be blamed as they blame Ramprasad Bismil that the condemned cell wrought a change in his ideology, but this is not true. I am the same man as I used to be, and have the same ideas. It is my considered opinion that bombs cannot serve our purpose. This is proved by the history of the Hindustan Socialist Republican Association. Throwing bombs is not only useless, but is often harmful as well. They are to be used on certain occasions only. Our chief aim should be to mobilise the toiling masses. The military wing should collect material for war for use on special occasions.

Finally, I would appeal to the youths to work fervently for the establishment of a socialist republic. If they carry on the struggle relentlessly, then they can attain the objective, 'not within a year' but after heavy sacrifices and passing through very gruelling trials."

While Bhagat Singh was in the condemned cell, he was allowed an interview with Bejoy Kumar Sinha, who was awarded transportation for life. It is a historical fact, whether one believes it or not, though there was a country wide agitation to get Bhagat Singh released, and all sorts of attempts, legal and illegal, were in the offing to rescue him from the clutches of the hangman, while he himself wished to be hanged. This was not out of despondency or frustration or a will to die. But a manifestation of a simple mathematical calculation as to how far under the circumstances he was useful alive or otherwise when hanged for the country.

Views of Sinha

Bejoy Kumar Sinha writes about the interview : "Even after such a long time, I remember vividly the interview which I had with Sardar Bhagat Singh in Lahore Central Prison. From almost his deathbed Motilal Nehru had entreated through a special emissary, that we should not stand in the way of legal appeal. He wanted to gain some time. He thought that the compromise talks were on the way, and he hoped that the Sardar could be saved."

In parenthesis, let us note that Motilal Nehru in all probability (He was never dogmatic) wished try everything possible to save the Sardar, but Gandhi, as we shall later on see, was reluctant.

Bejoy Kumar Sinha further says : "But he viewed this problem from a different angle. He confided to me in great anguish. 'It would be a calamity, would it not, if I am spared the rope' I told Bhagat Singh very plainly, that the government had to two-edged policy, namely, on the one hand, it was trying to befriend the Congress and on the other, was crushing all the revolutionary elements and so, there was no chance of the rope eluding him. I told Bhagat Singh that if the hangings are delayed or the sentence commuted, there would be more time for revolutionary propaganda. At long last he agreed to put his signature to the appeal, but this he did most unwillingly. Thus, the appeal was forwarded, but we did not say in it that our sentences should be reduced. We demanded that the whole case should be quashed and declared *ultra vires* as we had been tried under an ordinance. The whole country was clamouring to save the Sardar, but he himself wanted to be sacrificed on the altar. He maintained that he could serve the revolution better this way. The moments that I spent with him are unforgettable. People cling to life so badly, but here was a man just a little above 20 years, who wanted to ring down the curtain of life, to have a rendezvous with death, for the good of the country."

All this brings into bold relief the fact that Sardar Bhagat Singh was not only a believer is socialism, but at the same time he believed, like Mazzini, that it is the martyr's blood that ripens ideas. This is where a real revolutionary vary from the brand of socialists and communists that with world has been seen mushrooming in all countries, specially since the Second World War. They adore soft life, they address meetings, they lead any type of strikes and they think that they can incorporate socialism without a revolution.

Sardar Bhagat Singh embodied in himself true socialism. He wrote in a letter just before being hanged :

Koi dam ka mehman hun ai ahle mahfil
Cherage sahar hun bujna chahta hun,
Meri hawa men rehegi khyal ki bijli
Yah mushte khaq hai fani, rahe na rahe.

'O friends of the tavern, I am just a fleeting guest, being the morning lamp about to burn out. The atmosphere bequeathed by me its surcharged with the electricity of ideas. This my body is only a lump of dust, it may be there or may not be.'

One of the men who had a glimse Bhagat Singh when he was confined in the condemned cell was Shri Prannath, whom I met later on and did a programme along with him on Bhagat Singh for television. He writes :

"On that day I was privileged to stay near Sardar Bhagat Singh's condemned cell for nearly an hour. I had met him many times at the same place. I had witnessed him as a hunger-striker, and had seen him in action in the courts, but I had never felt that he was that courageous and so great. He and I both knew that he was walking through the valley of the shadow of death, the hands of the clock were moving fast towards the zero hour of hanging, but I found him cheerful. His face glistened as always. When I approached his cell he was pacing it like a tiger in a cage. As soon as I stepped inside the cell he asked : 'Did you bring the book?' I handed over the book quietly, *Krantikari Lenin* (Revolutionary Lenin) to him. He was very pleased at the sight of the book. I told him. "Would you give some message to the country?" He said, 'Down with Imperialism, Long Live Revolution.' I asked him. "How do you feel today?" He said briefly, 'I am feeling fine.' I persisted and asked, 'Have you any last wish?' He answered, 'May I be reborn and serve the motherland again.' He conveyed his thanks to the leaders, who had taken interest in the case and expressed his good wishes to his friends, specially the absconding ones. In that atmosphere of death I felt shaken, but he seemed to be entrenched firmly in the faith that looks through death. He seemed to be so much at peace with himself, he was so much free from fear and unattached that he appeared to be divine."

During these last days Bhagat Singh wrote to a friend :

"It is but natural that I should desire to live. I do not want to conceal this, but it is conditional in the sense that I do not want to live with my freedom curbed. My name has become a symbol of revolution and the ideals and sacrifices of revolutionary parties have placed me on a high pedestal. It is such a high pedestal that I may not be able to do justice to it as a living being. My weaknesses are not known to the public. If I am saved from the gallows, they would become known to everybody. Thus, the symbol of revolution would fade and even dissolve, but if I die wreathed with smiles, Indian mothers would wish their children to emulate Bhagat Singh, and thus the number of formidable freedom fighters would increase so much that it would be impossible for the satanic forces of imperialism to stop and stem the march of revolution. Of course, there lingers a hidden hankering in my heart that I have not accomplished even a thousandth part of what I proposed to do. Could I live, may be I could get the opportunity to fulfil the tasks and thus be happy.

Apart from this there was never any temptation to be saved from hanging. Otherwise I am the luckiest man. Nowadays, I think too much of my self. I have no lurking desire. Now I am impatiently waiting for the last test. I wish it could be nearer.

Yours comradely,

Bhagat Singh".

Politics is but a part of life. It would be interesting to know what Bhagat Singh ruminated sitting on the dividing line between life and death. I had seen Rajendra Nath Lahiri (hanged on the 17 December, 1927) under the influence of Shachindranath Sanyal, a theist revolutionary, turning from agnosticism back to the border of theism. Sanyal was responsible no doubt, but death sentence, which was round the corner, may have been accountable to an extent for this volte face. Anyway when we were exchanging presents just before judgement day, he presented me with a copy of *Madhuchhander Matramala* (a translation of some Vedic hymns supposed to be unravelling the mysteries of life and death). The question erupts not out of just an idle curiosity what was Bhagat Singh thinking on life, death, God and allied subjects? Fortunately, the editor of *Pratap* Jalandhar, Virendra was in that jail and he has recorded an even which throws direct light on the subject.

Just the day before the hanging, the Sikh chief warder Chatter Singh approached Bhagat Singh. Chatter Singh was given re-employment in the jail department after retiring as havildar from the British army. Knowing that Bhagat Singh had only a few hours to live, as a devout Sikh he thought it is his duty to help him prepare properly for the next world. According to his religion Chatter Singh was doing a very pious work. He went to Bhagat Singh and said, 'My son, death, the journey's end is round the corner. I am just like your father. Listen to me.'

Bhagat Singh was a little surprised, he asked, 'What is the matter?'

Advice of Chatter Singh

Chatter Singh said, 'I have only one request to make. The end is very close. Now you take the name *Wahe Guru* and read *Gurbani* (Sikh Gita). Here I have brought the *Gutka* (the little book) for you.'

Bhagat Singh let out a laughter and said, 'Old man, I would gladly comply with your request, but now that the journey's end is very near, if now I pray to God, people would say that Bhagat Singh was chicken-hearted. I never prayed, and now that I am feeling the icy breath of death on my neck if I started praying people would misunderstand me. It would be better to let me go my own way. I might be abused because I am an atheist and do not believe in God, but nobody would say that Bhagat Singh was dishonest and flinched at the slight of death.'

This report coming from very reliable source confirms the fact that Bhagat Singh did not put on his scientific socialism as a shirt worn only on the platform like our communists. He remained true to dialectical materialism, which is as much a part of socialist philosophy as the head is a part of the body. It is a daily happening in India that persons claiming to have a monopoly of Marxism, in matters of religion conduct if their private life like their forefathers. Of course, when asked they say they do not believe in the Sikh, Muslim or Christian rites, which they only perform to appease their senile parents, wife or some such person. But Bhagat Singh refused to behave like a Sikh even in the face of death.

This is accounted for by the latest research on him. Sohan Singh categorically writes : "In discussions with him, I found that Bhagat Singh did not believe in any religion. Some Arya Samajists have claimed after his martyrdom that he was an Arya Samajist. Some Sikhs have claimed he was Sikh. In fact, he was neither. 'I am an ordinary human being, that is all,' he would say."

This coupled with his conversation with the Sikh Warder, proves conclusively that Bhagat Singh was an atheist and remained so even inside the condemned cell.

Prannath had given to him a book by Lenin or on Lenin. Years later I asked Prannath to confirm, but he could not recall whether it was a book on Lenin or by Lenin. When asked to mount the scaffold Bhagat Singh was reading this book. He continued his reading and said : 'Wait a while. A revolutionary is talking to another revolutionary.' There was something extraordinary in his voice which made the excutioners wait otherwise befuddled as they are with drink (officially the excutioner was given his thirty pieces of silver and a bottle of wine during British rule) backed by brute-force, they hardly care for anybody.

Khudi Ram

Bhagat Singh continued reading. After a few moments he flung the book towards the ceiling and said, 'Let's go.'

While Khudi Ram had climbed the gallows with a copy of the *Gita* slung round his neck and Ashfaq had gone to mount the gallows on the 19 December, 1927, with a copy of the *Quaran*, Bhagat Singh was lost in a book by Lenin or on Lenin. The trio Bhagat Singh, Sukhdev and Rajguru were hanged together. Bhagat Singh was in the middle, Sukhdev was on his right and Rajguru on his left. It is said that Bhagat Singh recited this couplet before going to his death :

Dil se na niklegi markar bhi watan ki ulfat
Meri mitti se bhi khushboo-e-watan aegi.

'Even after death the love of motherland shall linger in my mind. My dead body shall emit the fragrance of my motherland.'

After he had sung the couplet he told the magistrate with a smile, 'You are really fortunate that you are witnessing how Indian revolutionaries march to their death.'

After this they were hanged and they became history.

All the martyrs before and since Bhagat Singh have been hanged the morning, but in the case of these three an exception was made and they were hanged at 7.33 in the dusk on the 23 March. This was carried out to maintain secrecy, but the ordinary prisoners of the jail raised slogans. Fearing that if the bodies were taken out of the jail gate, some hiding scout of the revolutionaries might notice, the high wall was breached at the back of the jail and the bodies were taken out for summary disposal to Ferozepur. There under cover of darkness a collective pyre was prepared. After some time, the half burnt bodies were thrown in the waters of the Satluj. After the police party had left, the villagers came to learn of dead bodies burnt with the connivance of the local police, they hit upon the truth. They retrieved the bodies from the river, made a pyre and cremated them properly according to their own conception. When I visited the place some 30 years after the occurrence, there were some villagers who remembered everything and they showed me the spot.

Death and Reaction

The news of these hangings was retaliated with strikes and protest meeting all over the country. The *hartal* at Kanpur took rather an ugly turn. A few days earlier, on the death of Muhammad Ali (the death was natural, he was not hanged or beaten to death), some Muslims had called for *hartal*, but Hindus had not responded. The Ali brothers were topmost leaders in 1921, but since then, Shaukat Ali had turned into a rank communalist (his farmous dictum—'In my eyes the worst Muslim in better that the best Hindu, Gandhi'), Muhammad Ali, however, had only separated from the national mainstream.

The Muslims of Kanpur refused to join the *hartal* at Bhagat Singh's death. At this some youths began force the Muslim shops to close. The agents provocateur came out to create trouble. Some policemen disguised as ordinary Muslims travelled very swiftly on tongas through the populous parts of Kanpur publicising Muslims were being killed. It was completely untrue, but this started the fracas. By evening of the 23 of March, fifty people were wounded, on the 24 and the 25 it grew into a huge riot. The forces of reaction triumphed. What could be the first glow of revolution got converted into a fratricidal riot. The police did not act. Ganesh Shanker Vidyarthi who had rescued many Muslims from Hindu areas was assassinated in a Muslim area while rescuing Hindus. His dead body was discovered after 4 days. It was recognised because he had worn Khadi clothes. From his pockets was found an article on the Karachi Congress. Thus, India lost one of her bravest sons. His death finally proved that the solution of the religious problem through sloppy sentimentalism and hypocritical mutual admiration could not succeed. But conventional leaders, including Gandhi, had nothing else to offer, that is why the problem still persists in independent India.

The striking power of the waves let loose by Bhagat Singh's supreme sacrifice, was very much reduced by these riots. Imperialism scored a great victory at Kanpur.

Bhagat Singh in Communist Eye

One of the accused remitted in the Lahore case was Ajoy Ghosh. Later on, he became the secretary of the CPI (then united). For many years, till the day of his death he held its supreme position. He wrote about Bhagat Singh. Here is an extract :

"I think I met Bhagat Singh for the first time some time in 1923. Then I was fifteen. Bhagat Singh was also, I believe, of the same age. Batukeshwar Dutt of Kanpur introduced me to him. Bhagat Singh was tall and slim. He was rather clumsily dressed. He appeared to be very shy and spoke with great effort. He was not smart and seemed to lack self-confidence. He was a typical village boy. At that time I did not find anything remarkable about him. When Bhagat Singh left, I conveyed my evaluation to Dutt.

I met him the second time before long and we had a longish talk. Those were the days when we used to dream of revolution childish dreams they were. It so appeared that revolution was round the corner, might take just a few years, that's all. But Bhagat Singh was not so complacent. I do not now remember his words, but he again and again referred to the prevalent somnolence and apathy in the country. He said that the path of awakening the masses bristled with difficulties. This meet confirmed the impressions created during the first interview.

Our conversation devolved on the past attempts to bring about revolution. We talked about the martyrs of the 1915-16 period. But as soon as the name of Kartar Singh came, Bhagat Singh become altogether a different man. Bhagat Singh had not met Kartar Singh, nor had I, Kartar Singh had been hanged when we were children. But we both knew that at the age of 19, he had become the undisputed leader to the group of men that had come from the USA to spearhead the revolution. This group contained such stalwarts as Sohan Singh Bhakna, Baba Rur Singh, Prithvi Singh Azad. Kartar Singh was a fearless freedom-fighter and a first class organiser. Friend and foe, all admired him. When somebody admires the idol you have loved and cherished for a long time, it gives you real pleasure. So when Bhagat Singh praised him, I was very pleased because he happened to be my idol as well. Immediately I felt something like love oozing within me towards Bhagat Singh. By the time Bhagat Singh left Kanpur, there was a strong bond of friendship between him and me. I' however, never spared him for what appeared to be a streak of pessimism in him.

In 1928, a young man burst into my room and wished *namaste* to me with a lot of flutter. I wondered who this fellow was. Well, it turned out to be no other than Bhagat Singh. But this was a different Bhagat Singh, very different from the one I knew. Here was a tall, well-built, handsome man with crimson lips and soft glittering eyes. We talked and I came to the conclusion that he had not only grown in years, his mind had also matured.

Now he was one of the two leaders of our party. The other leader was Chandrashekhar Azad. The goal of our party had become to establish a socialist society. The structure of the party had also changed. At the apex was the central committee of the revolutionary party, next came the provincial committees consisting of representatives from the district committees. All decisions were arrived at democratically. The members of the party were bound to obey all the decisions.

With regard to the man task, as to how to fight for freedom and socialism, our immediate strategy remained the same. That had undergone no change, and it was the method of armed group action. It was our considered opinion that there was no alternative but the revolutionary methods with which to fight the system that had bound us hand and foot. The idea was to strike at selected nerve-centres of the government again and again and thereby release the blocked energy of the masses, which when released would sweep away imperialism. At that stage, the idea was to join the mass upsurge, work, as its armed vanguard and give the torrent of lava, a socialist direction.

At the period and after, all those who met Bhagat Singh, have testified to his sharp intellect. His words forced conviction. Not that he was a good conversationalist, but when he spoke, all resistance seemed to liquefy vis-a vis a clear path thought through to the end. We talked till 'night's candles were burnt out and jocund day stood tiptoe on the far flung horizon'. When we went out together for a stroll, and I saw the sun shedding its first shafts, of light, it appeared to me that a new grey dawn was breaking.

Such was the conception of socialism those days. Eminent public leaders had forfeited our trust. Their legalistic methods, their empty boast to explode the system from within and change the raven of imperialism by painting its feathers, annoyed and irritated us. As a contrast, we wanted to present ourselves as models to forge a new pattern of leadership. Socialism was our ultimate goal. This was to be materialised after capturing power.

Bhagat Singh was singularly free from the symptoms of a traditional terrorist leader. We had serious differences of opinion and there were some stormy conferences. Bhagat Singh had to adopt certain paths and take up certain actions, which he, let to himself, would not have adopted or taken up. His was a restless soul. He lacked the quiet repose of Chandrashekhar Azad. Sometimes Bhagat Singh would flare up and hit hard at waverers, but seldom did he hurt anybody's feeling. If ever, in spite of this, he hurt somebody, or he thought he had, he came out with such profuse and sincere apologies that it was impossible to be sore with him. By nature he was loving specially towards people who were unhappy or ill. He was free and frank in his behaviour. The inner structure of his mind ruled out all triviality.

He was crazy about books. As a prisoner he spent all his time in studying socialism. He was perhaps the first among us to be drawn towards socialist ideas. He was a confirmed atheist and untouched by the religious beliefs of his predecessors in the revolutionary movement. It would be however sheer exaggeration to say that he had become a full-fledged Marxist, but impelled by his studies, the discussions that we all had, and the stormy events that were happening, for instance that Sholapur rising, the Peshawar upheavals leading to the brave mutiny by Grahwali soldiers under the leadership of Chandra Singh, he began to emphasise more and more on this point that our 'armed action' should be in conformity with, land form an integral part of the needs and demands of mass action.

Impact of Soviet Union

"We were great lovers of the Soviet Union. The studies in prison made this love penetrate deeper. We sent greetings to the Soviet Union on Revolution day (Nov. 1930) in which we extolled successes and victories of the Soviet people and pledged support to her against her enemies."

This evaluation by Ajoy Ghosh, when he was the all powerful secretary of the CPI (not yet split), it tantamount from the viewpoint of understanding the revolutionary movement and its great leader Bhagat Singh. It clarifies communist thinking also. Though he extolled Bhagat Singh to the skies, Ajoy Ghosh had a dig at him that he could not be agreed upon as full-fledged Marxist. The question is, if he was not a Marxist, who is? Ajoy Ghosh hit at him from a pedestal, at that time a monolithic body, but now torn into many fragments. Even if we forget this, it may be queried : is a party, confined to parliamentary activities entitled to call itself Marxist-Leninist? Can we call such people communists, who put on the sacred thread, call the Mulla, pundit, padri and granthi to sanctify their marriage, death and birth? Is it essential that revolution in every country should exact the same pattern as the 1917 revolution? Was not the 1917 revolution itself an unorthodox revolution, and is it not a fact that give it credence. Lenin had to invent the weakest link theory, unfamiliar to the two great founding fathers of scientific socialism ? What about the Chinese Revolution? Did it happen the orthodox way, even granting that the 1917 way was the orthodox one ? And what about Cuba? Did communism come there through the communist party? In reality, the Cuban communist party limped behind Castro, who was nearer to Bhagat Singh and Chandrashekhar Azad than any Indian communist believing only in parliamentary work can be. Is not a fact that all communist parties in developed countries have gone for the comfortability of parliament-arianism, although few parties have unhesitantly admitted this by abandoning loyalty to the dictatorship of the proletariat. Of course, since the Chinese Revolution the term 'proletariat' was redefined to encompass the full gamut of the toiling masses.

These are basic questions. There are other questions that are not that fundamental, but they are still important. For instance, did Mao continue to be a Marxist in spite of his ultra patriotic foreign policies? What is going to be the volition of history? Marxists (and not their enemies) have only themselves to thank for the confusion that has engulfed the world to socialism. Ajoy Ghosh had no knowledge all this, but he should have been less arrogant while writing about a man, who dragged him from his petty-bourgeois existence, and made him man of substance. Bhagat Singh's services to socialism is greater than of any Indian. Even now 'Inquilab Zindabad' is the battle cry of all leftists in India. Whether one likes it or not, Bhagat Singh has become the epitome of the fight for socialism more than any person or a party has.

Mistakes of Sohan Singh Josh

Sohan Singh Josh, a great freedom-fighter, writing some three decades after Ajoy, had committed almost the same mistakes in evaluating Bhagat Singh. The mistakes committed in this regard by Ajoy may be forgiven, but events of the last thirty years, specially trends in Euro-Communism should have made Sohan Singh humbler.

11 Proceedings in Privy Council

The Privy Council further demonished the cause of Indian revolutionaries. Revolutionary Bhagat Singh epitome, had lost all interest in legal proceedings after the Tribunal's verdict. But he was pushed, that a petition for special leave to appeal to the Judicial Committee of the Privy Council in London would surely yield of political advantage, whatever its eventual fate might be. The Defence Committee, especially its members Lala Duni Chand and Dr. Gopi Chand Bhargava, were very expectant on moving the Privy Council. Same thought lawyer Pran Nath Mehta and a counsel of national eminence, Motilal Nehru. He delivered a message from his sick bed in Simla. He was to die on February 6, 1931 just five days before the Privy Council did not even give it to a regular hearing.

Opening of Petition

Like in any other petition to the Privy Council, issues of fact were eschewed. The only issue was the legality of the Ordinance. It is unlikely that Bhagat Singh's counsel, the young D.N. Pritt, K C., actually knew about his client's popularity in India or the political significance of his trial. To him, it was just another banal brief in the Privy Council where only legal issues are contested. He had not quite made the transition "From Right to Left", the sub-title of his *Autobiography*.

Though published in 1965, it gives no reference of Bhagat Singh at all. Incidentally, his colleagues were also joined as parties to the petition. The petition was heard on February 11, 1931, four months after the Tribunal gave judgment, by a Board consisting of Viscount Dunedin, Lord Thankerton, Lord Russel of Killowen, Sir George Lowndes and Sir Dinshah Mulla.

Luckily a full transcript of the argument can be availed in the National Archives of India. Rather than consign it to the ghetto of an Appendix, it is given here in full. The reader who is not interested in them can turn the pages.

D.N. Pritt, K.C., Horace Douglas, C. Sidney Smith instructed by Messrs Douglas Grant & Dold, appeared for the petitioners.

A.M. Dunne, K.C. and W. Wallach, instructed by the Solicitor, India Office, appeared for the Respondent.

View's Pritt

Pritt : May it please your Lordships. In this case I appear with my learned friends Mr. Horace Douglas and Mr. Sidney Smith for the Petitioners, and my learned friends Mr. Dunne and Mr. Wallach appear for the Crown. If we can make good to your Lordships the proposition which we seek to advance, I hope I may submit with some confidence that it is a case that does not meet with the usual difficulties.

Viscount Dunedin : I think you may take that. It would strike at the whole jurisdiction. What you have to make out is that Section 72 does not authorise what was done.

Pritt : Yes, my Lord. Possibly the best thing will be to go straight to Section 72 and submit my arguments to your Lordships on the effect of that section. It is a section which has been in the statute for some time; it is a section of an Imperial Act of Parliament; there is no doubt whatever of its force and validity, but I do not think anyone would deny that it creates a somewhat striking power, and is one, at any rate, which any Court will construe with care.

Viscount Dunedin : It creates an absolute power.

Pritt : Yes, when the conditions are fulfilled.

Viscount Dunedin : Yes, I do not suppose Parliament has ever done anything more absolute than in passing the old Acts of Attainder.

Pritt : No, my Lord. The power it creates is a limited power of delegated legislation: "The governor-general may, in cases of emergency, make and promulgate ordinances for the peace and good government of British India or any part there of, and any ordinance so made shall, for the space of not more than the months from its promulgation, have the like force of law as an Act passed by the Indian Legislature; but the power of making ordinances under this section is subject to the like restrictions as the power of the Governor-General in Legislative Council to make laws".

I do not think I need trouble your Lordships with the words after the last semi-colon. The substance of the matter here is in my submission, that before any ordinance can be valid three things must happen, and at least two of those are of some importance to this Petition. In the first place, there must be a case of emergency, whatever "emergency" may mean; the second is that the ordinance must be an ordinance falling within the description that it is an ordinance for the peace and good government of British India or some part thereof; and the third point is that it must in addition to being for peace and good government, fall within the restrictions of the legislative powers of the Indian Legislature which I think are to be found mainly, if not wholly, in Section 65.

My Lords, these three points fall into two classes, the first is that something must happen before the power comes into force at all; and secondly, when it has come into force, that is to say when there is an emergency and the Governor-General may do something, there are two limits, so far as we are concerned, to what he may do. May I state my submission in outline, in relation to this very striking power. My submission firstly is that if the exercise of the power be challenged, it is necessary to establish affirmatively that there is a case of emergency; it is not for the Executive, if I may so describe the Governor-General, to say there is an emergency; it must be proved; like any other question of fact lying at the root of a jurisdiction, it has to be established before the Courts, in my humble submission.

Viscount Dunedin : You mean really the Court is to have the power of reviewing the view of the Governor-General that there was a case of emergency?

Pritt : I do not put it in that way; I would put it in that way if I were forced to do so. I put it in this way: the Courts in British countries are places where the facts are decided. At the root of the Governor-General's right to make an ordinance lies in every case the question of fact: Was there an emergency? If it becomes material to know whether there was an emergency or not, that is a matter which has to be proved before the Court.

Viscount Dunedin : Is it your proposition that before the Governor-General can promulgate an ordinance he would have to bring a declaratory action in the Courts for a declaration?

Pritt : No, my Lord.

Viscount Dunedin : What do you mean by "the Courts"?

Pritt : I mean this, my Lord, that anybody, however eminent, who has power to act when certain facts exist, must make up his mind whether they exist or not and then act, and that when his power is challenged and it is suggested that those facts did not exist, the question whether those facts exist or not is a question like any other question lying at the root of any jurisdiction and must be decided by the Courts.

Viscount Dunedin : Your contention comes to this, that this Board which is the only place to which you can come, shall have an inquiry into the facts and review the view of the Governor-General that there was a case of emergency. That is what it comes to, is it not?

Pritt : In the same sense as happens when any other executive makes up its mind that there is a riot and exercises powers which it has when there is a riot, and which it does not have when there is not a riot, and then subsequently at their leisure the Civil Court decide whether there was a riot or not.

Viscount Dunedin : I do not know quite what you mean by that. I am not aware of any clause in an Act of Parliament like Section 72 which has to do with riots.

Pritt : Not in an Act of Parliament but it is a question that often arises in English common law when the Civil Executive applies to the Military.

Lord Thankerton : You say this is a pure question of fact. I should have doubted that. Surely the trouble about an emergency is what it may lead to, as much as, if not more than, what has already happened. Does not this assume somebody having an opinion not as a question of fact?

Pritt : It is a very difficult question of fact.

Lord Thankerton : I should have said it was a question of opinion.

Pritt : Even a question of opinion is a question of fact.

Lord Thankerton : It is so treated by the Courts, I agree; but that leads to a consideration as to who is the proper person to judge of it, on the construction of this section; it is not the ordinary question of fact.

Pritt : The state of a man's mind is as much a fact as the state of his digestion.

Lord Thankerton : This is a question of administration, is it not?

Pritt : In my humble submission, Section 72 is not a matter of administration; it is a matter of substituted legislation

Lord Russel of Killowen : What is the test to be applied in ascertaining whether an emergency exists?

Pritt : The usual test as to whether Johnson has told a lie, or drove a car negligently.

Lord Russel of Killowen : This seems to be more a question of opinion. The question is: Who is best qualified to form an opinion?

Pritt : That brings me back really to my submission. I am putting my submission in two ways : firstly, that merely construing that section, the words "in case of emergency" meant not that the Governor-General is the sole judge as to whether there was an emergency or not, but that there had to be in fact an emergency. The second limb that I am going to put on that is this. A proper method of construing one section of a statute is to see what words it uses in other sections, and a comparison of this section with half-a-dozen other sections in this Act makes it, in my submission, overwhelmingly clear that the Imperial Parliament, when conferring this very great power by Section 72 on one individual, however eminent in the Executive of British India, was deliberately refraining from entrusting to him the right to decide, either as fact or opinion, whether there was an emergency or not.

Sir George Lowndes : I should have thought there was a personal element here.

Pritt : Many personal elements have to be decided by a Court afterwards. There is a personal element in every running-down case. May I call your Lordships' attention to Secton 67(b) of the Government of India Act; "Where either chamber of the Indian legislature refuses leave to introduce, or fails to pass in a form recommended by the Governor-General, any Bill, the Governor-General may certify that the passage of the Bill is essential for the safety, tranquillity or interests of British India or any part thereof". Those are plainly words that leave the matter in the hands of the Governor-General alone. Then it says the Bill shall become an Act by certain means which I need not trouble your Lordships with. Then sub-section 2 says : "Every such Act"—that is the Bill turned into an Act—"shall be expressed to be made by the Governor-General, and shall, as soon as practicable after being made, be laid before both Houses of Parliament, and shall not have effect until it has received His Majesty's assent". Then lower down your Lordships see: "and upon the signification of such assent by His Majesty in Council, and the notification thereof by the Governor-General, the Act shall have the same force and effect as an Act passed by the Indian legislature and duly assented to". Then in case the matter has to be dealt with so swiftly that even this is too slow, we get the proviso: "Provided that where in the opinion of the Governor-General a state of emergency exists which justifies such action, the Governor-General may direct that any such Act shall come into operation forthwith". Perhaps I can put the matter shortly in this way: There are at least eight other passages in that Statute of varying strengths and varying kinds. I do not pretend that I have not given your Lordships the best of them, but there are others as good and others not much worse, in which it is shown overwhelmingly that the Imperial Parliament, when it wants to entrust a matter to the Governor-General, has sufficient command of the English language to be able to put it beyond the range of doubt. Section 72 has existed for a long time, and some of the other Sections in which the sort of thing is dealt with have existed for a considerable time, and my first submission to your Lordships accordingly is that the Governor-General has power here to substitute himself to a certain extent and for a short period of time for the legislature in order to move more swiftly than the legislature can in Legislative matters . ..

Viscount Dunedin : I quite understand the point, but I must bring you to this: What is the remedy according to you?

Pritt : The remedy, in my humble submission, is a remedy for the Crown.

Viscount Dunedin : Is it not a remedy for the subject?

Pritt : The remedy for the subject is that when an Ordinance is sought to be applied to him, he shall submit an argument to some of His Majesty's Courts, or if one is being established by the Ordinance, I think there is authority for the proposition that he may submit it to that tribunal or he may submit it to another tribunal and say : Here is the Crown doing something which I say it has no power to do.

Viscount Dunedin : Assuming we grant leave to appeal, what would you say to the Board when the appeal was heard?

Pritt : I should say to the Board three things. The first thing I should say to the Board is: I challenge this Ordinance; it is made under a definite limited power; I say that the conditions of the exercise of the power do not exist, and never have existed.

Viscount Dunedin : What would happen after that?

Pritt : My submission on the whole of the facts would be this: The power is limited; in order to show that it has been validly exercised and that the conditions are fulfilled, there must be some proof that there was a case of emergency. I have challenged that, once before this very tribunal and once before the High Court at Lahore, and in neither instance did the Crown adduce one title of evidence that there had ever been a case of emergency.

Viscount Dunedin : Then you would say that the matter must be gone into, I suppose?

Pritt : I am not sure I should not take a higher line and say : The Crown having had two opportunities to establish that they had this power because there was an emergency, and having refrained on both occasions from adducing any evidence ...

Viscount Dunedin : The Ordinance had been promulgated long before this?

Pritt : Long before what, my Lord?

Viscount Dunedin : Long before the matter came into Court.

Pritt : This Ordinance was promulgated six or seven months after my clients first stood their trial.

Dunne : That is not the point.

Viscount Dunedin : It was promulgated before the trial took place before the special Tribunal?

Pritt : Yes, my Lord.

Viscount Dunedin : That is all that was done, is it not?

Pritt : As soon as that was done, we challenged it by *habeas corpus* proceedings, and the Crown adduced no evidence of any description.

Viscount Dunedin : And you failed on that?

Pritt : We failed on that, I think I ought to tell your Lordships at once that when the matter came before me I took the view, on behalf of my clients, which may be right or wrong, that they really ought to present to your Lordships at some stage an appeal from that decision. That was put in train at once and leave is now being applied for to the High Court at Lahore to appeal from that Judgment, and ultimately, if your Lordships think fit to grant us leave to appeal here, then either by the High Court at Lahore granting me leave, if it thinks right, or by me asking your Lordships in a supplemental petition if the High Court does not think right to grant me leave and your Lordships thought right to grant it, then ultimately by consolidation the matter would come before your Lordships in the dual form, namely, an appeal from the Judgment in the *habeas corpus* proceedings and a direct appeal from the decision on the Tribunal.

Coming back to the substance of the matter, I should most certainly submit on behalf of my clients that the Crown, having twice had the opportunity of establishing a case of emergency and not having even attempted so to do, that the decision of the Court ought to be declared by your Lordships to be entirely void, whereupon the condition of my clients, as I understand it, would be that my clients would be people as to whom there had been a preliminary hearing before the Magistrate, if that is the right description at Lahore, which was entirely void and they would be people whose trial was entirely void; and they could, if it was thought right, be re-arrested and tried according to the ordinary process of law which was mysteriously interrupted at the beginning of last May.

The second submission I should make to your Lordships, if I was granted leave to appeal and the substantive appeal came on, would be this—I am still only dealing with the emergency and not with the other difficulties which I desire to raise—let it be granted that I am wrong in asserting that it is for the Governor-General to establish that there was a case of emergency, or at any rate, let it be granted that I am wrong in asserting that it is for the Governor-General to establish that by evidence, and let me approach it in the way which one of the Courts below approached it at one stage and say: I see a statement by the Governor- General; the Governor-General is so important a person that if he says something in his Gazette, I will take it as evidence. It was not put in that crude fashion, but that is the substance of what one of the Judges said in the *habeas corpus* proceedings. Then I should submit to your Lordships' Board that we have only to look at the Governor-General's statement to come to the conclusion that there was no emergency.

Lord Thankerton : That is to say, we are to come to the conclusion that the Governor-General was wrong?

Pritt : When he said there was a state of emergency, he may not have regarded it as a matter of opinion.

Lord Thankerton : The preamble of the Ordinance gives the reasons, does it not? You say he should not have come to the conclusion that there was an emergency?

Pritt : It is not the preamble. One must be very accurate here. The preamble does say something about an emergency. It appears in the same number of the Gazette as a statement by the Governor-General; but in my very humble submission, in spite of the eminent position of the Governor-General, the statement by him proves nothing.

Viscount Dunedin : Either you look at his statement and say: Those are his reasons and he has come to a wrong conclusion that there was an emergency; or else you say : Those are not his reasons : I do not know what his reasons were; how can I say whether there was an emergency or not in the opinion of the Governor-General? Which do you say is the correct construction for the purpose of this argument?

Pritt : I put it alternatively. In the first place, I say there must be proof of an emergency; secondly, if it is suggested that is evidence, then I say, when it is looked at, there must be some limits to the word "emergency", and that he can only act within those limits. May I put another alternative: One or two Courts in India, for reasons which I confess I do not follow as a matter of logic, have laid down expressly that it is for the Court to make up its mind and to investigate the questions of fact whether there is an emergency or not, but the Court has sufficiently investigated that when it has come to the conclusion that there is some evidence on which the Governor-General could decide, and I should submit to your Lordships, if leave to appeal was granted, that there was no evidence. This depends upon a consideration of the facts of the case and a consideration of the meaning of the word "emergency", and the question of the meaning of the word "emergency", although important and lying at the base of the whole matter, is not the whole argument that I would desire to put before your Lordships. I rely very much upon the definition of the power, or rather the definition of the power to legislate under circumstances of this sort, that it must be for the peace and good government of British India. I do not presume to challenge the proposition that "the peace and good government of British India" is a very vide phrase, but at some stage in my submission to your Lordships I do want to put it very strongly that this particular Ordinance is a privilegium of a very terrible description; whether it could possibly conduce to peace is a matter of some difficulty; that it could conduce either to good government or to government at all, I would invite your Lordships to consider very carefully indeed. My submission is that on the true construction of Section 72 it is plainly intended to empower the Governor-General in cases of general emergency or cases of a particular emergency area, or whatever it may be, to pass what may fairly be called legislation, but this is legislation which I think in every Roman law country and jurisprudence would indignantly deny to be legislation at all.

Lord Thankerton : Why?

Pritt : Because it is a privilegium. It makes no law that and has to obey, except the civil servants of the Crown and the members of the Tribunal. It lays down no liberty to any man to anything; it lays down no provision by way of criminal law or anything else that any man shall not do anything.

Viscount Dunedin : What about the old Acts of attainder? What did they do?

Pritt : They were passed by the supreme Imperial Parliament.

Viscount Dunedin : Certainly.

Pritt : This is not; this is dedicated legislation, and all that the Governor-General can do is to make and promulgate Ordinances for the peace and good government of British India or any part thereof, which are to have he force of law for six month. That is a privilegium, and I submit that cannot in any view be called legislation at all for peace, order and good government.

Lord Russell : Do you say that under Section 65 of this Act the Indian Legislature could not have passed an Act in these terms?

Pritt : Section 65 is not the only section which has to be looked at in order to discover the power and restrictions of the Indian Legislature, but it is much the most important. I concede reluctantly that the Indian Legislature could have done this, but then the Legislature is allowed to legislate within clauses (a) to (f), whether it is for the peace, order and good government of British India or not. It is, in my humble submission right to bear this in mind, that what this Statute actually does is this. It says: Here are a number of men; they are all in custody; they are not running about; they are under trial; that is to say, preliminary proceedings are being carried forward against them on specific charges. They have at the moment the right of citizens in British India to have a *prima facie* case made out against them, and before they are tried to know what that case is. They have a right to be tried before the ordinary Sessions Judge with assessors or a jury, and after the trial to appeal to the established High Court at Lahore, with which Court this Ordinance cannot interfere; that is another point to which I will come in a moment. The authorities say by this privilegium, in which there is not a word about other men, not a word about other offences, not a word about means of preserving law and order and peace and good government, we say that these particular individuals shall be deprived of the right to know the case against them, shall be deprived of the right to have a *prima facie* case made against them, shall be deprived of the right of trial before a Sessions Judge and a jury or assessors, shall be deprived of the right to go to the High Court at Lahore on appeal; and we say they shall be tried before a special tribunal without knowing what the case is against them except as and when it comes out of the mouth of approvers or independent witnesses, as the case may be. At any moment the tribunal may change its personnel, and when they come to the end of the case, it may be that these people will be sentenced to death without appeal by three gentlemen who, by reason of the changes in personnel, may none of then have seen a single one of the witnesses, and they may sentence these men to death on evidence of approvers whose demeanour they never have had the opportunity to observe. I submit to your Lordships that on any reasonable meaning of the word "legislation" this is not legislation at all.

Assessment of then Existing Legislation

Lord Thankerton : Why is it not legislation? You may think it is bad legislation. You have admitted that under Section 65 the Indian Legislature could have passed such an Act. Would you have said that was legislation?

Pritt : I should have said that to an Englishman brought up with the idea of Parliaments with unlimited powers and of subsidiary Parliaments with very limited powers, that that would be an administrative Act disguised in the form of legislation, but which is perfectly lawful, but when one comes to a section which does not say the Governor-General shall be invested with all the legislative powers of Section 65, but does say that he may make and promulgate Ordinances for the peace and good government of British India, that means that the Governor-General may make legislation which provides what people ordinarily call law; which provides something which applies to more than one person or one group of persons. Legislation that it shall be unlawful to wear a particular kind of hat that is insulting to one's fellow citizens would be legislature; but an administrative Act disguised as a piece of legislation dealing *ex post facto* with the trouble which has already arisen in the case of the certain individuals who are to be tried for specific offences, in my humble submission, if legislation is used in any ordinary sense or if it is used as power to make and promulgate legislative Ordinances for the peace and good government of the country, my clients ought to be given the opportunity to put before this Board on a full appeal the argument that such an Ordinance is invalid and cannot fall within the words "Ordinances for the peace and good government of anything".

The third point is important, but less important and perhaps less clear, namely, that the restrictions imposed by this Act upon the power of the Indian Legislature to make laws must also be proved. Your Lordships will probably know that in one case that has been challenged on the broad proposition whether this type of ordinance offends against the unwritten law or constitution of the United Kingdom of Great Britain and Ireland. I do not think I can advance that argument to your Lordships; that seems to be precluded; but there is another ground here, and that arises out of the consideration of Section 84 and a later one. I think Section 113. Section 65 is the main section imposing the power and placing restrictions on the power. Section 84 is in a department called "Validity of Indian Laws". The only one that matters here is : "A law made by any authority in British India and repugnant to any provision of this or any other Act of Parliament shall, to the extent of that repugnancy, but not otherwise, be void". That is partly an enabling section, because it prevents repugnancy destroying the whole thing, but in my submission the effect of that is this : If any act of the British Indian Legislature be challenged, and therefore in any ordinance under Section 72 be challenged, as operating repugnantly to any provision of this Act of Parliament, it will be void. My submission is that this is repugnant to the provisions of this Act of Parliament, it will be void. My submission is that this is repugnant to the provisions of this Act of Parliament because it deprives the High Court at Lahore of Jurisdiction in the matter. May I refer your Lordships to Section 113: "His Majesty may, if he sees fit, by letters patent, establish a high court of judicature in any territory in British India, whether, or not included within the limits of the local jurisdiction of another High Court, and confer on any High Court so established any such jurisdiction, powers and authority as are vested in or may be conferred on any High Court existing at the commencement of this Act; and where a High Court is so established in any area included within the limits of the local jurisdiction of another High Court. His Majesty may, be letters patent, alter those limits and make such incidental, consequential and supplemental provisions as may appear to be necessary by reason of the alteration." My submission on that point, whether it be sound or not, can be put comparatively shortly. It is simply this: The right to confer jurisdiction on what is now the High Court at Lahore is committed by this Imperial Statute to His Majesty to be done by letters patent. If the Indian Legislature, being a subordinate Legislature, seeks by any Act of its own to deprive the High Court at Lahore, established by His Majesty's letters patent, of jurisdiction, in whole or in part, the argument is the same. It is offending against Section 113, which has conferred upon someone else, and someone higher namely. His Majesty, by the executive act of letters patent to create the High Court. This particular Ordinance, in order to be valid, has to be such as not to infringe Section 113. If this particular ordinance took away the whole jurisdiction of the High Court at Lahore, it would, in my humble submission, equally offend against Section 113.

Sir George Lowndes : Is that provided for specifically in the Act?

Pritt : There is something about it in the letters patent; I have not found anything in the Act. Section 65 is the general section which gives the power to make laws. It is suggested to me that Sir George Lowndes may be may be thinking of Section 106. My suggestion about it is that Section 65 and Section 84 have to be read together. Section 65 confers a very wide, but nevertheless not universal, power on the Indian legislature, and then Section 84 says: "A law made by any authority in British India and repugnant in any provisions of this or any other Act of Parliament shall, to the extent of that repugnancy, but not otherwise, be void."

Lord Russell of Killowen : I am not sure that I follow your repugnancy yet. Where is the repugnancy?

Pritt : The repugnancy, I suggest, is this : Whereas His Majesty alone can create the High Court at Lahore, or limit, or amend, or alter, or take away from its powers, before this ordinance was passed the High Court at Lahore had jurisdiction to hear my clients on appeal, and that has been taken away by the ordinance which had said they shall not have any appeal.

Lord Russel of Killowen : The ordinance has constituted a special tribunal to try particular people.

Pritt : Yes.

Lord Russell of Killowen : Is that repugnant the Section 113? I do not see it.

Pritt : In my submission, yes, because my clients, when the ordinance was passed, were people who were being prosecuted on charges that were being formulated in the ordinary course, and the High Court had jurisdiction at the moment to hear an appeal, and the ordinance has entirely destroyed that exceedingly important portion of the jurisdiction of the High Court at Lahore.

Sir George Lowndes : The section I was thinking of is Section 65, sub-section (3), which limits the powers of the Indian Legislature. It cannot abolish a High Court. That clearly suggests that it has power to limit the jurisdiction of the High Court.

Pritt : My submission, in answer to that, would be that the Indian Legislature cannot abolish any High Court existing when the statute was passed, neither can it interfere with the operation of section 113, which says that His Majesty can appoint a new High Court and deal with its jurisdiction.

I ought to refer, because this matter was sufficiently in the minds of the draftsmen of the letters patent, to a very few words in the letters patent which establish the High Court at Lahore; they were made on 21 March, 1919. It is a relatively recent High Court. The following words were put in : The last paragraph, which is No. 37, says : "We, do further order and declare that all the provisions of any of our letters patent" etc. (reads paragraph). So it is quite plain that the Crown, as an executive Act, has sought in the letters patent to authorise the Governor-General to do that which, in my submission, if I am right, he cannot do, and that which, if I am right, in my submission, the draftsmen of the letters patent thought there might be some difficulty about doing. My submission is that nothing in clause 37 of the letters patent can affect the position, for the reason that the *Crown by letters* patent cannot create, or alter, or modify the power of the Governor-General or the Indian Legislature under the various sections of the Government of India Act.

Sir Dinshah Mulla : Is not that the same as clause [illegible] of the letters patent at the Calcutta High Court of 18[illegible]?

Pritt : I imagine that it must occur in at any rate any recent letters patent. I will find out for your Lordship.

Sir Dinshah Mulla : I wanted to know whether there was any distinction between the two. One is a very old High Court and the other is a new one.

Pritt : Clause 44 in the Calcutta letters patent reads as follows: (reads same). It is textually the same. I suppose that letters patents of the Calcutta High Court have been redrawn.

Sir Dinshah Mulla : The Calcutta letters patent are of 1869, and what is done is to substitute the sections of the Government of India Act of 1915 in the case the Lahore High Court.

Pritt : Yes, that is obviously what has been done. This clause was substituted for the original clauses by amending letters patent of 11 March, 1919. I am obliged to your Lordship for guiding me in the matter.

Now may I put before your Lordships some of the authorities upon the subject of the powers of the Court to investigate the question whether there was a case of emergency. There is no very direct English authority, although there is one which I think it would be right to refer your Lordships to, but there are several in India, where the matter has been expressly discussed, and the trend of Indian decisions is that the Courts have power to investigate that question, and must investigate it. They must investigate the question and see whether there was any reason on which the Governor-General could arrive at his conclusion.

Viscount Dunedin : Were these cases which arose under Section 72?

Reaction of Pritt

Pritt : One of them was this very *habeas corpus* case, and another arose under the same section. The particular one that I want to draw your Lordships' attention to is as recent as the 1st September last, and was a case in the High Court of Bombay, which dealt with Section 52.

Sir George Lowndes : Is that the Sholapur case?

Pritt : Yes. This is a case where there was legislation. There were riots on a widespread scale in Sholapur

Lord Thankerton : That does not matter for this point.

Dunne : We have prints of that judgment. (Handing same).

Pritt : I want to refer to the judgment of Chief Justice Beaumont, and I will begin where he quotes the section. A few lines after the quotation of the section, after discussing the Defence of the Realm Act and and the state of siege in France, he says: "As the question in this case, in my judgment, turns upon this section. I will quote it in full." I have already read that to your Lordships. "It is to be noticed that the section applies 'in cases of emergency'. The question whether the determination as to the existence of an emergency is an administrative act to be decided by the Governor-General alone, or whether it is a question of fact which can be inquired into by the Courts has been discussed by the High Court of Lahore in the case of *Desraj* v. *Emperor*, and the learned Judges who decided that case differed upon the point. In my opinion the judgment of Mr. Justice Bhide is correct, and the question whether an emergency exists or not is one of fact which the Courts can inquire into. But inasmuch as the Govenor-General is the person who must in the first instance, decide whether or not there is an emergency upon which he ought to act, and inasmuch as he may frequently have information which, in the public interest, he may be unwilling to disclose, and which no Court can compel him to disclose, I think that the Courts can do is to enquire whether there is evidence upon which the Governor-General may reasonably conclude that an emergency exists. If that question be answered in the affirmative, there is an end of the matter."

Lord Thankerton : That involves an inquiry into what the Governor-General does not want to disclose.

Pritt : Perhaps, May I submit several points in answer to what the learned Chief Justice says. There is in the first place the Governor-General : he may disclose to the Court what he thinks is enough.

Viscount Dunedin : The first point is whether the judgment of Mr. Justice Bhide is correct. Does he give any reasons?

Pritt : No, my Lord, I do not think he gives reasons.

Viscount Dunedin : Therefore, there is no argument upon that.

Pritt : It obviously was very fully argued.

Viscount Dunedin : I am not saying there was not an argument before him, but there was no argument in his judgment except to say : "I think Mr. Justice Bhide's judgment is correct". Therefore, it does not help us upon that point

Pritt : Only to this extent, that the argument that leaps to the mind, though I may be wrong, is adopted by this learned Chief Justice.

Viscount Dunedin : It does not help us, except the fact that he says so.

Pritt : That is so.

Viscount Dunedin : I do not think you need go into this matter.

Pritt : If your Lordship pleases. Then the judgment of Mr. Justice Madgavkar contains a certain amount of argument. I confess I find it a little difficult to follow, because while he is concurring it seems to me to be rather against me than for me, and therefore, it is natural, and inevitable, that I must read it. The passage I am referring to is at the top of page 6. He says : "On the third point"—that is this point— "I agree with the reasoning and the conclusions of the learned Chief Justice, and have little to add".

Lord Russell of Killowen : There are no reasons of the Chief Justice at all.

Pritt : They may have been given interlocutorily. "Unlike legislation in India, the validity of Statutes of Parliament cannot be questioned in the Courts of British India. Section 72 of the Government of India Act empowers the Governor-General to pass such ordinances in cases of emergency. It is argued for the petitioners that the omission of any such words as 'in the opinion of the Governor-General' after the word 'emergency' suffices to enable us to consider whether there was such an emergency as to justify the passing of the Ordinance and further to examine also its provisions to see how far they make 'for the peace and good government of British India'. Two learned judges of the Lahore High Court have considered the former question in the case of *Desraj* v. *Emperor*. Their difference of opinion seems to me more apparent than real. Section 72 as a whole hardly empowers the Courts to consider whether the Governor-General was right or wrong in his conclusion that an emergency existed, much less up examine how far the provisions of the Ordinance tend to the peace and good government of the country. That responsibility the statute has laid on the Governor-General and not on the Courts. Unless the Governor-General thought that there was an emergency, and he alone under the section is the judge thereof, he would not promulgate the ordinance to meet that particular emergency. The statute does not require that the Legislative Assembly should not be sitting as a necessary precedent to the exercise of the power of passing an ordinance. Therefore, the fact that in some cases the Act of Indemnity has been passed by the Central Legislature and not by way of ordinance by the Governor-General is immaterial".

Viscount Dunedin : That goes to another point, does it not?

Pritt : Perhaps it does.

Lord Thankerton : The next passage rather deals with your argument He points out that there is no law against it.

Pritt : There is no law in England against a privilegium.

Dunne : There is another passage on page 11 dealing with the third point.

Pritt : I am obliged to my learned friend. "The third point on which our decision really rests has been dealt with in detail in the judgment of the learned Chief Justice. I have already held that the ordinance is within the power of the Governor-General, and that it is, not open to us to examine its provisions and whether, it at all, they go beyond the necessities of peace and good government, within the meaning of Section 72 of the Government of India Act"; and yet he concurs, as I understand it, in the judgment which says the exact opposite. It is fair that I should read it. Then Mr. Justice Blackwell says, on page 13 : "It was contended by Mr. Thakore for the applicants that no case of emergency had been established. I do not agree with this contention. The reasons which moved the Governor-General are set out at the end of the Ordinance. On the materials placed before him the Governor-General was in my opinion clearly entitled to conclude that an emergency had arisen. I therefore think it unnecessary to decide whether the Court is empowered to enquire into the question whether in emergency existed, or whether that is a matter solely for the determination of the Governor-General. There has been a difference of judicial opinion upon this question in the Lahore High Court (see *Desraj* v. *Emperor*, A.I.R. 1930 Lahore, 781). I incline strongly to the view that the Court is entitled to enquire into the matter. Assuming that it is, the Court is not in my opinion entitled to enquire into the question whether the facts placed before the Governor-General were accurate or inaccurate. The Governor-General must obviously act promptly, and may sometimes have to make up his mind on information which may afterwards be found to be erroneous. In considering whether there was a case of emergency within the meaning of Section 72, the Court in my opinion is only entitled to require to be satisfied that facts were placed before the Governor-General which, if true, might reasonably lead him to conclude that an emergency existed."

Viscount Dunedin : The only way to do that would be by examining the Governor-General.

Pritt : May I draw your Lordships' attention to something that I think I mentioned when I was reading the Chief Justice's Judgment? The Governor-General is in this position. The matter is challenged and it is said that there was no emergency which justified his making the Ordinance. He cannot be compelled to come into Court: he can please himself and he may do one of three things. The first, which he would be very reluctant to do, is to say : Never mind the public interest; I am challenged; I will give you every fact. If that were his only course, there would be a difficulty. His second course would be to say : I can reconcile the general public interests and the particular interest of maintaining the Ordinance; I will show you quite enough to prove an emergency without showing you everything I know.

Viscount Dunedin : In order to do that he would have to be made a party to the case?

Pritt : If it is in the direct criminal proceedings, it would be the Crown, or if it is in the *habeas corpus* proceedings it would be the Crown again. The Crown, having access to public information, on applying to whatever Department is proper, would be supplied without much evidence and information as the Department thought proper. The Crown in England often has to do the same thing. The third course which the Governor-

General could adopt is a course which is adopted by the Executive in this country whenever a difficulty arises. He can go to his Legislature and say : I had to act in an emergency which I say is an emergency; I am not going to publish my facts to the Court in the disturbed state to this country at present. Give me an Act of indemnity.

Lord Thankerton : If it is an Act of indemnity, it is either at the time of the emergency or long after.

Pritt : Long after.

Lord Thankerton : I cannot understand the opinions of two of the Judges in this Bombay case. It may be that the reasons cannot possibly be disclosed. Do you say if the Governor-General does not disclose the reasons, the Ordinance is bad? If he does disclose the reasons, it may prove another emergency. The Court must either be seized of the whole of the facts or none of them.

Pritt : I respectfully agree.

Viscount Dunedin : Have you any other authority besides this that you can show us?

Pritt : Perhaps your Lordships ought to see the decision in this very *habeas corpus* case.

Viscount Dunedin : I think we know that. One judge said there was no inquiry at all; the other judge said that an inquiry was possible, but that he thought that the people had put themselves into such a position as to show that there was an emergency.

Pritt : Yes, and I think they relied as an alternative on the Governor-General's own statement. May I say in answer to Lord Thankerton I see the difficulties of the Executive. It would be impertinence on my part to say that I sympathise with them. The answer is : I did not draft this Constitution. This Constitution has said, in my humble submission, in the plainest possible terms that the Governor-General may do this very striking thing in cases of emergency, and he may do it in cases where he is of opinion there is a state of emergency for any time. Before he does it, there must be a state of emergency. That is the kernel of the case.

I was inclined to think that some of the English cases threw some light on the matter, but I do not want to weary your

Lordships with them if it is thought that they do not. Your Lordships remember the line of cases under the Defence of the Realm Act, one or two of which went to the House of Lords. This covers two points of my argument; it covers the question who is to decide a question of fact like this question of whether there is an emergency, and also the question of what is legislation in the direction of peace and good government.

Viscount Dunedin : We will listen to any case you choose to give us, but I do not myself see how any case would be much use, unless there was something equivalent to Section 72, which, so far as I know, there is not.

Pritt : I agree, and that is why, even when a number of my clients have been sentenced to death, I hesitate to read them. It is a true analogy, but the words may be still so different that it may not be of much use. I must put before your Lordships why I say it is an analogy. The analogy is complete in this sense. I submit they are both cases of subordinate legislation, and they came from the same body. In the one case, the Imperial Parliament has said certain persons may pass subordinate legislation for securing the safety of the Realm and for the better prosecution of the war—I have forgotten the exact words for the moment—in the other case, the same Imperial Parliament has said in cases of emergency certain persons may pass legislation for the peace and good government of British India. The essence of the cases on which I wanted to rely—indeed, perhaps it is sufficient to state it—is that there is an efficient body, the High Court of the Court of Appeal and, I think I may say, the House of Lords in this country, dealing with the Defence of the Realm legislation to see whether the legislation passed falls within the four corners of the Section of the Imperial Statute.

Viscount Dunedin : Obviously.

Pritt : The analogy is this : It is the duty of whatever court becomes concerned with the Lahore Case to construe whether the legislation passed by the Governor-General to establish this particular Court falls within the four corners of Section 72.

Viscount Dunedin : Nobody doubts that.

Pritt : The qustion is : Is there a case of emergency, and is it legislation for peace and good government?

Lord Russell : The analogy would be if you were able to say that this Statute exceeded the power of the Indian Parliament?

Pritt : That is only one limb.

Viscount Dunedin : It is only the argument that you have given us over again?

Pritt : Yes; I suggest that that argument is supported by some English authority. I think I can fairly leave these cases.

Viscount Dunedin : I do not think they help us at all. One is perfectly willing to concede you the proposition that obviouly it must be within the four corners of the section.

Lord Russell : It must be *intra vires?*

Pritt : Yes, and the *vires* depends on whether there is an emergency, and whether the legislation is for peace and good government.

Viscount Dunedin : That is your argument?

Pritt : Yes.

Viscount Dunedin : We are much obliged to you.

(Counsel and parties were directed to withdraw and after a short time were again called in.)

Viscount Dunedin : Their Lordships need not trouble you, Mr. Dunne. They are unable to advise His Majesty that leave to appeal be granted in this case for reasons which will be given later.

The reasons were given on February 27 in a judgment by Dunedin.

In brief, Pritt argued that before he could promulgate an Ordinance, the Governor-General had to establish affirmatively as a question of fact that an "emergency" did exist. Dunedin simply did not appreciate the point when he asked the preposterous question whether the Governor-General had to bring a civil suit in the courts for a declaration before making the Ordinance. It was a conditional power and fulfilment of the condition—existence of an emergency—had to be established if any one challenged the legality of the Ordinance. Pritt revealed that he had advised his clients to come to the Privy Council in appeal from the High Court's judgment in *Des Raj's* case, delivered seven months earlier in July 1930. Justice Bhide's judgment might have helped the petitioners.

But this Board would not have altered its opinion. Dunedin's brief judgment showed that the consideration that weighed with him was the finality of the Governor-General's view. He was the sole judge as to the existence of an emergecy. Even in the judicial clime of 1931, it was an extreme view that Dunedin propounded. "It is more than obvious that that someone must be the Governor-General and be alone. Any other view would render utterly inept the whole provision. Emergency demands immediate action, and that action is prescribed to be taken by the Governor-General. It is he alone who can promulgate the Ordinance."

Pritt's Contention that the G-G's opinion was open to judicial review was dismissed out of hand. "In fact, the contention is so completely without foundation on the fact of it that it would be idle to allow an appeal to argue about it."

Dunedin went so far as to hold that the Governor-General did not have to give any reason in support of his action : "Their Lordships must add that, although the Governor-General thought fit to expound the reasons which induced him to promulgate this Ordinance, this was not in their Lordships' opinion in any way incumbent on him as a matter of law."

Chamier and Mitchell

Watching the proceeding before the Privy Council in London was the Legal Adviser to the Secretary for India, Sir Edward Maynard Chamier. He had held the office since 1917 and knew India well. He had served as government Advocate in the North-West Frontier Province as far back as in 1875, in Oudh as Judicial Commissioner, and as Chief Justice of the Patna High Court (1911-15). He new the legal world in India and in London, in so far as it touched India. Hence the significance of an air-letter he dashed off to D.G. Mitchell, the Joint Secretary in the Law Ministry. Mitchell hastened to forward it to the Home Secretary, H.W. Emerson, on February 24. This suggests that Chamier wrote as soon as the Privy Council dismissed Bhagat Singh's petition.

The letters, now resting in the National Archives tell their own tale :

24th February

My dear Emerson,

I enclose a copy of an air-mail letter I have just received from Sir Edward Chamier. Crerar will be interested.

Yours sincerely,

D.G. Mitchell

Copy of an air-mail letter received by me today from Sir Edward Chamier.

My dear Mitchell,

I was agreeably surprised to find that Lord Dunedin presiding over the Board which heard the petition in the Lahore Conspiracy Case—with any other President I think the petition would have been admitted to a regular hearing—but Dunedin took a very strong line from the start and earned the others with him not that Lowndes (or Saunders?) and Mulla wanted any "carrying". They evidently felt that in the end the petition must fail and it was useless to prolong the agony.

I will send you with their "reasons" a transcript of the shorthand notes—you may be interested to see exactly what line the board took.

Yours sincerely,

E. Chamier

12 Martyrdom and Anger Reaction

The news of the final verdict of the tribunal spread like wild fire all over India. The one-sided and arbitrary decision awarding death sentence on Bhagat Singh and his comrades was greatly resented by one and all. Ways and means were devised to save the lives of these youths. But all efforts proved fruitless as the Viceroy and the Punjab government were ultimately of one opinion *i.e.* to send the three patriots labelled as conspirators by *The Pioneer*, to gallows in spite of efforts made at various levels. Popular attitude was expressed in a speech in Delhi by the Mayor of Calcutta on 20th March, three days before the execution. 'We demand with one voice and one will that the death sentence on Bhagat Singh and his comrades be commuted. Bhagat Singh is today not a person but a symbol. He symbolises spirit of revolt which has taken possession of country. We can condemn his methods, but we cannot help admiring his selflessness.'[1]

'Although accused refused to appear at many hearings of Tribunal, they were given opportunity to do so at every hearing. Their absence was due entirely to their own attitude.'[2]

On 20 March, at an extraordinary meeting of the Bar Association of Ludhiana passed the following resolution.[3]

'That in order to preserve the peaceful atmosphere that is obtaining at present in the country as the result of the Gandhi-Irwin settlement, the Bar Association of Ludhiana is of opinion that the death-sentences passed on Sardar Bhagat Singh, Rajguru and Sukhdev of the Lahore Conspiracy Case be commuted and requests His Excellency the Viceroy to exercise his special powers in the case of these convicts. It is further of opinion that the execution of death sentences of these persons is likely to bring about conditions not conducive to the welfare or the country'.

On 21 March, 1931, the members of the Naujawan Bharat Sabha organised a demonstration and procession in Lahore against the reported announcement of the jail authorities and the Tehsildar of Lahore to the relatives of Bhagat Singh, Rajguru and Sukhdev to have their last interview with the three condemned prisoners on 23 March. This news greatly stirred the public feeling in the city.[4] The procession started from Pari Mahal with red flags and banners and after passing through the principal streets and bazaars of the city, it terminated outside Mori Gate where a public meeting was held under the presidentship of Comrade Ram Chandra. The meeting was crowded and was attended by about three hundred ladies.[5]

Comrade Mangal Das moved a resolution strongly protesting against the reported decision of the government to hang Bhagat Singh , Rajguru and Sukhdev, demanding their release along with other political prisoners and opining that there would be no peace in the country until these prisoners, the Meerut Case accused, the martial law prisoners and the 1914-15 political prisoners were released. [6]

On 21 March the following letter was received by the relatives of Sukhdev from the Home Secretary, - Punjab Government, through the District Magistrate, Lyallpur. [7]

I have the honour to state that the Governor-General-in Council has rejected the mercy petition of the condemned prisoner Sukhdev. I, therefore, request that the relatives, whose address is given in the margin, may be informed to come interview him on the 23 March, 1931 at 11 a.m. This interview may be considered as final.

On 22 March, a huge mass meeting under the auspices of the Naujawan Bharat Sabha was held Jallianwala Bagh celebrate Bhagat Singh Day. Sardar Gurdit Singh was in the chair. Speeches were delivered by Sardar Pratap Singh, Baba Sohan Singh and others demanding commutation of death sentences of Bhagat Singh and others and release of all the political prisoners, no matter they were convicted of violence. [8]

Rai Bahadur Badri Dass, assisted by Lala Sham Lal, Advocate, appeared before Mr. Justice Bhide of the Lahore High Court to argue a petition for a writ of the *habeas corpus* and for leave to appeal the Privy Council. The Judge declined to hear the application for a writ of the *habeas corpus*, saying that he had already expressed his opinion on a similar petition.[9]

The Tribune commented, 'The Government will be committing a Himalayan blunder if they hang Bhagat Singh and his comrades. That is the feeling in the country.'[10]

The Gandhi camp also felt that if Bhagat Singh was executed, the country would be shaken to its foundations and the Karachi Congress itself might be swayed by the younger section. 'Mahatma Gandhi fears it will have unfavourable repercussion on the younger elements in the Congress....The country cries for mercy for these condemned prisoners.'[11]

On 20 March, 1931, Subhas Chandra Bose addressed an assembly of about 25,000 people in the Azad Maidan in Delhi.[12] The occasion was a mass meeting to protest against the imminent execution of Bhagat Singh and his comrades. The other leaders who attended this meeting were Mrs. Aruna Asaf Ali. Attaullah Shah Bukhari, Dr. Muhammad Alam, Sardar Mangal Singh, Sardar Sardul Sinch and Smt. Sarat Kumari Sinha mother of Bejoy Kumar Sinha.[13]

The main resolution of the meeting which deplored the imminent execution of these revolutionaries at that juncture as violating the spirit underlying the truce and prayed for commutation, was moved by Mrs. Aruna Asaf Ali.[14]

Subhas Chandra Bose during the course of his speech stated, 'The whole of India knows by this time that Bhagat Singh and his comrades, Rajguru and Sukhdev are going to be executed before long. I must say that the news came as a terrible shock to me when I alighted at Delhi station yesterday noon. . . . There is not the slightest doubt that the execution of Bhagat Singh and his comrades on the eve of the Karachi Congress will profoundly disturb the political atmosphere in India. . . . We demand with one voice and one will that the death sentences on Bhagat Singh and his comrades be at once commuted. Bhagat Singh is today not a person but a symbol. He symbolises the spirit of revolt which is abroad in the country We may condemn his methods, but we cannot ignore his selflessness.'

'Citing the instance of Mr. Mac-Swing, the Lord Mayor of Cork, who had gone on hunger-strike in jail and whom the

Government would not release despite the appeal of the people, and that of Seon Mackeon who had been sentenced to death and whom the Government released some time later in order that negotiations over the Irish question would begin in an atmosphere of peace and goodwill, Mr. Bose warned the Government that it was not acting up to the spirit underlying the truce and that it was undoing to the very great extent the atmosphere of goodwill which Mahatmaji had been able to bring about.[15]

On the same day, a deputation on behalf of the working committee of the Naujawan Bharat Sabha waited on Gandhi. They impressed on him that they could not be any party to the truce unless the death sentences of Bhagat Singh and his comrades were commuted.[16]

On 21 March, 1931, R.B. Badri Das, Advocate, filed an application for leave to appeal to the Privy Council under Clause 31 of the Letters Patent, against the order of Mr. Justice Bhide who held that Bhagat Singh and his comrades were being in legal custody.[17] It was prayed that the court might declare that the case was a fit one for an appeal to their Lordships of the Privy Council under Clause 31 of the Letters Patent.[18]

Besides, Badri Dass filed an application on behalf of Sardar Kulbir Singh, brother of Bhagat Singh for a writ of *habeas corpus* praying that Bhagat Singh, Shivram Rajguru and Sukhdev be brought up before this court and dealt with recording to the law.[19]

On 23 March, a deadlock had resulted the matter of an interview of the relatives of Bhagat Singh and his comrades owing to certain conditions imposed by the jail authorities, restricting the number of their blood relations.[20] With the stroke of ten, almost all the blood relations of three patriots reported themselves at the gate of the Central Jail. Sardar Kishan Singh was there with all the male and female members of his family, including the octogenarian grandfather and grandmother of Bhagat Singh, his brothers, the youngest being ten years old, sisters and about half-a-dozen blood relations with children. Chint Ram Thapar, uncle of Sukhdev came with two lorry-ful of blood relations from Lyallpur. a distance of about eighty miles. Owing to the shortness of time, two brothers of Rajguru were unable to be present, only his aged mother was present.[21]

The Superintendent of Central Jail permitted an interview only to the father, mother and two brothers of Bhagat Singh, the mother and brother of Sukhdev and the mother of Rajguru.[22]

Chint Ram Thapar who had written orders from the Chief Secretary, Punjab Government for interview, sister and other relations who had come from all over the province were not allowed as a result thereof, they refused to have an interview as a protest. The mother of Rajguru also did the same in sympathy.[23]

After about three hours fruitless waiting outside the jail gate in scorching heat, the relatives of Bhagat Singh and others returned home without having any interview.[24]

Soon after this unfortunate and unexpected episode, telegrams were sent to the Viceroy, Home Member, Punjab Government and others intimating developments which ran thus. 'Relatives of Bhagat Singh, Sukhdev, Rajguru went Central Jail for last interview. Authorities refused permission except father, mother, brother. Other blood relations unallowed contrary expressed Jail Manual rules. Pray interfere and allow interview to all near relations who came from distant places this being last occasion.[25]

Dr. Gopi Chand Bhargava sent the following telegram to the District Magistrate, Lahore, Superintendent, Lahore Central Jail, and the Chief Secretary to the Government of the Punjab.[26]

'Bhagat Singh, Rajguru and Sukhdev hanged this evening. Where and when should we present for taking the dead bodies? Wire. Sardar Kishan Singh, father of Sardar Bhagat Singh and mothers of Rajguru and Sukhdev are at Lahore.'[27]

Sardar Kishan Singh and Lala Chint Ram, uncle of Sukhdev with a few others went to see a high official of the Central Jail, Lahore for claiming the dead bodies and it is said though he was at home he sent word that he was not at home. At the Central Jail too he was not found. Thereafter, a high local official who ought to know, was phoned to; and he began speaking on the phone, but when he knew what it was about he gave no reply and closed the phone.[28]

A responsible official in the Secretariat was contracted on telephone. His peon replied that he was at home, and an Englishman attended to the phone. But when he heard who it was that was phoning he replied that Mr.–was not in at all and he did not know when he would come back. This was at about 3-30 or 9 p.m.[29]

At this, the relatives of the prisoners went to the gate of the Jail and though a number of jail officials and wardens were standing about, nobody was willing to give any definite reply.[30]

On 24 March, 1931, at about 1 a.m. notices signed by the District Magistrate, Lahore were pasted in various parts of the city announcing that the bodies of Bhagat Singh, Sukhdev and Rajguru had been cremated according to Sikh and Hindu rites on the banks of the Satluj.[31]

The issue of *The Tribune* dated 25 March, 1931 reported on the front page : 'Bhagat Singh, Rajguru and Sukhdev executed. No last interview with relations. Shouts emerge from Jail. Dead bodies secretly disposed of. Removed to distant place.'[32]

Jai Dev Gupta narrates a shocking incident connected with the death of Bhagat Singh and his associates. 'After the hanging, when the bodies had not been given, the fear was that they were taken out somewhere for cremation. The situation was very tense. Everybody was sad, sullen and angry. People were moving here and there and also watching the outskirts of the city. At Bradlaugh Hall, one information centre had been formed. I was incharge there. His sister Amar Kaur was there. The daughter of Lala Lajpat Rai was also there and so were a few persons, two or three, not more than that. It was decided that if anything came to their knowledge, it would be communicated to the information centre at Bradlaugh Hall. Early in the morning of 24 March, two volunteers came from Ferozepur and informed that the bodies had been cremated on the banks of the river Satluj. These two volunteers, one more person and I, we four, without giving any rise to suspicion started after telling Amar Kaur to inform her father that they should follow us, just after an hour or so, so that there might not be any crowd which might give rise to suspicion to the police.

We four of us boarded the train at Lahore and got down at Ganda Singhwalla railway station. . . We got down there and from there the volunteers took us to the river. First we went to the upper side of the river, then climbed down to the banks where the river was flowing. They told us that that could be the place because they had seen fire at a distance. . . . So we decided to take off our shoes and after that we began to walk over the sand. One place was warm—rather hot. We dug there a big round hole and after digging about a yard, there arose a very strong stench of kerosene and we found a bone here. Some bones here, some bones there; some flesh here and some flesh there. In the meantime, Amar Kaur also came there with many other people and whatever was available, was taken out. But there was one bone, probably it could be the forearm from the elbow to the wrist, it was out in a diagonal form at the wrist. The bone was not charred nor was it showing a sign of burning. 1 could not understand the matter. . . . The bone was rather very long. Probably, it was Bhagat Singh's because he was tallest of the three.

'....I did not give that bone to anybody. I kept that bone with me. We all returned and a large procession was taken out and that bone was given to Dr. Gopi Chand Bhargava and Dr. Satyapal. . . . They examined it. Of course, they were also surprised. . . . Ultimately, the enquiry commission came to the conclusion that the cut was not intentional, it was incidental.[33]

The Tribune commented in a befitting manner, on 26 March, 1931, 'India deeply moved over Bhagat Singh's execution. Demonstrations all over the country. Prayers, Processions and *hartals*. Funeral procession in Lahore. Cremation on bank of Ravi.[34]

The news of the execution of the three patriots spread like wild fire throughout Lahore. Youngmen took out processions throughout night shouting '*Inqilab Zindabad*' and Bhagat Singh *Zindabad*. There was again *hartal* on 24 March. Even fruit shops and Sabzi Mandi also remained closed. The local colleges and schools including the D.A.V. College, S.D. College, Dayal Singh College, Law College and F.C. College remained closed.[35]

The spacious parade ground was filled with bareheads from end to end and the gathering looked like a seething mass of humanity. Over 30,000 people, Hindu, Sikhs and Muslims, including about 5000 women joined the prayers. As Sardar and Sardarni Kishan Singh accompanied by other relatives entered the meeting place, they were received amidst thundering shouts of Bhagat Singh *Zindabad*, Bhagat Singh *Suragbas*'... Similar ovations were accorded to the next-of-kins of Rajguru and Sukhdev. Men and women sobbed and wept bitterly, several of them fainted and others quietly removed tears trickling down their eyes. Maulana Zafar Ali Khan offered prayers amidst solemn silence. He invoked the blessings of the Most High for the peace of the souls of Bhagat Singh, Rajguru and Sukhdev. He also appealed for communal unity and national solidarity. Many students were wearing black bands on their left arms as a sign of mourning. Instead of tri-colour national flag two huge black flags were waving at the place of prayer meeting.[36]

Over 40,000 persons including about 5,000 ladies, mostly dressed in black *saris* and wearing black scarves joined the demonstration in connection with the executions of three patriots.[37] A two mile long procession with black flags started from Nila Gumbad and passed in solemn silence through Anarkali Bazaar, Lahori Gate, Shahalmi Gate Bazaar, Rang Mahal, Lange Mandi, Hira Mandi, Ravi Road and terminated on the banks of the Ravi. As far as the eye could reach, a vast sea of bare heads was visible. The younger sections of the processionists refused to follow the programme of the Congress regarding a silent procession and they now and then broke the silence by raising shouts of '*Inqilab Zindabad*', 'Bhagat Singh Zindabad,' Rajguru Zindabad' and 'Sukhdev Zindabad'.[38]

When the procession was passing through Paper Mandi, news was brought that the ashes and chaired remains of Bhagat Singh, Rajguru and Sukhdev had been brought by their relatives from the banks of the Satluj near Ferozepur and that they would be carried in *arthis*[39] bedecked with flowers. At about 3-30 p.m. three flower bedecked *arthis* carrying the remains of three patriots were brought out from Pan Mahal amidst unparalleled enthusiasm. Prominent Congressmen, members of the Naujawan Bharat Sabha and students of local colleges carried the *arthis* on their shoulders and everybody in the procession made frantic efforts to touch the *arthis*. Flowers and rose water were showered on the *arthis* by men and women throughout the route. Mothers of Bhagat Singh, Sukhdev and Rajguru were conspicuous figures in the procession.[40]

The procession reached the banks of the river just after sun-set. Here arrangements had already been made for a public meeting. The vast gathering reminded the people of Lahore of similar scenes on the death of Lala Lajpat Rai.[41]

The meeting began at about 7-30 p.m. Mehta Anand Kishore was in the chair. A resolution was moved from the chair strongly condemning the executions of the three patriots characterising them as illegal and expressing indignation at the manner in which the dead bodies were disposed of at midnight far away from Lahore. There were no speeches and the resolution was passed amidst repeated shouts of 'Bhagat Singh Zindabad, Pandit Parshu Ram Sharma then read the messages of Mahatma Gandhi and Jawaharlal Nehru on the executions.[42]

Sardar Kishan Singh who on rising to speak received a thundering ovation, related in detail how the dead bodies were carried in lorries from the Lahore Central Jail and cremated on the banks of the river Satluj near the village Ganda Singhwala with kerosene oil. When he stated that several lorries full of British soldiers acompanied the dead bodies and before they were cremated, their bodies were dismembered and the charred remains thrown away in different places, the vast audience, particularly the relatives of the three patriots and the ladies began to sob and burst into tears. Many men and women actually fainted and there were numerous touching scenes in the audience. There were loud cries of 'Shame, Shame' from all sides of the vast gathering. Maulana Zafar Ali Khan then recited a poem composed for the occasion. What were described as the charred remains of the dead bodies were then cremated with due religious ceremonies.[43]

Bejoy Kumar, one of the close associates[44] of Bhagat Singh paid a befiting tribute to his memory.[45] 'Bhagat Singh laid down his life for the great socialist cause. He was, above all, a crusader for the socialist cause....His eventful revolutionary life dramatically symbolised the rising temper of the fighting Indian people. . . In personal life, Sardar Bhagat Singh was noted for his lovable nature. He had the temperament of an artist and has eyes would not miss to see the subtle side of things. He was an intellectual and it was his deep intellect blended with his extremely sensitive nature, to make him one of the finest specimens of India's revolutionary youths. As for the spirit of self-sacrifice, he had it in abundance. He was ever ready to die for the cause of the revolutionary movement.

Comrade Shiv Varma[46] another associate of Bhagat Singh, called him a true symbol of martyrdom. He believed for instance. that he task of leading and carrying forward the freedom struggle would fall to the workers and peasants, to the common people led by the proletariat and a party based on the masses and relying on the teachings of Marx.[47]

Under the auspices of the City Congress Committee, Amritsar Subhas Chandra Bose paid tributes to Sardar Bhagat Singh on 8 April, 1931.[48] He advised the youngmen. 'Their fight would be resumed shortly and therefore they should keep in readiness for that.... In the end the speaker remarked that Long Live Revolution. The people, he said, would have to change their views and would have to take the revolutionary ideas. This was the struggle of the youngmen but the general public would also have to change their view; therefore, their programme was to create revolutionary views in India. When this was done, they would be securing *Swaraj* soon. The youngmen had done it and they had to suffer considerably.'

To perpetuate their memory in a most befitting manner, an All-India Bhagat Singh—Rajguru—Sukh Dev Memorial Committee with headquarters at Anarkali Paisa Akhbar Street, 'Lahore' was formed. Anand Kishore Mehta was its General Secretary. In a letter, which was intercepted by the police, to Jamna Lal Bajaj, the General Secretary narrated the aims and objects of this committee. 'I have the honour to inform you that on 28 April, 1931 a meeting was held in the Bradlaugh Hall, Labore, in order to form an All-India Martyrs Memorial Committee. Invitations were sent to the All-India Leaders and other public workers to attend the meeting. Besides others the following gentlemen attended the meeting.

1. Dr. Satyapal. 2. Baba Nihal Singh. 3. L. Pindi Das. 4. Mehta Anand Kishore. 5. Sardar Kishan Singh. 6. G.S. Mangal Singh. 7. Sant Mangal Singh. 8. Maulvi Abdul Ghani. 9. L. Pirthi Chand of Ferozepur. 10. Dr. Mohammad Alam. 11. Dr. Dharam Vir. 12. S. Gopal Singh. 13. S. Sardul Singh.[49]

Besides these, telegrams and letters were received from Dr. Ansari, Satya Murti, Sen Gupta, expressing full sympathy with the Memorial and praying for its success.

Proposed by Dr. Satyapal and seconded by Mr. Abdul Ghani, Baba Nihal Singh was unanimously elected as President of the meeting.

The following resolutions were passed :

1. That in order to immortalise the memory of the martyrs an All-India Memorial be established, and a Committee be formed to collect funds and to give a form and shape to the Memorial. That the name of the Committee will be the All-India Bhagat Singh—Rajguru—Sukhdev Memorial Committee.
2. All those persons who pay the sum of Rs. 50 to the Memorial fund either from their own pocket, or by collection from their friends, can become members of the Committee.
3. That an appeal for Rs. 10 lacs be made to the country for this Memorial.
4. To carry on the work of the memorial a provisional working committee was formed.
5. A publicity bureau was formed consisting of the following gentlemen.

    1. Dr. Satyapal Convener. 2. Pt. Mani Lal Kalia. 3. Sardar Gopal Singh Kaumi. 4. L. Pindi Dass.

6. The following office-bearers were selected:

    (a) Mehta Anand Kishore, General Secretary; (b) Maulvi Abdul Ghani; (c) Sardar Kartar Singh; (d) Shrimati Sushila Ghosh—Secretaries.

7. All the accounts of the Memorial Committee should be kept with 1. The Punjab National Bank Ltd., Lahore. 2. The Central Bank of India Ltd., Lahore. 3. The Peoples Bank of Northern India Ltd., Lahore.
8. Mehta Anand Kishore, Dr. Satyapal and Baba Nihal Singh were appointed as operators; any two of those operators must sign a cheque in order to draw it from the bank.

To give a form to the Memorial the following proposals have been received.

1. To build a workers' home and a lecture hall. 2. To found library and a reading room. 3. To maintain a permanent fund with the interest of which to relieve the sufferings of the political prisoners and to help their families. 4. To maintain another permanent fund with the interest or which to conduct the defence of political cases. To publish political literature.[50]

When approached by Anand Kishore for help, assistance and guidance in this task, Gandhi wrote, 'I have your letter of the 13th instant. Your reasoning does not appeal to me at all. A memorial erected in honour of anybody undoubtedly means that the memorialists would copy the deads of those in whose memory they erect the memorial. It is also an invitation to posterity to copy such deeds. I am, therefore, unable to identify myself in any way with the memorial.'[51]

The Punjab Government had prescribed two or three appeals issued in connection with the proposal and it had also seized a number of printed copies. 'They are keeping a close watch for any opportunity to prosecute any person who comes within the mischief of law in regard to the proposal.'[52] H. Williamson of the Home Department took a serious note of these activities and wrote, 'At the same time it is obvious that there is a definite plan to erect buildings etc. in honour of men whose sole claim to fame is that they murdered police officers. I do not think any Government in the world should allow this and I am of the opinion that if there is no provision of law to stop it, some special provision should be made. It would, I think, be unwise to wait until funds have been collected and building has started, and I suggest that the Punjab Government be consulted as to the measures which should be taken to prevent the eretion of any memorial and, preferably, to break up this Memorial Committee. It is possible, of course, that the people who are out to collect funds are themselves on the money-make and that nothing much will materialise, but I still consider that this is the time to decide what action should be taken in the event of the work of the Committee materialising.[53]

Five days after the Gandhi-lrwin Pact, Nehru made a speech at Allahabad on 10 March, 1931 in which he clarified a few significant issues about Sardar Bhagat Singh. It signified Nehru's sense of optmism.[54] 'We made every effort for release of such prisoners as Bhagat Singh and we have every hope that our effort will be successful. If we had been obstinate in asking for the immediate release of Bhagat Singh, he would perhaps have been hanged by now. If he is alive still, it is because of Mahatma Gandhi's effort, and if he and other prisoners guilty of violence are eventually released it would be due to Mahatma Gandhi's effort.[55]

On the eve of the execution of Bhagat Singh, Rajguru and Sukhdev, Nehru expressed his sense of grief in an All India Students' Convention assembled at Karachi in the historic session of the Indian National Congress.[56] He felt much perturbed by the tragic happenings in the country and frankly confessed that the execution of Bhagat Singh and his comrades was a reminder of their inability to protect brave and patriotic young-men. I have also heard in the afternoon of the tragic happenings at Cawnpore, culminating in a large number of death....The tragedy at Cawnpore is an abject lesson that violence, though we may use it with the best of motives is apt to recoil on us and lead to internecine conflict. . . . Youngmen must envisage a new order of things and remove the evils which make progress impossible. Youngmen must remember that 'freedom' and 'independence' are mere words till a new order is fashioned which ends inequalities, exploitation and religious bigotry.[57]

The Hindustan Ghadr Party, San Francisco branch in a pictorial, 'Message of the Martyrs : A Call to Arms', paid glowing tributes to the three patriots.[58]

Another black and bloody chapter has been added to the already criminal record of the British imperialism in India. On the 23 March, 1931, the inhuman and heartless British bureaucracy ruthlessly guillotined, nay murdered in cold blood, our three young patriots, Bhagat Singh, Rajguru and Sukhdev. All entreaties and petitions for mercy were haughtily rejected and the beloved of the land were separated from us forever, without the least regard for the feelings of 350 millions of Indians and the enlightened world.

'If we really want to put an end to these dastardly outrages to humanity at large and to Indian man and womanhood in particular, if we have the least desire to see our Motherland freed from the bloody foreign yoke, there is only one way left to us. It is to 'wake up and hearken to the clear and unmistakable clarion call of the martyrs— 'A Call to Arms' a call to shake off indolence and cowardice, a call to come to close grips with the British Imperialism and drive it to the wall at the sharp point of the sword; a call to live like free men or perish in the struggle of freedom, because a heroic death is far, far better than the life of a slave.'[59]

In an interview with the Viceroy on 18 February, 1931, Gandhi discussed about Bhagat Singh. I talked about Bhagat Singh. I told him. "This has no connection with our discussion, and it may even be inappropriate on my part to mention it. But if you want to make the present atmosphere more favourable, you should suspend Bhagat Singh's execution." The Viceroy liked this very much. He said, 'I am very grateful to you that you have put this thing before me in this manner. Commutation of sentence is a difficult thing, but suspension is certainly worth considering.'

I said about Bhagat Singh "He is undoubtedly a brave man but I would certainly say that he is not in his right mind. However, this is the evil of capital punishment that it gives no opportunity to such a man to reform himself. I am putting this matter before you as a humanitarian issue and desire suspension of sentence in order that there may not be unnecessary turmoil in the country. I myself would release him but I cannot expect any Government to do so. I would not take it, if you do not give any reply on this issue."[60]

On 7 March, 1931, while addressing a mass meeting attended by over 50,000 persons at Delhi, Gandhi stated, 'The next question is about Bhagat Singh and others who are under sentence to death. How can there be peace, I am asked, when a sentence of death is hanging over the heads of these patriots? It is unfortunate that the youngmen distributing these pamphlets should not understand such a simple thing. They ought to understand that we have entered into no peace treaty. It is a provisional temporary settlement we have arrived at. I beseech the youngmen not to bid good-bye to common-sense, to cool courage, to patience, to reason. I have claimed to be a youngman of 62. But even if I were to be labelled as a dilapidated old fogey, I have a right to appeal to your good sense. I do not want you to take for granted all that old men say to you, but I want you to consider it and weigh it, and it you find that we 'old' men have bungled, that we have been guilty of weakness get us to abdicate, and assume the reins yourselves. But that presupposes cool courage and solid common sense.

But let me tell you why Bhagat Singh and the rest have not been released. May be, if you had been negotiating you might have secured better terms from the Viceroy, but we the Working Committee would secure no more than what we have. I may tell you that throughout the negotiations, I was not acting on my own, I was backed by the whole Working Committee. We brought all the pressure we could to bear on our negotiations and satisfied ourselves with what in justice we could have under the provisional settlement. We could not as negotiators of the provisional truce forget our pledge of truth and non-violence, forget the bounds of justice.

But it is still open to us to secure the release of all you have named—and that can be done if you will implement the settlement. Let 'Young India' stand by the settlement and fulfil all its conditions, and if, God willing, Bhagat Singh and others are alive when we have arrived at the proper stage, they would not only be saved from the gallows but released.

But I will address to 'Young India' a word of warning. These things are sooner asked for than obtained. You want to secure the freedom of those condemned of violence. There is nothing wrong about it. My creed of non-violence does not favour the punishment of thieves and dacoits and even murderers. I cannot in all conscience agree to anyone being sent to gallows, much less a brave man like Bhagat Singh. But I tell you, even you could not save them unless you fulfil the conditions of the settlement. You cannot do so by violent means. If you pin your faith to violence, take it from me that you will not only not secure Bhagat Singh's release but will have to sacrifice thousands of Bhagat Singh. I was not prepared to do so, and hence I preferred me way of peace, of non-violence. The way that you have adopted has been on trial for centuries and history records numerous instances of the truth that those who use the sword perish by the sword. You will not stop at using the violent weapon against your rulers, you will use it against your brothers and sisters too, and others of your way of thinking.

I beseech you then, if you want the release of prisoners, to change your methods, to accept the settlement, and then come and ask me about the Garhwalis and Bhagat Singh. Come to me six months hence, after you have implemented the settlement and gained in strength, and ask me the question you are asking today and I promise to satisfy you.[61]

In another interview between Gandhi and Irwin,on19 March, 1931, the latter mentioned thus, 'As he was leaving, he (Gandhi) asked if he might mention the case of Bhagat Singh, saying that he had seen in the press that intimation of his execution for March 24. This was an unfortunate day, as it coincided with the arrival of the new President of the Congress at Karachi and there would be much popular excitement'.

I told him I had considered the case with most anxious care, but could find no grounds on which I could justify to my conscience commuting the sentence. As to the date, I had considered the possibility of postponement till after the Congress, but had deliberately rejected it on various grounds :

(i) that postponement of execution, merely on political grounds, when orders had been passed seemed to me improper;

(ii) that postponement was inhuman in that it would suggest to the friends and relatives that I was considering commutation; and

(iii) that Congress would have been able legitimately to complain that they had been tricked by Government.

'He (Gandhi) appeared to appreciate the force of these arguments, and said no more.'[62]

In a press interview on 21 March 1931, Gandhi was asked about his views on execution of Bhagat Singh and the safety of his life. To a question, 'Do you expect to hold the National Congress to the terms of the truce with Lord Irwin,' he replied, 'Yes, but if Bhagat Singh is hanged, as it now seems almost certain, it may have highly unfavourable repercussions upon the younger element in the Congress who may attempt to slip the Congress.' And to another question in the same interview, 'Do you entertain any hope that Bhagat Singh may be saved at the last minute?' he replied, 'Yes, but it is a very distant hope.'[63]

The next day, Gandhi wrote a letter to the Viceroy and pleaded for Bhagat Singh and his associates. He stated, 'It seems cruel to inflict this letter on you, but the interest of peace demands a final appeal. Though you were frank enough to tell me that there was little hope of your commuting the sentence of death on Bhagat Singh and two others, you said you would consider my submission of Saturday, Dr. Sapru met me yesterday and said that you were troubled over the matter and taxing your brain as to the proper course to adopt. If there is any room left for reconsideration to the following.

Popular opinion rightly or wrongly demands communication. When there is no principle at stake, it is often a duty to respect it.

In the present case the chances are that, if commutation is granted, internal peace is most likely to be promoted. In the event of execution, peace is undoubtedly in danger.[64]

Seeing that I am able to inform you that the revolutionary party has assured me that, in the event of these lives being spared, that party will stay its hands, suspension of sentence pending cessation of revolutionary murders becomes in my opinion a peremptory duty.

Political murders have been condoned before now. It is worthwhile saving these lives, if thereby many other innocent lives are likely to be saved and may be even revolutionary crime almost stamped out.

Since you seem to value of my influence such as it is in favour of peace, do not please unnecessarily make my position difficult as it is, almost too difficult for future work.

Execution is an irretrievable act. If you think there is the slightest chance of error of judgment, I would urge you to suspend for further review an act that is beyond recall.

If my presence is necessary, I can come. Though I may not speak I may hear and write what I want to say.[65]

To this letter, the Viceroy replied, 'I have again thought very carefully over everything that you have said—and the last thing 1 should wish to do would be to make your task, especially at this juncture, more difficult. But I am afraid, for the reasons I sought to explain fully to you in conversation, I cannot see my way to feel that it would be right to take the action you request.'[66]

It seems from the tone of his letter that the Viceroy was not to heed to any kind of request, not even of the greatest leader of India *i.e.* Gandhi, of suspending or commuting the sentence awarded to Bhagat Singh and his associates. Under these circumstances the law was to take its own course.

On the day of execution of Bhagat Singh and his two associates, Sukhdev and Rajguru, Gandhi gave a statement in which he paid glowing tribute to the young revolutionary leaders who sacrificed their lives while waging an open war-violent in its nature, contents and effects—against the British Raj.

Bhagat Singh and his companions have been executed and have become martyrs. Their death seems to have been a personal loss to many. I Join in the tributes paid to the memory of these youngmen. And yet I must warn the youth of the country against following their example. We should not utilise the energy, our spirit of sacrifice, our labours and our indomitable courage in the way they have utilised theirs. This country must not be liberated through bloodshed.

About the Government I cannot help feeling that it has missed a golden opportunity to win over the rebels to its side. At least from the point of view of the settlement, it was its duty to postpone indefinitely the carrying out of the death sentence. The Government has by its own act dealt a severe blow to the settlement and has shown its capacity to disregard public opinion once again and to exhibit the great brute strength it possesses.

The reliance on violence is perhaps ominous and it suggests that inspite of high-sounding and pious proclamation, it does not want to part with power. But the people's duty is clear.

The Congress must not swerve from the path it has chalked out for itself. According to my view, notwithstanding the gravest provocation the Congress should endorse the settlement and test its capacity to secure the result hoped for.

We must not put ourselves in the wrong by getting angry. We must realise that communication of the sentences was not a part of the truce. We may accuse the Government of violence but we cannot accuse it of breach of the settlement. It is my conviction that the grave blunder committed by the Government has increased our power to win freedom and Bhagat Singh and his comrades have embraced death therefore. Let us not throw away this opportunity by doing anything in anger. It is beyond dispute that there will be a general strike and we cannot honour the deceased patriots better than by taking but absolutely peaceful and dignified procession.[67]

In the *Navajivan* dated 29 March, 1931, Gandhi gave vent to his sentiments in an article, entitled 'Bhagat Singh'.

Bhagat Singh and his two associates have been hanged. Many attempts were made to save their lives and even some hopes were entertained, but all was in vain.

Bhagat Singh did not wish to live. He refused to apologise; declined to file an appeal. If at all he would agree to live, he would do so for the sake of others; if at all he would agree to it, it would be in order that his death might not provide anyone to indiscriminate murder. Bhagat Singh was not a devotee of non-violence, but he did not subscribe to the religion of violence; he was prepared to commit murder out of a sense of helplessness. His last letter was as follows : 'I have been arrested while waging a war. For me there can be no gallows. Put me into the mouth of a cannon and blow me off.' These heroes had conquered the fear of death. Let us bow to them a thousand times for their heroism.

But we should not imitate their act. I am not prepared to believe that the country has benefited by their action. I can see only the harm that has been done. We could have won *swaraj* long ago if that line of action had not been pursued and we could have waged a purely non-violent struggle. There may be two opinions on this conjecture of mine. However, no one can deny the fact that if the practice of seeking justice through murders is established amongst us, we shall start murdering one another for what we believe to be justice. In a land of crores of destitutes and crippled persons, this will be a terrifying situation. Those poor people are bound to become victims of our atrocities. It is desirable that everyone should consider the consequence of this. Further, we want a *swaraj* which is theirs and for them. By making a *dharna* of violence, we shall be reaping the fruit of our own actions. Hence, though we praise the courage of these youngmen, we should never countenance their activities.

By hanging these men, the Government has demonstrated its own brute nature, it has proved fresh proof of its arrogance resulting from its power by ignoring public opinion. From this hanging it may be concluded that it is not the intention of the Government to part with any real power to the people. The Government certainly had the right to hang these men....On this occasion, the Government would have brought credit to itself if it had not exercised its rights and this would have been highly useful in maintaining peace.

'....While negotiating the settlement, Bhagat Singh's hanging was weighing upon us. We had hoped that the Government would be cautious enough to pardon Bhagat Singh and his associates to the extent of remitting the sentence of hanging. We should not break the pledge, we have taken just because our hopes have not been fulfilled, but should bear this blow which has fallen upon us and honour our pledge....Hence our dharma is to swallow our anger, abide by the settlement and carry out our duty.[68]

Under the title, 'The Cult of Violence,' Gandhi wrote an article in *Young India* on 16 April, and condemned the deed performed with the philosophy of violence.[69]

The deed was condemned. The spirit of bravery and sacrifice was praised. The hope behind was that we would thereby be able to distinguish between the deed and the motive, and ultimately learn to detest deeds such as political murders, no matter how high the motive might be.

In a letter to Darcy Lindsay from Sabarmati Ashram on 8 May, 1931, Gandhi gave his opinion thus :

'....The matter you refer to is very delicate. There is romance around the life of Bhagat Singh. He was no coward. From all enquiries made by me I find that he was a man of spotless character and of great daring. Somehow or other he had developed a belief that political association had its use. It was impossible not to notice the execution, I believe quite unwise, of Bhagat Singh and his comrades, whom the execution made martyrs. I have no doubt whatsoever that the execution has surrounded these lives with a halo which they would no otherwise have had. The only thing therefore that was possible and that the Congress was bound to do was to pass a resolution condemning murderous deeds as also the execution and at the same time appreciating the bravery and sacrifice underlying such deeds. I however quite agree with you that there is undoubtedly a great deal of thoughtless approval of political murder. But many of us are doing everything we can to counteract the growth of the violent revolutionary movement.'

In June 1931, Gandhi wrote an article in *Young India* and gave vent to his feelings on revolutionaries.[70]

'I have already expressed my doubts as to the propriety of my having drafted and sponsored the Bhagat Singh revolution not because it was wrong in principle, but for the misinterpretation it has but itself to. But the reader must know that it was neither the fear of the Naujavans nor my love for Pandit Jawahalal that prompted me to initiate the resolution. Not that I should be ashamed of yielding to Naujavans or placating Jawaharlal. I should be foolish if I did not yield to Naujavans, if yielding advanced the interest of the country and involved no sacrifice principle. And I should go a very long way to please Jawaharlal and retain his affection which I have the privilege of possessing in abundance. But there was no prompting required in this case. I had interested myself in the movement for the commutation of the death sentence on Bhagat Singh and his comrades. I had put my whole being into the task... I had to come in contact with his devoted father and those who were attached to Bhagat Singh not for his deed but for his character. I am thus drawn to the resolution in the natural course. I am too sensitive not to be moved by circumstances demanding sympathy.' Bhagat Singh indeed became a symbol for the people of India.[71] His name and fame stepped into the portals of each and every dwelling.

Sardar Gulab Singh who had been an associate of Bhagat Singh reminised in connection with the scenes in Lahore Jail and the hangings of the great patriots.[72]

'The Three Comrades lay waiting for death in their cells. From the four corners of the country rose a roar in favour of commutation of the death sentences. Mahatma Gandhi, Pandit Motilal Nehru and other leaders were on their feet struggling to save the lives of these patriots. The dumb millions of our country gathered in thousands and thousands, in cities, in towns, in villages, and urged upon the government to stop the executions. There was no organisation left that had not put in an appeal with the authorities. Men of all creeds and persuasions, of all classes, professions and sects, joined in bringing pressure on the government. Innumerable appeals and wide sympathy poured in even from foreign countries. But here it was an alien government. It spurned the voice of the millions.

But hope is one of those clinging feelings that does not leave the human breast till the very end, and millions kept on hoping.

Our lives hanged by a thin thread and the increase in the number of police and military guards around us in the Central Jail repeatedly reminded us how chimerical were the hopes of our countrymen. There were growing signs that the executions were not far off.

A plum tree was there outside the gate of the condemned cells adding to the eerie atmosphere. Underneath it, we daily stood in solemn silence before going to the court. This is where we were searched both before being taken to the court or brought back. We became emotionally attached to the spot; it made us highly conscious of the proximity of our three condemned patriots. In the cells our eyes would search in vain for them, even the outer doors were shut at the time of our coming and going.

All of us had begun attending the court those days. Some would come back earlier than usual in the hope of getting a glimpse of our condemned comrades when they are taken out into the open courtyard for short spells in the day. Even this meagre contact was only rare. Any day, any hour, any moment might bring them the signal to offer their youthful lives at the altar of freedom.

A prisoner, who had to visit, in the course of his duties, our wards some time also acted as our messenger. One day we sent a message to Sardar Bhagat Singh, expressing our still lingering though faint hope that expectations of our countrymen might come true and they might be saved. Bhagat Singh sent back in reply a couplet of Iqbal written in Urdu on a piece of paper.

A few moments more and I go out like a wick of the lamp in the morning.

No false hopes, no weakening of the resolve to die with a smile, a steeled heart, a courageous mind, and anreous thinking, no illusions, no wavering, no flickering like a wick of the lamp, but a continuous flame emitting abundant heat and light till the last extinguishing blow that was what I read in the lines of the poet scribbled by Bhagat Singh.

What a tragedy it was, what a killing suffocation that none of us living so near could be allowed to see these youngmen-and know their thoughts, their views, their feelings in the hour of their impending death. A cruel machine was to crush them to death unfeelingly. They were allowed no human contact with the outside world during all this period when they waited for death in their cells.

And the day came—the evening of the March 23, 1931. It was just before sunset. Executions always take place in the morning. But this time-honoured practice was set aside in the case of these youngmen: All of us, all the prisoners, were locked inside the cells in the afternoon. A top officer was visiting the jail, we were told. It struck us that the officer might be coming to inspect the condemned cells. We listened.

No sound came from Ward No. 15. Not a soul moved in the jail. Such a weird silence was portentous. The invisible death was stalking the place.

Uneasiness, suspicion, curiosity filled the air. The warders stood mute outside the locked barracks and cells. The officers of the jail one by one, came and went round the place. Time ticked by. An hour-and-a-half passed. Then we heard the voice of Sardar Bhagat Singh informing his two companions "They have come!"

The three of them shouted thrice the "Long Live Revolution!" We from our cell echoed them.

Hardly five minutes passed and they were on the gallows. We could only hear the crashing sound of the falling plank. The million hopes dashed to the ground.

Hearing the thud of the plank, we in our furry began to shout revolutionary slogans and shake the barred doors of our cells. The people living in the bungalows across the jail road guessed from the noise and commotion inside the jail what had happened.

Several high-ranking officials attended the executions. The bodies were taken out but not through the main gate. They were removed through the smithy adjoining the building where the Special Tribunal trying us held its sessions. The bodies were not handed over to the relatives or friends of the martyrs but taken in lorries to the bank of the Satluj where even before they were fully cremated they were thrown into the river.

A pursuit party that followed in cars the lorries carrying the bodies found some charred and mutilated remains of the martyrs on the bank of the Satluj.

These facts about the treatment meted out to our brave comrades we learnt from the next day's papers.

Every jail employee who met us paid glowing tributes to the courage of the three patriots in the moment of the execution. There was none who had not had admiration, sympathy and a word of praise. Most of the prisoners fasted, many prayed for the martyrs. Not a soul left unaffected by the tragedy. Many a warder wept by relating the tales of these patriots' prison days. Some had been on duty in the condemned cells. Some had been near them during their undertrial period. The sympathies were typical of the common man.

'The whole nation was stirred to its very depths. The same helpless grief, the same burning indignation. A gloom set on India. The whole country went in mourning.'

REFERENCES

1. Quoted in Home Poll, Pile 4/21, 1931.
2. *Ibid.*
3. *The Tribune*, 24 March, 1931.
4. *Ibid.*
5. *Ibid.*
6. *Ibid.*
7. *The Tribune*, 24 March, 1931.
8. *Ibid.*
9. *The Tribune*, 25 March, 1931.
10. *The Tribune*, 24 March, 1931.
11. *Ibid.*
12. *Ibid.*
13. *Ibid.*
14. *Ibid.*
15. *Ibid.*

15. *Ibid.*
16. *Ibid.*
17. *Ibid.*
18. *Ibid.*
19. *Ibid.*
20. *The Tribune,* 25 March, 1931.
21. *Ibid.*
22. *Ibid.*
23. *Ibid.*
24. *Ibid.*
25. *Ibid.*
26. *Ibid.*
27. *Ibid.*
28. *Ibid.*
29. *Ibid.*
30. *Ibid.*
31. *The Tribune*, 26 March, 1931.
32. *Ibid:*
33. Transcript of Interview with Jai Dev Gupta, *op.cit.*
34. The Tribune, 26 March, 1931.
35. *Ibid.*
36. *Ibid.*
37. *Ibid.*
38. *Ibid.*
39. Biers.
40. *The Tribune*, 26 March, 1931.
41. *Ibid.*
42. *Ibid.*
43. *Ibid.*
44. He was also convicted in the Lahore Conspiracy Case.
45. Quoted in *The Tribune*, 23 March, 1967.
46. He was also convicted in the Lahore Conspiracy Case.
47. Quoted in Gopal Thakur, Bhagat Singh : The Man and His Ideas, Delhi, 1962.

48. Home Poll, File 33/11, 1931.
49. *Ibid.*
50. *Ibid.*
51. *Ibid.*
52. *Ibid.*
53. *Ibid.*
54. *The Leader*, 12 March, 1931.
55. *Ibid.*
56. *The Bombay Chronicle*, 28 March, 1931.
57. At Kanpur, on 24 March, 1931, 166 persons were killed and 480 wounded in a communal riot causod by differences aver a *hartal* to mourn the execution of Bhagat Singh and his comrades.
58. Home Poll, File 29/7, 1931.
59. *Ibid.*
60. The Collected Works of Mahatma Gandhi, Vol. XLV, p. 200.
61. *See Young India*, 12 March, 1931.
62. The Collected Works of Mahatma Gandhi, *op.cit.,* pp. 315-16.
63. See full text in *The Hindu*, 22 March, 1931.
64. Gandhi wrote this letter to Irwin a few hours before the execution of Sardar Bhagat Singh, Sukhdev and Rajguru. (The Collected Works of Mahatma Gandhi, *op.cit.,* pp. 333-47.
65. The Collected Works of Mahatma Gandhi, *op.cit.,* pp. 333-34.
66. *Ibid*, p. 334.
67. The Collected Works of Mahatma Gandhi, *op.cit.*, pp. 335-36.
68. See the complete article in The Collected Works of Mahatma Gandhi, *op. cit.*, pp. 359 tt.
69. See the full text of the article in *Young India*, 16 April, 1931.
70. *Young India*, 11 June, 1931.
71. Jawaharlal Nehru, *An Autobiography*, Delhi 1967, p. 175.
72. See 'The Last Moment's an artcle by Gulab Singh in *Link*, 22 March, 1981.

Bibliography

Ahmed, Muzaffar, *The Communist Party of India and its Formation Abroad*, Calcutta, 1961.

All India Congress Committee Papers, 1928-31.

Bakers, Dudley, Grivas : *Patriot of a Terrorist*, London, 1959.

Bandopadhyaya, Jayantanuja, *Indian Nationalism versus International Communism*, Calcutta, 1966.

Banerjee, Kalyan Kumar, *Indian Freedom Movement : Revoluntionaries in America*, Calcutta, 1969.

Basant, Annie, India : *Bond or Free*, Adyar, 1939.

Bhagat Singh' Diary in *Nehru Memorial Museum and Library.*

Bipan Chandra, *Rise and Growth of Economics Nationalism in India*, New Delhi 1966.

Bipan Chandra, *Nationalism and Colonialism in Modern India*, New Delhi, 1979.

Bisheshwar Prasad, *Bondage and Freedom : A History of India* 1707–1947, Vol. II, *Freedom*, 1858–1947, Delhi 1979.

Blunt, W.S., *My Diaries : Being a Personal Narrative of Events, 1888-1914*, Vol. II, London, 1917.

Bose, A.C., *Indian Revolutionaries Abroad, 1905–22*, Patna, 1977.

Bose, S.C., *The Indian Struggle, 1920–24*, New York, 1984.

Breen, Dan, *My Fight for Irish Freedom*, Tralee, 1964.

Brockway, A.F., *The Indian Crisis, London*, 1930.

Buch, M.A., *Rise and Growth of Indian Militant Nationalism.*, Bombay, 1940.

Caveeshar, S.S., *India's Fight for Freedom*, Lahore, 1936.

Chakraverty, Chandra, *New India*, Calcutta, 1951.

Chatterjee, Jogesh, *The Search of Freedom*, Calcutta, 1967.

Chintamani, C.Y., *Indian Politics Since the Mutiny*, Allahabad, 1947.

Chirol, Valentine, *Indian Unrest*, London, 1910.

Collier, Richard, *Sound of Fury*, London, 1963.

Colvin, Ian, *The Life of General Dyer*, London, 1929.

Coupland, R., *The Constitutional Problem of India*, Madras, 1934.

Craddock, Reginald, *The Dilemma in India*, London, 1929.

Crozier, Brian, *The Rebels*, London, 1960.

Das, C.R., *India for Indians*. Madras, 1921.

Das. R.P., *The Impact of the Russo-Japanese (1905) War on Indian Politics*, Delhi, 1966.

Debates, *House of Commons*, 1920–31.

Debates, *House of Lords*, 1924–31.

Debates, Legislative Assembly, 1920–31

Delhi Assembly Bomb Case and Judgment. These documents are available in National Archieves of India.

Deol, Gurdev Singh, *Shaeed Bhagat Singh: A Biography*, Patiala, 1969.

Digby, William, *Prosperous British India*, London, 1901.

Dutt, K. Iswara, *Congress Cyclopaedia*, Vol. I, New Delhi, n.d.

Etherton, P.T., In *the Heart of Asia,* London, 1925.

Fischer, Louis, *The Soviets in World Affairs*, London, 1930.

Fraser, Andrew, *Among Indian Rajahs and Ryots*, London. 1911.

Gandhi Papers

Gandhi, M.K., *Autobiography*, Ahmedabad, 1963.

Gandhi, M.K., *Satyagraha in South Africa,* Madrass, n.d.

Garnett, David, *The Golden Eco.*, London, 1936.

Ghosh, Ajoy, *Bhagat Singh's and His Comrades,* Bombay. 1945.

Ghosh, Kali Charan, *The Roll of Honour : Anecdotes of Indian Martyrs*, Calcutta, 1955.

Gokhale, G.K., *Speeches,* Madras, 1916.

Gopal, S., *Jawaharlal Nehru: A Biography, Vol. 1, 1889–1947*, London, 1975.

Griffiths, P. J., *The British Impact on India, London*, 1965.

Gupta, Manmathnath, *They Lived Dangerously*, Delhi, 1969.
. . . . *Bhagat Singh and His Times*, Delhi, 1977.

Gupta, Manmathnath, *They Lived Dangerously,* Delhi, 1969.

Halifax, *The Earl of, Fullness of Days*, London, 1957.

Home Department (Judical), 1920–31.

Home Political, 1920–31.

Horne, E.A., *The Political System of British* India, Oxford, 1922.

Hoyland, John S., *The Case for India*, London, 1929.

Hyndman, H.M., *The Awakening of Asia*, London, 1919.

Irwin, Lord, *Indian Problems*, London, 1932.

Iyer, C.S. Ranga, *India in the Crucible*, London, 1928.

Kaye, Cecil. *Communism in India*, Deihi, 1926.

Keer, Dhananjay, *Veer Savarkar*, Bombay, 1950.

Kenworthy, J.M., *India : A Warning*, London, 1931.

Kohn, Hans, *A History of Nationalism in East*, New York, 1929.

Kondapi, C., *Indian Overseas*, New Delhi, 1951.

Lahore Conspiracy Case and Judgement. These documents are available in National Archives of India.

Lawton. Lancerton, *Empire of the East, Part-11*, London, 1912.

Macmunn, George, *Turmoil and Tragedy in India*. Vol. II, Calcutta, 1935.

Majumdar, R.C., *History of the Freedom, Movement in India Vol.II*, Calcutta. 1963.

Manmthnath Gupta

Mehrotra, S.R., *India and the Commonwealth, 1885-1929*, London, 1965.

Mehrotra, S.R., Towards Indian Freedom and Partition, New Delhi, 1979.

Meston, Lord, India and Meston, Lord, *The Empire*, London, 1924.

Meston, Lord, *Nationhood for India*, Oxford, 1934.

Modern Review

Moraes, Frank, *Jawaharlal Nehru*, Bombay, 1957.

Motilal Nehru Papers

Mukherjee, *Haridas and Uma*, *Bipin Chandra Pal*, Calcutta, 1953.

Nehru Papers

Nehru, Jawaharlal, *An Autobiography*, Delhi, 1962.

Pal, B.C., *Nationality and Empire*, Calcutta, 1916.

Pande, B.N., *Nehru*, Delhi, 1977.

Payne, Robert, *Red Storm Over Asia*, New York, 1951.

Permanand, Bhai, *The Story of My Life*, Lahore, 1934.

Prabodh Chandra, *Sixty Years of Congress*, Lahore, 1964.

Pratap, Raja Mahendra, *My Life Story of Fifty-five Years*, Delhi, 1947.

Rai Lajpat, *Young India*, Lahore, 1927.

Reports of the Sessions of the Indian National Congress, 1928–1931.

Sandhu, Virendra, *Shaheed Bhagat Singh*, Delhi, 1974.

Sanyal, Jatindra Nath, *Sardar Bhagat Singh*, Allahabad, 1931.

Sarkar, Sumit, *The Swadeshi Movement in Bengal, 1903–08*, New Delhi, 1973.

Satyagraha in *South Africa*, Madras, n.d..

Selected Works of Jawaharlal Nahru, S. Gopal. (ed.) Vols. III-IV.

Shastri, Bal Hardas, *India's Armed Struggle for Freedom*, Poona,1958.

Singh, Durlab, *Famous Letters and Ultimatums to the British Government*, Lahore, 1944.

Sitaramayya, B., Pattabhi, *The History of the Indian National Congress*, Vol. I, Bombay, 1946.

Tara Chand, *History of the Freedom Movement in India*, Vols. II and III, Delhi, 1967, 1972.

Thakur, Gopal, *Bhagat Singh : The Man and His Ideas,* New Delhi 1962.

The Bombay Chronicle

The Collected Works of Mahatama Gandhi, Volumes covering the period 1925-31.

The Hindu

The Hindustan Times

The Leader

The Pioneer

The Punjab Jail Enquiry Committee Report, 1929.

The Searchlight

The Times of India

The Tribune

These recorded interviews are available in Nehru Memorial Museum and Library, Teen Murti House, New Delhi

Wint Guy, *The British in Asia*. New York, 1954.

Young India

INDEX

D

E

I

J

K

L

M

P

Q

R

S